Chicken Soup for the Soul.

Making "Me Time"

Chicken Soup for the Soul: Making Me Time
101 Stories About Self-Care and Balance
Amy Newmark

Published by Chicken Soup for the Soul, LLC www.chickensoup.com
Copyright ©2021 by Chicken Soup for the Soul, LLC. All Rights Reserved.

The publisher gratefully acknowledges the many publishers and individuals who granted Chicken Soup for the Soul permission to reprint the cited material.

Front cover photo of coffee mug courtesy of iStockphoto.com/baibaz (©baibaz)
Back cover and interior photo of woman courtesy of iStockphoto.com/Viktor_Gladkov (©Viktor_Gladkov)
Photo of Amy Newmark courtesy of Susan Morrow at SwickPix

Cover and Interior by Daniel Zaccari

Distributed to the booktrade by Simon & Schuster. SAN: 200-2442

Publisher's Cataloging-In-Publication Data
(Prepared by The Donohue Group, Inc.)

Names: Newmark, Amy, compiler.
Title: Chicken soup for the soul : making me time : 101 stories about
     self-care and balance / [compiled by] Amy Newmark.
Other Titles: Making me time : 101 stories about self-care and balance |
     Making "me time"
Description: [Cos Cob, Connecticut] : Chicken Soup for the Soul, LLC,
     [2021]
Identifiers: ISBN 9781611590746 | ISBN 9781611593143 (ebook)
Subjects: LCSH: Time management--Literary collections. | Time management--
     Anecdotes. | Self--Literary collections. | Self--Anecdotes. | Self-
     care, Health--Literary collections. | Self-care, Health--Anecdotes. |
     LCGFT: Anecdotes.
Classification: LCC BF637.T5 C45 2021 (print) | LCC BF637.T5 (ebook) | DDC
     640/.43--dc23
Library of Congress Control Number: 2020947977

PRINTED IN THE UNITED STATES OF AMERICA
on acid∞free paper

30 29 28 27 26 25 24 23 22 21   01 02 03 04 05 06 07 08 09 10

Chicken Soup for the Soul.

Making "Me Time"

101 Stories About Self-Care and Balance

Amy Newmark

CSS

Chicken Soup for the Soul, LLC
Cos Cob, CT

Chicken Soup for the Soul

Changing the world one story at a time®
www.chickensoup.com

Table of Contents

Introduction...1

❶

~Mind, Body and Spirit~

1. My Name, *Melissa Face* 5
2. Hello, Me, *Cosmo DeNicola* 7
3. Tanning Lotion and Trails, *Lauren Barrett* 11
4. Check Your Sole... Um, Soul, *Anne Russ* 13
5. Me Time Zone, *Anneliese Rose Beeson* 15
6. Hold That Thought, *Monica A. Andermann* 17
7. From Loss to Freedom, *Laura M. Martin* 20
8. A Splash of Insight, *Lynn Kinnaman*............................24
9. Rest in the Present, *John Kevin Allen* 28

❷

~To-Do and You~

10. The Birds and the Bees, *Kat Gottlieb* 32
11. Stop Juggling and Put Something Down, *Ann Morrow*.........35
12. Never Disappointed, *Jon Peirce* 39
13. The Discipline of Doing Nothing, *James C. Magruder*.........43
14. A Daily Hour Just for Me, *Barbara Lehtiniemi* 45
15. Dinner with Kay, *Brenda Beattie* 48
16. Remember to Remember You, *Joshua J. Mark* 51
17. Fifty and Fabulous, *Tyann Sheldon Rouw* 54
18. Shinrin-yoku Is Good for You, *JC Sullivan*......................58
19. Not Mad, but Madly Happy, *Gina Gutzwiller* 61

❸
~Accept Help~

20. No Superheroes Here, *Brynn Mahnke* 65
21. Sharing the Load, *Judy Salcewicz* 69
22. Recharging Batteries, *Jonet Neethling* 72
23. An Unexpected Gift, *Wendy Kennar* 75
24. Put On Your Mask First, *Carole Brody Fleet* 78
25. All Things Food, *Diane Stark* 82
26. Surviving and Thriving, *Terry Hans* 86
27. The Ladies' Breakfast Club, *Phyllis Cochran* 89
28. Finding Time for Me, *Wendy Portfors* 92

❹
~Self-Discovery~

29. Running the Race for Me, *Amber Curtis* 97
30. A Lost Librarian, *Lori Shepard* 100
31. The "Me" That I Am Left With, *Jack Byron* 104
32. What Do You Need, Son? *Ankit Raghuvir Rao* 108
33. Letting Go of the Reins, *Stephanie Nikolopoulos* 111
34. Alone at the Kabuki Baths, *Lynn Sunday* 114
35. A Case of Shaken Identity, *Marilyn Haight* 117
36. Deep Breath In, Deep Breath Out, *Dana Drosdick* 121
37. Learning to Take Care of Me, *C. Ede* 125
38. Slow Cooking, Slow Living, *Pam Gibbs* 129
39. Trail of Hope, *Annette Gulati* 133

❺
~Self-Care Isn't Selfish~

40. Somewhere In-Between, *Kim Hanson* 137
41. Permission to Joyride, *Rebecca Radicchi* 140
42. Farmer's Hours, *Kristiana Pastir* 143

43. One Day, *Wendy Hairfield* 145
44. Grace over Guilt, *Diane Stark* 149
45. Finding My Footing, *Joan Bailey* 153
46. Better Reader, Better Mother, Better Me,
    Courtney McKinney-Whitaker 156
47. Refilling the Bucket, *Wanda Strange* 159
48. The Day I Saved Myself, *Kristin Baldwin Homsi* 163

❻

~Declutter, Detox, Defend~

49. Giving Thanks by Letting Go, *Maggie John* 167
50. The Day I Banished Busy-ness, *Kim Forrester* 171
51. A Working Man's Chuck-It List, *Timothy Martin* 175
52. A Little Housekeeping, *Connie K. Pombo* 178
53. No Service Means No Worries, *Noam Paoletti* 181
54. Forever Changed, *Jonney Scoggin* 184
55. The Cleanup, *Judee Stapp* 187
56. Learning to Read Again, *Robert Kingett* 190
57. Me First Beats Martyrdom, *Barbara Davey* 193
58. Out of Breath, *Dawn Marie Mann* 197
59. The Six Months Test, *Pauline Youd* 200

❼

~Giving Your Time with Joy~

60. Patched-Together Positives, *Jeanne Zornes* 204
61. The Cheerleader, *Susan Jelleberg* 207
62. Self-Care Found in a Library Basement, *Jill Keller* 210
63. Redefining Doing It All, *Haley Moss* 214
64. Being Intentional about Self-Care, *LaQuita Jean Starr* 218
65. Counsel Walking, *Sister Josephine Palmeri* 221
66. Reaching Out, *Margaret Lea* 224
67. Finding My Way Back, *Connie Kaseweter Pullen* 227

❽

~You Deserve It~

68. My Own Beat, *Stephanie Doerr*..............................232
69. Should Today Be a Pajama Day? *Marlys Johnson-Lawry* 235
70. Just Us, *Amy Newmark*.....................................238
71. Imaginary Holidays, *Ann E. Oakland*.......................242
72. The Face in the Mirror, *Crystal Schwanke*.................245
73. Doing It for Me, *Jennie Ivey*.............................249
74. Time to Play, *Tanya Janke*................................252
75. Girl's Trip, *Monica A. Andermann* 255
76. Cereal for Dinner, *Shannon McCarty* 258
77. It Was a Belly-Binge Kind of Day, *Dr. James L. Snyder*....262

❾

~Personal Space~

78. The Best Mother's Day Gift Ever, *Karen Sargent*............266
79. The Best View, *Anna Jensen* 269
80. Let It Go, *Cassie Silva*...................................272
81. A More Balanced Life, *David Hull* 276
82. Cozy Corner, *Lisa Leshaw* 278
83. One Piece at a Time, *Jennie Ivey*..........................281
84. The Glad Game, *Polly Hare Tafrate*.........................284
85. Adventures in Meditation, *Phyllis Abate Wild*..............288
86. Three O'Clock on Phantom Lake, *Ilana Long*.................291

❿

~Pursue Your Passion~

87. Escaping Insomnia, *Debby Johnson*..........................294
88. Wanted: Me, *Butch Holcombe* 296
89. My Holy Hour, *Lola Di Giulio De Maci* 300
90. Digging Holes, *Barbara Sue Canale* 302
91. Me Again, *Meeg Pincus Kajitani* 305

92. Reconstructing Me, *Betsy S. Franz*................................308
93. Dancing with the Anxiety Monster, *Juliet Huang*.................311
94. Not Available, *Jayne Thurber-Smith* 314

⑪

~We Time~

95. A Suitcase and an Adventure, *D'ette Corona* 317
96. Alone Together, *Diane Stark*.................................321
97. How Do You Want to Spend Your Time?
    Melissa L. Weber 325
98. Looking Forward to Those Lily Pads, *Kristine Byron*...........328
99. The Sneeze, *Anne Wandycz*..................................330
100. Cabin Life, *Tamra Anne Bolles* 333
101. My Ladies of the Lake, *Louise Butler* 336

Meet Our Contributors.......................................339
Meet Amy Newmark 353
Thank You..355
About Chicken Soup for the Soul 356

Chicken Soup for the Soul

Introduction

If there's anything we've learned during this pandemic, it's that life is unpredictable and nothing is guaranteed. You've got to live it with joy while you can. And you've got to spend as much time as possible with your favorite people while you can, devoting those hours to the people who mean the most to you and add the most value to your life.

This new collection of stories focuses on how you can live your life most joyfully, by deliberately creating time for yourself — me time, time with your most important loved ones (we time) — and by taking care of yourself. Self-care, work/life balance, pursuing your passions, decluttering your home and your calendar, and treating yourself as well as you would treat a guest are all covered in these pages. They're all things you know you want to do; we're going to help motivate you by showing you how other people did it — and the consequences of not doing so!

One of the themes that you'll see in these pages is the importance of getting outside in nature. I know that's what I've been hearing about the most from my friends and family and neighbors. Everyone's been saying things like "Wasn't that the most beautiful spring you ever saw?" or "Weren't there more birds singing this year?" or "Were there more flowers on the trees this year?"

Maybe the spring of 2020 was unusual, or maybe we were just noticing it because we were finally forced to be less busy. I know that the shutdown gave me time to really look at the trees on my property, and the bird nest outside my front door where I monitored a robin couple as they raised two sets of babies. I even got to watch the babies fly for the first time. Yes, I was there for that very event! And I got to watch the family of tiny birds on my rear patio, too, seeing the first flight of every single baby from that nest one summer Sunday.

Then, in the fall, I was transfixed by the activity in a large hickory tree at the beginning of our driveway. One day I stood under the tree and little green bits of hickory nut shells floated down around me as if it were raining. I could actually hear dozens of squirrels gnawing the shells off the nuts up in the tree. It was truly fascinating. That was something I wouldn't have experienced if I hadn't been "stuck at home" instead of going to the office and returning home after dark.

Getting outside means freely moving our bodies, gaining the perspective of being a tiny life inside a much larger world, and breathing the same air as the ancient trees that have seen it all and will still be standing when we're gone. It's the most powerful tool I know to reset your heart and soul. You'll read a lot about the transformative effect of walking out your front door no matter the season of the year or the season of your life.

This pandemic is going to leave a legacy, not just of loss and economic problems, but of renewed focus on what matters. We hope you'll take some "me time" to enjoy the stories in this new collection and to implement some good habits of your own as you move forward in life.

—Amy Newmark—
November 16, 2020

Mind, Body and Spirit

My Name

*Caring for your body, mind, and spirit is your greatest
and grandest responsibility. It's about listening to the
needs of your soul and then honoring them.*
~Kristi Ling

No one had called me Melissa in months. Hearing my name
was something I took for granted before the COVID-19
pandemic. But now I wasn't spending time with the
people who know me as Melissa: my co-workers, fellow
writers, and friends.

I had been at home with my two children for months. Evan, age
nine, and Delaney, six, call me Mom or Mama. I really don't have a
preference between the two as long as they aren't whining when they
say it. And I realize that I am fortunate to have wonderful little people
in my life who call me Mama — even at 2:00 a.m. when one of them
is sick.

Something happened when I stopped hearing my name, though.
It became a whole other type of isolation, separate from the pandemic
itself. Before I became Mrs. Face or Mama, I was Melissa. My name is
of Greek origin and means "honeybee" according to a cross-stitch that
used to hang on the wall above my mother's dresser.

My parents named me after Melissa Manchester. "We loved the
name, and there were no other Melissas around at that time," my
mom said. Then I began kindergarten, and there were three Melissas
all seated in the front row of Mrs. Whitley's class. From that moment

until the start of middle school, I was Melissa S. That's what I wrote on my graded work, what my teacher called during attendance, and what was written on the chalkboard — often with a checkmark beside it for talking too much in class.

Even though I didn't love having to attach my last initial to my name in school, I never really had a problem with my name. I never contemplated a name change. Even as an adult, I have never thought a different name would suit me better. I am Melissa, and my name is a big part of my identity. Except during the pandemic, when a big part of myself went missing.

After a few months at home, I decided to do something just for me. I signed up for a writing class that I'd wanted to take for a long time. Before COVID-19, I couldn't get to the class because of childcare concerns. But now that the course was being offered online, all I had to do was make sure my husband was home to watch the kids while I locked myself in my room for two hours on Tuesday nights. I was so excited to be enrolled in the class. I ordered a new journal, dug out my best pens, and organized my desk.

At our first session, the instructor began class by addressing us all by name and introducing our first prompt. "I want you to start by writing 'Right now, I am,' and then continue with whatever follows that," she said. She explained that this is often a good way to get out the "ick" — everything that might be in the way of what we really need to write.

I started writing my piece. Ten minutes later, she asked us to begin sharing.

"Melissa, we'll start with you," my teacher said.

I cleared my throat and read my first line.

"Right now, I am happy," I said. "I'm happy to be interacting with other adults, happy to be writing, and especially happy to hear my name."

— Melissa Face —

Hello, Me

Knowing yourself is the beginning of all wisdom.
~Aristotle

April 1, 2005. Cheers all around. Fifty years of life, success and achievement. Surrounded by family, friends and co-workers congratulating me on my life. The photos show me smiling, basking in the glow of my birthday celebration. I should be feeling great on the inside too. However, when I looked in the mirror that evening I saw a different person and felt an emotional letdown.

My fifty years included twenty-nine years of what I thought was all about me — 24/7 work, independence and the freedom to focus on my goals. Even though I had a great personal life and all the material trappings of success something was missing. A thought crossed my mind. If I were to die that evening, an accurate epitaph for me would read "unfinished business." But what exactly was missing and how could I find it?

It took a long time. The next ten years saw me chasing many new identities while raising my profile. Serial entrepreneur, sports team owner, traveler... and a heavy social calendar. It was fun and exhilarating, and my wife and I were having the time of our lives. Most times I felt that I was on a self-inflicted schedule playing a role rather than relaxing and enjoying each moment. I had become a *what* is he instead of *who* is he.

I was troubled by constant questioning: "Don't you ever relax?"

"Are you always working?" "What are you running from?" "Where are you running to?" I needed to find the real me and answer all those questions.

Finally, year sixty and beyond changed everything. Family health issues, death of loved ones, selling companies, reducing business responsibilities, and the end of my football team jolted me right off my hamster wheel. I had more time to reflect on my evolution as a complete person. I realized I was more of a work in progress than I had ever imagined. I started to refocus on being in the moment, but it scared me because "me time" felt more like alone time. I revisited that epitaph and reimagined it reading "herein lies Cosmo, after a life well lived," but would that be true?

For decades each day had started the same way. Up early, shower, dress, jump in the car, McDonald's drive-through, and then speed to the office. Things were about to change. Clearly it was time to let loose and become a better me, but how?

I started slowly by carving out time for me. Rather than establishing goals for the rest of my life I started searching for simple joys. First I had to stop talking and start listening. I started attending daily mass and found it to be a great source of reflection, meditation and peace. I could feel my heartrate lowering and my breaths deepening. It stimulated a spiritual transformation within me that led to fundamental changes in what I considered important. I was gradually able to eliminate thoughts that led to a false sense of fulfillment and concerns that fed anxiety and isolation. Interestingly the more I paid attention to my emotions the more compassion I had for people less fortunate.

My mind was clear and my heart was open, giving me the confidence to take the next step — literally. Each day after mass I walked across the street to a diner and sat at the counter. It is a charming owner operated restaurant. Seven stools at the counter and two tables with seating for eight. With a capacity of fifteen customers it is the definition of intimate. We sat close to each other, with no privacy, and all conversation available for everyone to hear and judge. This was a very uncomfortable step for me. I may present as a very outgoing person, but I am also extremely discreet and I value privacy. If given the choice I'd always sit at a table in the back of any restaurant. I would never sit at a bar or counter where the person next to me could hear, or even worse, engage me in conversation.

However, at the diner I placed myself in the middle of these strangers and conversations. Full disclosure, I did initially choose the stool against the wall; but over time I moved to a spot with more interaction possibilities. I was always a talker, but every conversation in the past had to have a purpose, and I needed to have an audience. Now, I found myself listening and engaging with others and enjoying the interaction. I felt free and was more open with my new group of friends than even my longest relationships.

Who is this new me? I'm actually savoring the nutritional and emotional nourishment. I went there for the coffee but stayed for the companionship. No strings attached — just me finally being me.

People always would say, "Cosmo, you need a hobby." Was I that one-dimensional or did people just not understand me? As it turns out I did have two hobbies, but I was going about them in the wrong way, treating them more like work tasks.

One of my hobbies is reading newspapers. Even though I own technology companies I eschew electronic readers and prefer hands-on old-school newspapers. The black ink on my hands is my badge of honor. I read four to six papers a day.

I had turned my newspapers into part of my work life, reading only the articles that would contribute information to further my business interests in healthcare, technology, professional football and the entertainment industry. I was skipping the other articles even if they looked interesting. How did I turn something I loved into yet another work project?

Once I recognized how much I was missing by rushing through the newspapers, I changed how I read them. In the process I felt more relaxed and informed, and it even turned out that those not-directly-relevant articles did in fact broaden my knowledge and help my businesses.

My other hobby, caring for chickens and show pigeons has its origin in my youth. As the son of two Italian immigrant families I raised pigeons in the back yard. Chickens were added as we raised our children. As an empty nester I decided to indulge myself and build an aviary, with pigeons on one side and chickens on the other. It brought back amazing memories of my childhood and my children. It's work, but I love getting dirty and being hands on.

I've always had hobbies but now I know how to enjoy them better. They're my hobbies, on my time and I'm better for them and because of them.

Taking time for myself has resulted in a happier and relaxed me. Slowing down (without sacrificing) my life has made me a better husband, father, son and person. I now enjoy my grandchildren in a way I never thought was even possible. I also carved out the time to start a charitable foundation with passions including World Health, Cultural Diplomacy, Humanitarian Recognition and Conservation. Making more time for me has benefited others as well.

Like Dorothy in *The Wizard of Oz* I always had the power. It just took me sixty years to realize that there is no shame in taking time for me.

— Cosmo DeNicola —

Tanning Lotion and Trails

*Often you will end up loving the new things you try,
and even if you don't love it, you've given yourself
a new experience.*
~Alli Simpson

Currently, my skin is a blend of different shades. My face is one color, and my neck is a shade lighter with streaks running down the front. That is where I am right now, and I don't care. It is the time to try new things. Get adventurous. Live life on the edge. The time to try that tanning lotion that has been sitting in my cart for months. The time to explore new trails.

I bought the tanning lotion a couple of weeks into the COVID-19 quarantine. "Hey, why not? No one is going to see me," I reasoned. It came in the mail, and I lathered it all over. My ankles and shins came out super tan. My feet remained ghostly pale, and my thighs and calves appeared to be mildly darker. I have always wanted to be multiple shades of orange, so I purchased the tanning face lotion for the cherry on top.

Meanwhile, I began mapping out new trails to run and walk all over my city. Daily, I hit these trails with my son in his stroller. We covered every inch of the trails, no matter the terrain. Flat. Hilly. Paved. Unpaved. Smooth. Rough. Didn't matter. My son and I would go bouncing along the trails, having the time of our lives. He on the edge of his seat and I running home to track where we went on the map and to find our next destination.

A few days later, my face lotion arrived. No sooner had I mastered the art of making my legs and arms look evenly tan than I decided to mess around with my face. Sure enough, the next day I woke up looking like Trump, with white circles around my eyes. I was that high-school girl in the 2000s who couldn't figure out how to blend her make-up so that her face and neck were not two starkly different colors. But this time I was the high-school teacher with a two-toned face, teaching girls who have beautiful, even skin.

"I'll blame it on the lighting in my house," I told myself. "No one will know over video chats."

And no one did notice. My face is now looking quite bronzed I feel inclined to add. Not to mention, my legs and arms are getting buff (my husband would probably laugh at this) from all the trails we have been exploring.

This time for me is all about trying new things — things that I might have been fearful to do before. Things that had a million reasons why I didn't have time to do them. I'm writing blogs that I have always wanted to write. I am making the killer website that's always been on my to-do list. I'm reading the books that have been on my want-to-read lists. I'm taking on a pull-up challenge and then quitting it two weeks later. I'm lying on the floor with my son as we laugh and play games. I'm going into the unknown, one tanning lotion and one trail at a time.

— Lauren Barrett —

Check Your Sole... Um, Soul

*Sometimes, our stop-doing list needs to be
bigger than our to-do list.*
~Patti Digh, Four-Word Self-Help:
Simple Wisdom for Complex Lives

Not too long ago, I experienced a day when I was extraordinarily clumsy. It came on very suddenly. I'm never a picture of grace personified, but on this particular day, I seemed to be tripping over everything—including the lines in the linoleum floor of the fellowship hall at my church.

It's an old church, and the floor is uneven in some places, so my stumbling was easy to brush off. It was the floor's fault. But when I tripped going into the grocery store, again on my way out to the car, and yet again in my own home, I began to grow concerned.

My life had been really busy and stressful over the past few days... okay, the past few weeks. Had I let myself get so rattled that I had literally become unbalanced?

Having been raised by devoted Christian parents who also worked in the mental-health field, I tended to look for spiritual and emotional reasons before I headed to the local family practitioner when my body started acting weird. But what if I truly needed to see a doctor? Maybe I had an inner-ear infection or was developing vertigo. Could I be having a stroke?

I took some time to stop and center myself before I decided what to do next. I have this calming practice that combines a yoga pose with a breath prayer. I realized I hadn't made much time for prayer recently, much less this particular practice. I went to change into more comfortable clothes for the exercise, and as I removed my shoes, I was cured!

I hadn't distracted myself into dizziness. I wasn't off-balance at all. I had completely worn out my favorite pair of sandals. The soles of both shoes were split completely in two! I wasn't having a stroke. I had been walking around all day in broken shoes that were tripping me.

I had been running my brain ragged (and most likely sending my blood pressure through the roof) trying to figure out what was causing my clumsiness. It never occurred to me to check my soles.

But isn't that always the way? At least, if you love a good homonym.

So often when our lives aren't going the way we want and things seem off-balance, we look for ways to make it better. We embark on a home-improvement project, lose ten pounds, buy a new outfit or log on to LinkedIn to search for a better job. But just as it never occurred to me to check the soles of my shoes, our own souls are the very last thing we think to check. We tend to exhaust all the possibilities outside of ourselves before we ever turn inward to look for answers.

The next time things are going badly, life seems out-of-balance, or you start to feel overwhelmed, take a moment to remember the last time you sat still, were silent or took the time to pray or meditate. If you can't remember when that was, it might be a clue.

This weird and wacky world can really throw us off-balance. Taking time to center ourselves is never indulgent or wasteful. It is essential to our ability to navigate life without tripping all over ourselves.

The local cobbler said the soles of my shoes were irreparable. We had a good run, but it was time to let them go. Fortunately for us, our souls can be mended and restored — once we realize they are in need of repair.

— Anne Russ —

Me Time Zone

It's okay to be a "me-time mom."
~Author Unknown

The day has ended yet only just begun
for I have two lives — one that hides behind the sun
You may not see my secret life — the one lurking in the dark,
the one that eagerly awaits its time to spark
Daytime me puts the other me aside
Daytime me doesn't get to hide
Daytime me washes all the clothes
Daytime me kisses the injured toes
I am a teacher, a maid and a cook
I hand out the cuddles and the disconcerting looks
I referee the arguments, the teasing and the fights
I fasten the helmets to go ride the bikes
Nighttime me relaxes in the chair
Nighttime me reads books without a care
Nighttime me watches comedy shows
Nighttime me eats the treats that I chose
I sometimes wonder whether I used to be bored
when I had just one life and hardly any chores
I want to do all the things that I did before
but how do I fit them in now there's so much more?
I read books, played piano and swam
I cycled and socialised and ran

I wrote poetry, played video games and went to bars
I knew popular culture and all the famous stars
Now my me time has become so small
sometimes I feel it's hardly there at all
When the children will not settle but the sun has gone away
I throw my arms in the air, for daytime me has to stay.
I count to ten and breathe in deep
Why oh why won't they go to sleep?
Me time is a ship that has sailed past
How could I be so foolish to think that it would last
I tuck their hair behind their ears
and then I begin to feel the tears
Am I crying for my me time? That seems a little mad
Surely it's something else that's making me sad
Crying for my me time does seem a little daft
As I leave the children's room I begin to laugh.
I'm trying to put me time into a time slot
I precariously balance it on the top.
But I realise my me time comes in different forms
to be enjoyed even while daytime storms
I read a book whilst I make the tea
I play ukulele whilst the children dance with me
I swim in the sea with the children under my wings
I run around the park between pushing them on swings
And there are famous stars that I know,
even if they come from the children's favourite show
Yes the ultimate me time is when I'm on my own
but me time can also be enjoyed when you're not alone
My me time is a state of mind
When I'm in the me time zone who knows what I'll find?

— Anneliese Rose Beeson —

Hold That Thought

We can complain because rosebushes have thorns
or rejoice because thorns have roses.
~Alphonse Karr

Okay. I'll admit it. I can be a complainer. After all, there's so much in this life to gripe about: the dirty clothes that don't make it into the hamper, that annoying neighbor's loud music, my husband's shoes left splayed at the front door, rainy days, traffic...

Complaining is a habit I cultivated since childhood, a skill I honed through the years. My family didn't seem to mind — they were great complainers, too — though I do recall some eye-rolling and long-drawn sighs from friends and schoolmates when I would voice my negative opinions. In fact, I can distinctly recall the exact moment when I first realized my complaining habit reached its expert level.

I was sitting in my college boyfriend's car on our way to the beach one hot summer afternoon — no air conditioning, the wind messing my hair, my thighs sticking to the vinyl car seat. I'm pretty sure there was some of the above-mentioned traffic as well, though I couldn't confirm it this many years later. In my disdain, I mumbled something about the situation under my breath. Probably for the tenth time. My usually mild-mannered boyfriend turned to me and snapped, "What are you complaining about now?"

The college boyfriend without air-conditioning and I amicably parted ways at the end of that summer. Shortly thereafter, I met a man with a much better car and attitude. We married three years later and lived together happily. Sure, there was still plenty to complain about, but he never seemed to mind. Or so I thought.

One day, as I reminded him once again to remove his bills from the dining-room table, put away his shoes away, and lower that dog-gone stereo, he put up his hand. "Stop! Stop your complaining. It's driving me crazy."

I looked at him blank-eyed.

He took a deep breath. "You never hear me complaining, do you?"

"Well," I answered, "you're complaining about my complaining, so actually, yes, I am hearing you complain right now."

His eyes widened. A bead of perspiration formed on his upper lip. Then he grabbed his car keys and ran out the door.

Perhaps I'd gone too far, I thought. Maybe I really did complain too much. But, what to do about it? After all, it had been a lifetime habit. And habits are hard to break.

I took a breather and sat down to think about solutions. I could quit cold turkey. No, that wouldn't work. When I felt annoyed, I could lock myself in the bathroom and scream. No. The neighbors would probably hear me. Phone a friend? She probably wouldn't be a friend for very long. Then it hit me.

I'd been in the habit of keeping a journal for most of my life. It provided a sort of timeline for me, and I liked to review past entries occasionally to reminisce or review the path I had been on at that point. Journaling kept me sort of honest with myself, and I liked it for that reason. Perhaps, I thought, a complaint journal might be the answer I was seeking.

That day, I decided to give it a try. Each time I found myself feeling the urge to voice a petty irritation, I promised myself to write it in my complaint journal that evening — no holds barred. At first, I couldn't wait to get that pen in my hand and really unload onto the paper. It felt so good, so freeing, to say exactly what was on my mind without anyone judging me or my thoughts.

The initial benefit was immediate. Without fear of recrimination, my generally reticent husband opened up to me more. Other benefits took more time to become apparent, yet I eventually became aware of them all the same. Old friendships became deeper, and new friendships appeared. Neighbors became more neighborly. Overall, I started to just feel better — happier and less stressed.

When I look back on some of my initial entries, I have to laugh out loud. Some of my gripes appear truly ridiculous when read in hindsight. I still keep that journal, though. Those few moments each day when I can sit down, take a breather from the pressures of the day and free myself of whatever is bothering me made a big difference for the better in my life. And, if you ask my husband, probably in his life, too.

— Monica A. Andermann —

From Loss to Freedom

Change is freedom, change is life.
~Ursula K. Le Guin

I promised myself I would quit at thirty, but I didn't. By then, it seemed like the sort of task that required nearly impossible levels of drive and commitment, like learning to figure skate or speak Japanese. Cigarettes were essential to me, like the keys, phone, and wallet that I never left home without. Smoking allowed me to resist a second helping of dessert, gave me an excuse to escape infuriating moments — "I need a cigarette!" — and provided intervals of silence during which I observed nature, like a sunset fractured by violet lightning or a fog of tiny white aphids falling like snow.

I told myself I wasn't hurting anyone else. My dulled senses couldn't detect the scent that followed me everywhere. I'd roll my eyes at conversations about secondhand smoke even as new studies showed that cigarette toxins clung to walls and furniture, and that this third-hand smoke could be reabsorbed through the skin.

On my own, I might never have quit. But during my second year in a creative-writing graduate program, the incoming class included a woman named Kera, a thirty-something former New Yorker who had walked away from a successful career and messy personal life to spend three years writing in rural Georgia, just like I had. We had great stories between us. Once, the FBI had shown up at my apartment on Christmas Eve looking for my ex. Once, she had slept in the apartment of a genuine Kuwaiti princess. Smoking was the last trace of our prior glamour and wildness.

Kera was already settling into new patterns: baking, hiking, and spending evenings in her king-sized bed named Gustav. I was still struggling to find an identity that wasn't tied to my past.

She brought up quitting on the drive home after our weekly dinner date at a surprisingly good Thai restaurant in the strip mall next to Walmart. Kera lit our after-dinner cigarettes and passed one to me. "We should quit," she said.

Smokers have conversations like this the way people complain about their significant others to their friends: affectionately and without any intention of acting on their grievances.

I exhaled a cloud of smoke and nodded. "Definitely."

Then she suggested a date. She was serious.

The next morning, I sat on my porch drinking black coffee and relishing each drag, made alert by the impending change the way we suddenly notice our surroundings when we're about to move.

* * *

My first cigarette was at a New Year's Eve party my freshman year of high school. I was too frightened by my family's rumored history of addiction and the threat of being permanently grounded to drink, but I couldn't afford to be seen as a puritan.

I'd been told that cigarettes tasted terrible and would make me feel sick, but that first drag off a half-smoked Camel Light made my lips tingle and my head buzz. The sip of Coke I took after tasted exceptionally sweet.

Smoking looks ugly from the outside, but it was a divine experience for me. I felt Lauren Bacall elegant, Margot Tenenbaum cool. It was magical breathing out swirling clouds, becoming a maker of mist, a dragon.

***

In the weeks leading up to our quit date, I filled my time Googling the symptoms and benefits I was about to experience. I read but ignored advice to announce my plans on social media and tell my friends and family what I was doing. I didn't want to be cheered on, especially by people who had never been through what I was about to experience. There was also my pride; if I failed, I wanted to do so as quietly as possible.

Quitting felt like breaking up with someone I loved but knew was bad for me. I kept my last half-pack stashed in the bottom drawer of my nightstand like an old love letter. I went back to it twice, holding and smelling it, before I flushed the contents down the toilet. Within a few hours, I started fantasizing about buying another pack.

Withdrawal took many forms. My mouth tasted sour. My guts twisted and stabbed. My skin broke out in hard, pea-sized cysts. I had a constant runny nose and slept poorly. When I went out, I felt a nagging confusion as if I'd misplaced my keys or forgotten to pay a bill. I tried to fill the craving for cigarettes with other indulgences, but the second I finished a chocolate bar or a juicy burger, my mind yearned for some new source of comfort. I ate boxes of butter mints and gnawed toothpicks to splinters. My thoughts looped like a bad pop song: *I want I want I want I want I want.* I dreamed of smoking. In the dreams, I'd reach for my wallet or lift my hand to wave and find that I was holding a cigarette, as if it was an inescapable part of me.

I missed the mental dialogue I'd have with myself about smoking, convincing myself to endure, looking forward to that small reward. Time, no longer broken into manageable segments by cigarette breaks, stretched on interminably.

Quitting affected Kera differently. When we went out for dinner now, we were both ravenous, still adjusting to the absence of appetite-suppressing nicotine. But at the end of the meal, as I was fantasizing about what I'd have for dessert, she'd comment on how satisfied she was. She seemed more content in general, giving away the doughnuts she fried on the weekend and turning down dinner invitations to save up for a trip to Joshua Tree.

The only thing that kept me from feeling useless to her was our morning workout. The gym was my most comfortable form of stress management. I went six days a week, and after we quit, Kera began accompanying me. I planned our workouts and monitored our progress. When everything else in my body seemed to be getting worse, getting stronger and having more stamina felt important.

One morning as I was dropping her off after our workout, Kera told me to put the car in Park. I thought she might have a story to tell me. Instead, she said that she was leaving. She had decided that our graduate program wasn't a good fit for her, and she was moving the following day. She tried to soften this final blow by telling me that she had waited until the last minute because she knew I'd try to talk her out of it — which was probably true but didn't take away the sting.

The next day, as she drove north in her U-Haul, I almost started smoking again. Instead, I skipped the gym and went for a run. I was surprised to find that I enjoyed having the time to myself again. I ran the following morning, and the one after that, surrendering to the comforting rhythm of my own footfalls.

One day, at the end of my usual three miles, I realized I wasn't winded and decided to keep going. I ran four miles, then five. When I finally stopped after almost an hour, I was exhilarated to find that I was stronger than I'd thought. Now, the space around me felt like freedom instead of emptiness.

— Laura M. Martin —

A Splash of Insight

The ability to be in the present moment is a major
component of mental wellness.
~Abraham Maslow

I was stumped. The question posed on social media wasn't difficult, at least for most people, but it was like being hit with a bucket of cold water for me, shocking me into a realization.

What do you do for fun?

I couldn't come up with a single answer.

Had my existence become so empty? Living alone, with an office in my home, work time had overflowed like lava, consuming more and more of my days until there was no boundary safeguarding my personal time. It was all work, all the time.

The worst part was that, at the end of the week, I could not successfully justify it. What had I accomplished? Ryder Carroll says, "Inevitably we find ourselves... spreading our focus so thin that nothing gets the attention it deserves. This is commonly referred to as 'being busy.' Being busy, however, is not the same thing as being productive."

I was not productive, and I was not happy. However, I was endlessly busy.

Something needed to change. I had no idea how to make it happen or where to begin. That is, until a four-legged fluffball entered the picture, upended the status quo, and made it clear that there was so much in the world yet to be discovered.

Dogs had always been a part of my life. For this next dog, I had specific requirements. My someday dreams included doing some traveling in my RV, visiting new places, and meeting new people. I needed a dog that would be happy with that. My last dogs had been Jack Russells, bright and energetic, but needing a lot of stimulation and challenges. Besides the Terriers, I'd owned Labradors and Belgian Tervurens. They were all lovely animals, but each bred with a purpose. They had active, outside-focused motivations and were driven to stalk, retrieve, or herd.

I wanted a dog that had been created to be with me. I wanted to know that, when she cuddled next to me, she was fulfilling her purpose and was satisfied. After much research, I settled on the breed: Havanese.

When I got my puppy, she was eleven weeks old and the smallest dog I'd ever owned. She weighed a mere four pounds and moved like a wind-up toy. I wanted to start her off right, as a socialized pup who was comfortable around other dogs and humans, so I took her to weekly playdates hosted by a local dog trainer.

I remember walking into the room, my tiny puppy cradled in my arms, and watching the rambunctious puppies jumping, running, and roughhousing. My eyes began to fill with tears. "I can't do this," I mumbled, turning to go.

"Wait." One of the puppy moms stopped me. "Just sit here beside me and let her stay in your lap."

I sat next to her. Her pup was a Cavalier King Charles Spaniel about the same age and size as my Trixie. Both our puppies were a little shy. However, my initial panic eased, and I returned week after week. In a short time, Trixie was running around, dodging the bigger puppies and finding a spot on a piece of equipment or a box where she had height equality. She was having a blast.

Then Ziggy came.

He was also a Havanese, three months older. Before long, Trixie and Ziggy were obsessed with each other, wrestling without a sound and ignoring the other dogs.

It wasn't long before Ziggy's mom and I decided we could hold our own playdates since our puppies only had eyes for each other. The first time we met at Jane's house, we drank tea and watched the puppies tumble nonstop for nearly three hours. It was Zen-like for me, calming and mesmerizing, taking me to a new level. When I left that day, my stress level was nonexistent, and I felt like I'd had a relaxing two-hour massage.

Our friendship grew, and we found we had more in common than just our good taste in dogs. We both wanted to visit places in Montana and the surrounding areas, and we both liked to cook. That led to a regular and sacrosanct tradition of Friday playdates. We'd try new recipes while the dogs entertained each other, or we'd take day trips with them.

Trixie and Ziggy will be five years old this year, and our pack of four has had many adventures. We've expanded our travel time, taking the RV on extended trips to Yellowstone, Glacier National Park, Canada, and shorter jaunts around our state. We share an interest in birds and other wildlife, and we've photographed bears, moose, eagles, and waterfowl.

The dogs, true to their natures, are happy to be part of the activities and never fail to bring us joy and laughter.

We keep a running list of new places to go, things to see, and recipes to tackle. I find the planning to be just as much a delight as the actual events. My weeks no longer pass by, indistinguishable from one another, without meaning. My Fridays are my oasis, a place where the whole day is simply about having fun and celebrating being alive.

As I recall my past habits, I realize I am accomplishing as much, if not more, by changing my focus from being busy to being present. That question, that splash of cold water, made me aware of how much I'd been missing by not carving out time for the things that really matter.

Now, I treasure every minute. By creating clear boundaries and giving myself designated time for fun, I have an easy answer to that question that once baffled me: *What do you do for fun?*

Where do I begin?

— Lynn Kinnaman —

9

Rest in the Present

*You are worth the quiet moment. You are worth
the deeper breaths, and you are worth the time
it takes to slow down, be still, and rest.*
~Morgan Harper Nichols

Last summer, I was suffering from too much stress. I had just graduated from a challenging doctoral program and was exhausted from the years of research, study and writing that led to my walking across that stage. My wife and I took a vacation after graduation to celebrate, but the academic intensity had become a habit and my brain couldn't seem to shut off. I felt like I should be reading, studying, or writing. My job as an educator didn't help. I had finished teaching a summer program and was gearing up for the fall semester that was coming too soon.

We vacationed on Mackinac Island in Michigan, where the pace of life slows considerably. Ordinarily, the clip-clop of horses, the lack of cars and the quaint shops would have relaxed me, but I could not slow down. I was too wound up, tired, and distracted. I had to check one more e-mail. I had to make one more fall schedule adjustment. I had to communicate with one more fall student about his concerns.

We took a day away from the crowds and sat on the beautiful back lawn of our hotel where we could appreciate a gorgeous view of the famous Mackinac Bridge. I had my phone with me to look at e-mails and then put it down. "Enough," I murmured. I needed to relax, but why couldn't I? My lovely wife sat next to me on a rattan loveseat. I had a cool glass of lemonade to enjoy. The deep blue sky was full of puffy clouds. A breeze stirred up whitecaps on the lake. Yet my shoulders were tense, raised up to my ears, and I could not put them down.

A dragonfly buzzed around us. Those creatures are special to me because they are a symbol of living in the present. They live most of their lives underwater as larvae and emerge with only months ahead to enjoy an iridescent adulthood. This one's brightly colored wings reminded me of the dragonfly tattooed on my wife's right ankle. With each movement, this creature's wings changed color—blue one moment, green the next. Dragonflies usually fascinate me with their quick movements that remind me of acrobats in the wind, but I was not in the mood that day. I needed stillness, not movement. As if on cue, the dragonfly came to rest on a blade of grass in front of me.

I need to do that, I thought. I needed to hold onto something and slow down. Take shelter from the persistent wind of life and just relax, if only for a short while. I watched that dragonfly carefully for many minutes and listened to that message. And then it flew away. Ah, I thought. Back to the grind.

I looked out over the bridge, the grass, gazed at the clouds and took a breath. Maybe I could slow down. I turned to my wife to tell her about my revelation when I felt a tickle on my leg. I looked down and saw colorful wings. The dragonfly was perched on my right ankle in the exact position of my wife's tattoo, facing upward and forward at a forty-five-degree angle.

I could have sworn that dragonfly looked at me and communicated. "It's not a matter of relaxing," it seemed to say. "It's a matter of appreciating the now, the here. Life is so short, so fleeting. Be here in the moment and let the future take care of itself." This beautiful creature that only had months to live reminded me of the preciousness of life. I would never again have this moment with my wife, this cool breeze, this moment of quiet. I was trying too hard to relax. Instead, I could appreciate what was here now and let that appreciation guide me into a sense of peace. I felt my shoulders descend to their normal place. The dragonfly seemed satisfied that its message had been delivered. It sprang off my ankle and flew away. I did not see it again. I decided not to tell my wife about the experience. I needed to let it sit for a while so it could sink in. I spent the rest of our time on Mackinac appreciating what we had in the moment.

Months later, I finally told my wife about it. I added that I wanted to get my first and only tattoo — a dragonfly on my right ankle, facing upward and forward at a forty-five-degree angle. I have it now, and every time I see it, I take a breath and smile. "Just be," it says. "Be here now. Life is so precious."

— John Kevin Allen —

Chapter
2

To-Do and You

10

The Birds and the Bees

Adopt the pace of nature. Her secret is patience.
~Ralph Waldo Emerson

he timer was set for ten minutes. I sat down on a soft pillow and crossed my legs with hands resting on my knees, palms up, eyes closed. "Okay, time to center myself, inhale, exhale. Relax… Re-lax… RELAX!"

I cracked an eye to check the timer. Thirty seconds had passed. Oh boy, this "me time" was going to be difficult!

As a working mother, my years passed in a blur of family-oriented activity without time for relaxing. When the kids were finally out of the nest and I was able to retire from my full-time career, I thought, *Now I can take some time for ME!*

Of course, as a lifelong list maker, I did my research. There were many possibilities. There were relaxation activities like yoga, meditation, getting pampered at a spa, exercise, socializing… I was determined to find the one thing that truly filled my soul. And so began my not-so-smooth journey to finding myself.

Meditation was the first to come and go. I never fully understood how to shut my mind off for any length of time. I always felt like I was just waiting for it to end.

Next, I tried "Teatime as Me Time." At first, I was very enthusiastic about this dainty endeavor. I envisioned sitting across from a dear friend, sipping from delicate cups and nibbling tiny sandwiches, but that is as far as it ever went. I have the fancy tea set (never used) and a pantry shelf full of tea packages that I will never consume. (I prefer the electric jolt of coffee in the morning.)

The pampering stuff isn't for me either. I like being productive. Sitting around feeling special doesn't feel special to me. So, I immediately scratched the spa ideas off my list.

Exercise is a highly recommended me-time activity. I liked to exercise, so why not double up my workouts and plan some exciting fitness goals? But after a week or so of training, exercise time felt more like torture time.

Many other me-time experiments left me wanting less of them, not more. I felt like a failure at this relaxation thing, especially when I found myself procrastinating to begin a me-time routine. I would chastise myself for "wasting" precious hours daydreaming on my front porch with my two dogs, watching the big, fuzzy bumblebees buzz about my garden. In those moments, time stood still. I could while away the morning watching the bugs, birds, and critters do their thing. I would delight in the seasons — Mother Nature birthing and dying in her perennial cycle.

A profound perspective is gained when noticing the small details of this miraculous world. My self-absorbed human concerns were really nothing in the grand scale of things. Taking the focus off myself was a relief. I realized that all the shoulda-woulda-couldas of living my best life placed more expectations on me, my relaxation and my performance. Ironically, I discovered that I truly desired less emphasis on *me* altogether.

Maybe the experts had this me-time thing all wrong, and it had little to do with "me" or "time" as I was defining it. Perhaps we are too concerned with how we spend our time instead of enjoying the nothing-ness of simply being. Instead of viewing it as a void, a hesitation between activities, we can shift our consciousness into embracing timelessness. Witnessing simple, humble moments of nature re-centered my soul better than anything else. Maybe a better version of "me time" is simply "be time"… or, better yet, "bee time"!

I just watched a young robin sunning its outstretched wings in the afternoon warmth. He closed his eyes as if to fully appreciate the moment, and I wondered if he was taking a little me time for himself. I watched until he flew away, and I am not sure how much time transpired. It could have been a minute or ten, but I enjoyed every second of it. However, I wonder, "Does it count as me time when I watch a bird enjoying his?"

I think back to all those busy years when I did not take a moment to appreciate our intricate natural world. Even when I rushed to make the 5:00 yoga class, to learn how to stretch and ground myself, the Earth's bounty was dancing outside the door. Now, I realize that me time is highly overrated if it makes me feel more pressure to fit one more thing into my schedule, especially if it takes away from the time I would have to simply… be.

— Kat Gottlieb —

11

Stop Juggling and Put Something Down

If you prioritize yourself,
you are going to save yourself.
~Gabrielle Union

When I left corporate life and started my own business, I thought I had it all figured out. When I made the decision to change my lifestyle and get fit, I thought I was on the right track. And when I purchased a second business, I knew I was doing the right thing. Slowing down never occurred to me. I was all about making things happen.

Over the course of three years, I programmed my brain to be in a state of perpetual motion. Even when I wasn't working, I was thinking about work. There was never enough time to get things done, and I feared I'd let someone down if I stopped long enough to relax. But the busier I got, the less I seemed to accomplish.

When the fatigue and brain fog set in, I told myself I just needed to work harder and get organized. But something was wrong. I was emotionally and physically exhausted. My Apple watch buzzed repeatedly in the night, warning me that my heart rate was over one hundred. My body ached, my head pounded, and no matter how much I exercised,

I was losing strength.

When I visited the doctor, the first thing she asked was "How's your stress level?" I shrugged. "Same as usual. Nothing new or out of the ordinary." But something was happening in my body. A multitude of tests and bloodwork revealed I had Graves' disease, an autoimmune disorder that causes hyperthyroidism, with symptoms that include accelerated heart rate, high blood pressure, physical anxiety, fatigue, and muscle weakness.

As Dr. Joy sat next to me to discuss the treatment, I said, "This doesn't seem fair. I've worked so hard on my health. I quit drinking, changed my diet and lifestyle, and lost weight. Things are supposed to get better, not worse."

She smiled sympathetically. "We'll get it figured out. Do some reading up on Graves' disease and take care of yourself." She wrote prescriptions for heart and thyroid medications and referred me to a specialist.

I scoured the Internet for information, articles and personal stories. I learned that autoimmune diseases cause the body to attack its own healthy cells. Disorders can be hereditary and are more common among women. In many cases, they are triggered and aggravated by stress. *How is your stress level?* I asked myself.

The following day, that question resurfaced when I bumped into an old friend. We hadn't seen each other for a while but were connected on Facebook. After exchanging hellos, Cindy said, "I just love following all the things you're doing. Wow, you've taken on a lot; you've got quite a juggling act. I don't know how you do it all, but you make it look good."

I smiled. "I have to admit, some of those projects I'm juggling are starting to get heavy."

"So, stop juggling and put something down. It's okay to tell people 'no.'" As we parted ways, she added, "It was good to see you. You look like you've lost weight; take care of yourself." She waved and disappeared around the corner.

For the next week, I thought about our short conversation. I re-read online articles indicating that stress management played a part in controlling Graves' disease. And I made a list of everything I was juggling. I was running two businesses — each requiring a multitude of different tasks. My calendar was filled with online marketing, photo shoots, website design, copywriting and planning a huge regional event. On a good day, I'd squeeze in thirty minutes of writing the book I was working on. I barely had time to blink, let alone relax. But, somehow, I was managing to do it all. My commitment to do more, be more and serve more was too much. I examined the list. It was clear I didn't *want* to do it all. Something had to give.

Prioritizing was hard. I examined the juggling act and tried to decide what to let go of. I bid farewell to clients, explaining I was cutting back and lightening my workload. When asked to speak at events or take on new projects, I said "no." And I found someone to help me plan that big event. My calendar got a makeover, and I reminded myself it was perfectly acceptable to have white space on my schedule.

Until then, I didn't realize how much I'd missed the simple joys — little things that helped me relax and recharge, like long hikes, taking my dog to the park, visiting my favorite bookstore, and sitting on the back porch to watch the sunrise. Those things belonged on my calendar, so I started using an orange highlighter to block out time for myself. Those orange blocks are mine. They represent time to unplug, let my imagination wander, and focus on what's important.

Along with scheduled downtime, creative work found its way into my day. I blocked snippets of time for my writing and photography projects. Once I'd prioritized, it didn't take long for everything else to fall into place. I didn't know how, but I was more productive by doing less.

My calendar is still full, and my workload is still heavy, but I'm not buckling under the weight. I know my limits and when it's time to stop juggling. I've learned to be kind to myself. I start each day with meditation and end with gratitude. And somewhere in the middle, I savor a quiet block of time, reserved for just me. These little things play a big part in my wellbeing.

Perhaps this disease wasn't triggered by stress. Then again, maybe it was. Either way, the diagnosis has helped me reclaim my life. Dr.

Joy was right. We're getting it figured out. Gradually, I'm becoming a healthier, happier, more relaxed version of myself.

—Ann Morrow—

12

Never Disappointed

By failing to prepare, you are preparing to fail.
~Benjamin Franklin

My dear friend is a poet — quite a fine poet, actually. Some years ago, when she was first starting out as a poet, she and I were in a writing critique group together. Even then, early on in her career, her work showed great promise. Her images were always powerful and moving.

But Janina had one habit that I found disconcerting. Particularly in her longer poems, she would often give two alternate word choices, separating the two by a slash. Occasionally, the choice was obvious. One word would fit well, while the other would be simply wrong or at least seriously out of place. They were like forks in the road, leading in two (at least in theory) equally desirable and productive directions. And sometimes we would be faced with several of these either/or choices in a single poem.

Having to make so many choices between alternate wordings made it difficult to get the overall sense of the poem. At least, I found it difficult. On one occasion, confronted by my third or fourth set of slashed options for the evening, I told Janina about my frustration with her system. These were choices, I said, that she needed to make for herself, however difficult she might find them, before bringing the poem to us for critique. She provided a fairly plausible explanation for her methods, and I did not press her further. But I noticed that the "build-it-yourself" slash options were fewer and farther between in future sessions.

But while the "either/or" slash option may not be a great way to make poetry, it does offer considerable promise in other areas of life, notably in scheduling events. Often, those of us who are fairly busy will have two (or occasionally more) events that we could be doing at the same time. Typically, at least one of the events (say, a tennis match or a theatre rehearsal) will be dependent on factors beyond one's immediate control, such as the vagaries of the weather or the availability of other people. In the past, I was often bitterly disappointed at the cancellation of an outdoor tennis match, something that happens quite often in the humid climate of Nova Scotia where I live. Sometimes, this disappointment would last into the next day, ruining it as well as the day of the actual rainout.

That disappointment can be greatly reduced or even eliminated through the judicious scheduling of a "Plan B" event — something that is not dependent on weather or the availability of busy people. For instance, on a Thursday evening in summer, I may wish to play men's doubles tennis at my club. But if that event is rained out, as it is close to 50 percent of the time, I have a "Plan B" event ready to hand, namely my Acoustic Song Circle at Dartmouth North Library, an event in which we go around the circle having everyone take turns leading the group in a song. Faced with a choice between two equally desirable if quite different sorts of events, I am in a "can't lose" situation.

It is much the same with social and cultural events. If, for example, there is an "early-stage" play rehearsal set — I often act in community theatre plays — and I don't know whether it will come off because the play hasn't been fully cast yet, I will move in advance to mitigate the disappointment and irritation at possibly having my time wasted. I will deliberately choose another event, such as a concert, play, or movie, at exactly the same time slot. I may even "triple-book" two alternative events if one of the alternatives is weather-dependent (e.g., an outdoor play). This, in fact, is exactly what I've done for this coming weekend. There is supposed to be a rehearsal for a Halifax Fringe play I'm in. But as of today (four days before the scheduled rehearsal), the play has not yet been fully cast. So, I have taken the precaution of signing up for a mixed doubles event at my tennis club on Saturday afternoon. And if that doesn't happen due to weather, there's always an Acoustic Song Circle on the go down in Musquodobit Harbour, a short drive from where I live in Dartmouth.

Nor need the notion of "either/or" double-booking scheduling be confined to single events. For instance, as an actor, I often audition for plays. Being cast in a play means, usually, a commitment to three rehearsals a week. Not being cast means being disappointed, often bitterly, sometimes to the extent of feeling emotionally disabled for some time afterwards. I'm sure any reader who has ever acted will know this feeling without my having to explain it further.

Starting this fall, I won't show up for an audition without an alternative plan in mind in case I am not cast. The alternative will have something to do with theatre. It may be taking private lessons or a group course or signing up for improv sessions. It may even be something as big as signing up for an out-of-town playwriting work-shop. Whatever happens, I'll still be doing something with theatre. While this will not completely eliminate any disappointment I feel at not being cast, it should reduce it significantly by not making me feel I have a huge block of time to fill.

And the idea even works at home while one is watching TV. Suppose I am watching a tennis match. I know that there's always a break after the odd games (3, 5, etc.). In the past, I was irritated at having to wait two minutes for the game to resume. Now, I simply run out to the kitchen and work on the sinkful of dishes that is almost always there. By the end of the match, if I am faithful in going to the kitchen every commercial break, those dishes will all be done.

This whole idea started with something as simple as always making sure I had a book to read whenever I had a doctor's appointment. In the past, like most others, I would fret and stew any time I had to wait more than a few minutes past the scheduled time to see the doctor. But once I started bringing a book, those delays haven't mattered. Much of my best reading lately has been done while waiting in doctors' offices.

For all of us, but particularly for those of us who are Type A and can't stand to see any of our time wasted, always having an alternative ready during times of potential interruption or delay is crucial to preserving our mental health. Women who knit or sew have long been in on this secret. But with good planning, the secret is available even for those of us who don't sew or knit.

Bottom line: While the "either/or approach" may not be the best way to write poetry, it could just be a pretty good way to help organize a life.

—Jon Peirce—

13

The Discipline of Doing Nothing

You cannot pour from an empty cup.
~Author Unknown

I can't think of any benefits of this pandemic, but if there was one, it might be how it forced me to slow down. Eventually, I will return to the rat race with all its demands and deadlines. But I hope I never forget the one lesson I learned: to consciously "insert pauses" into my day by developing the discipline of doing nothing.

Many years ago, Coca-Cola ran a brilliant advertising campaign about "The Pause That Refreshes." They were on to something. Pauses refresh us because they allow us to stop, refocus, and rest.

The older I get, the more I've intentionally inserted pauses into my day. Some pauses are only a few minutes long; others are hours. It may be a walk to a faraway copier at work instead of the one in my department. Or driving an alternate route home. Or a day at the beach. The idea is to relax, rejuvenate, and rest by diverting my thoughts from what stresses me to what refreshes me.

Rest replenishes us. And I rest best by, well, doing nothing. I recently read a little book by Sandy Gingras called *How to Live at the Beach*. I love this lighthearted, five-minute read. It's a metaphor that conjures up images of the mentality we have when we're at the beach — and why we need to transport this beach mentality to our non-beach lives.

My son, his wife, and my grandson live near the beach in Santa Barbara, California. Next to Hawaii, it's one of the most beautiful places in the United States. When I head to the ocean with them, I'm awed by the benefits of the beach. It invites us to a state of serenity and calls us to a life of simplicity.

The beach near their home is where I naturally reduce speed and forget about the complexity of the world. The beach may be the only place where I can return to my child-like self by building sandcastles with my grandson or sitting in the surf and letting the waves massage me or float me like a piece of driftwood.

For me, a day at the beach epitomizes the discipline of doing nothing. It's a pause. A prototype of a simpler life. I'm learning how to bring a beach mentality, and all its benefits, back home with me. A beach mentality slows me down, allows me to ponder only what's in front of me, diffuses stress, and allows me to fully appreciate what surrounds me in my nine-to-five world.

During this time of "country closure" (and doing nothing), I've noticed what I typically fail to notice, some of which is in my own back yard: the graceful arc of a hawk; the song of the cardinal, red-winged blackbird, blue jay, robin, or killdeer; the power and precision of the red-headed woodpecker; the wobbly legs of a newborn fawn; the majesty of a doe up close; and the artistic curl of an ocean wave just before it breaks at the shore. Ironically, I notice more when I "invest the time" to do nothing. Who says doing nothing is boring? Doing nothing calms, recalibrates, enlightens, and refuels me.

I've realized that by pausing more, I've seen more, listened more, heard more, and felt more. Yet, pausing is a discipline all its own. It's much more difficult to slow down than speed up.

By developing the discipline of doing nothing, I've learned that a life of clarity, simplicity, and rest awaits.

It's like a day at the beach.

—James C. Magruder—

A Daily Hour Just for Me

Self-care is one of the active ways that I love myself.
When you can and as you can, in ways that feel loving,
make time and space for yourself.
~Tracee Ellis Ross

For most of my working life, I hated getting up in the morning. The alarm always seemed to go off while I was in deepest slumber. My first thought upon waking was, "How soon can I crash into bed again?"

I'd stagger, blurry-eyed, to the kitchen to start a pot of coffee, and then hop into the shower. Between being an employee, mother, spouse, student, and volunteer, I felt like I was on a hamster wheel — just non-stop forward motion until each day ended. Many times, I wished there was just one more hour in each day so I could get things done.

Then I found out there was a way to get an extra hour — and I didn't have to share it with anyone.

While helping at a community fundraiser, I fell into conversation with another volunteer who used to have the same problem with getting up in the morning. He said getting up an hour earlier solved his problem. The idea was that a person should spend the first hour of the day in a positive way and in solitude.

Getting up an hour earlier seemed counter-intuitive to me. Dragging myself out of bed at 6:30 a.m. five days a week was difficult enough. How could I possibly get up one hour earlier? If I set my alarm even ten minutes earlier, it was only so I could have the guilty pleasure of hitting the snooze button before having to get up.

Nevertheless, I thought I should give waking up earlier a try. There were many things I never seemed to find time for, like exercise, meditation, and reading, and those could be incorporated into a quiet hour before everyone else got up.

At first, it was difficult. When my alarm went off at 5:30, I was tempted to hit the snooze button and pull the covers over my head. But I forced myself to get up. If I found it important enough to get up to work for someone else each morning, it surely was important enough to get up to devote time to me.

Initially, I planned to spend thirty minutes doing aerobics and then relax with a cup of tea while reading some enriching books. But exercise didn't prove to be sufficient motivation to get out of bed early — at least not every day.

I experimented with how best to spend my "extra" hour each day. Did I want to learn a new craft? Take an online course? Start doing yoga? Now I had an extra hour five days a week to indulge in activities that were just for me.

I began looking forward to getting up each morning. When my alarm sounded, I'd bounce out of bed, already anticipating the steaming cup of tea I'd be enjoying in a few minutes.

Instead of feeling more tired by losing that hour of sleep, I ended up feeling more energized, more in control of my life. Even though I used to be tired all the time, I realized it wasn't sleep I was lacking. I had been deficient in self-nurturing.

It didn't matter how I spent my hour. The value in the time was it gave me a full hour of pure peace. No demands on my time, no obligations, no conversation. Most importantly, it meant that instead of jumping out of bed and rushing to prepare for work, I was easing into the day at a comfortable pace.

Soon, I was getting up early on weekends, too. I found it effortless to get up at an early hour when I knew the first hour would be mine alone to savor any way I wished.

My daily hour habit got me through many challenging periods in my life. When I was a working mother of a young child, that daily hour was my sanity saver. During periods of upheaval, the daily hour was the one constant—a reliable, stress-free zone.

Even after I began working freelance from home, my daily hour continued. Decades after beginning the practice, I still can't wait to get out of bed.

Nowadays, my hour is spent journal-writing while I sip tea and watch birds at the feeder. Even though my life has become more manageable, I still look forward to getting up each morning and spending a quiet hour by myself.

How I've spent my daily hour changed with my interests and needs at any given time. But one thing hasn't changed in all these years: The first hour of the day belongs to me alone.

— Barbara Lehtiniemi —

15

Dinner with Kay

I know what I bring to the table, so trust me
when I say I'm not afraid to eat alone.
~Author Unknown

Being a parent is hard enough, but being a single parent is overwhelming. After twenty years of marriage and two kids, I found myself a single mother. When my husband left, I was all the kids had. I had no family to help me where I lived, so I did what any mother would do. I rose to the occasion and worked my fingers to the bone to provide for them.

At times, I was working sixty-plus hours a week. I had as many as three jobs at a time. It wasn't easy, but my kids never went without. I never missed a bill, never had a late payment, and all without child support. The only problem was that I was working myself to death.

One Easter weekend, I worked thirty hours from Friday to Sunday, with little to no sleep. On Sunday night, I fell into bed exhausted. My next memory was waking up in an ambulance with two paramedics holding me down. I had no memory of how I got there, and I had a splitting headache. They kept asking me what kind of drugs I was on. Seriously? I'd never taken drugs in my life. All I remember is being angry and confused.

They took me to the hospital, and over the course of a couple of days, they deduced that I had simply collapsed from exhaustion. Apparently, I'd gotten up in the middle of the night and had a seizure. I had bitten my tongue and hit my head on the doorknob of my bedroom closet. The saddest part was, I didn't even know my own children. My daughter said I looked right at her but didn't recognize her. Yet, I kept telling the paramedics to call another employee to open the business because I couldn't get there. That's ridiculous, don't you think?

When I was released from the hospital, I began to rethink everything. As a single parent, I had to provide, but I was going to have to find a better way to do it. I needed to be home more for my kids, work fewer hours, and still make ends meet. The only way was to find a better-paying job, which wouldn't be easy.

In time, I did find a better job, and I was able to once again think about taking care of me. I had been taking care of everyone else for so long that I'd forgotten about myself. Growing up, my mother was always sick, and I had to take care of her. After I got married at eighteen, I soon had the two children and a husband to take care of. I had never been a priority, and the thought of doing something I enjoyed seemed foreign.

The first thing I did was take up jogging. It helped me get back into shape and forced me to eat right. I then began teaching aerobics classes so I could help other women get their lives back. I did everything I could to talk with other single moms about taking care of themselves so they'd be better equipped to take care of their children. However, my favorite thing to do was to go out to dinner with Kay.

Every two weeks, Kay and I would go out to dinner. My children were old enough to stay home alone for a couple of hours, and I always made sure they had their favorite dinner to eat while I was gone. Kay and I just relaxed, forgot our troubles, and enjoyed the time out. We never went anyplace expensive. My daughter always asked why she never got to meet Kay. I just told her, "Someday."

Time passed quickly, and my children grew up and moved on with their lives. One day, my daughter asked me again about Kay. "Who was she?" she asked. Finally, I explained that Kay was my middle name, and those nights I went out I was alone. It was a time to just be me and treat myself. It was my me time. She was shocked to find out that Kay wasn't a real person. However, Kay was a real person. She was the part of me who needed to feel special once in a while.

It's easy to get lost as a mother because we love our kids dearly. Sometimes, we just need to find ourselves. Kay is still one of my favorite dinner companions.

— Brenda Beattie —

16

Remember to Remember You

*The Universe will never require you to set yourself
on fire to provide heat for others.*
~Clyde Lee Dennis

I hung up the phone and returned to scrubbing the kitchen floor. My brother Jason had just invited us over for dinner. Again, I had to tell him we couldn't make it; I had too much to do. Every morning, I made my to-do list. Every evening, each line was crossed off as done. The list was essential because there was always so much to do. But no matter what I did, a new list grew in the morning.

It was June 2016, and my wife Betsy had been diagnosed with liver cancer a month earlier. This was not our first journey with cancer. She was diagnosed with breast cancer in 1997, and it returned in 2008. Both times, I was her primary caregiver, and we'd beaten the disease. In the summer of 2016, I felt I was reprising a role I knew well. But this time, for some reason, I could not remember my lines or what to do once I stepped on stage each morning. I could've used some strong direction and a little stage managing.

But that's where the lists came in. I never needed the lists with the earlier cancer journeys. I just did whatever needed to be done next and then whatever came after that. This time, though, her diagnosis was more serious, and there was less she could do. The best advice I got as a caregiver was to remember the instructions regarding oxygen masks on airplanes: Put yours on first before trying to help someone else. But I forgot it that summer, and the next summer, and the next. I had helped save Betsy twice before, and I was determined to do it again. I was so determined, in fact, that I forgot about myself entirely.

In the evenings, we watched whatever shows on TV she wanted to watch and went to the films she wanted to see in theaters. I scheduled her chemo appointments and doctors' visits, CAT scans, blood draws, car inspections and repairs, and eye doctor and dentist visits. I had always taken care of the housework so that was nothing new, but now I was also taking care of the cat boxes for the four cats, scheduling vet visits, going over our daughter Emily's student loans, and struggling to do the bills — all tasks Betsy had routinely taken care of. Betsy always took care of so much and so well that I felt like an inferior replacement, an understudy to a much greater artist whose range I could never match.

By December 2016, the chemo had done its job, and she was improving. Throughout 2017, she was so healthy that I would have forgotten she had cancer if I hadn't been driving her to Friday chemo sessions and doctors' appointments. Even so, I had become used to my new role, and I continued to perform it, though not nearly so regularly.

Then, in May 2018, she woke up one morning with abdominal pain so severe that she couldn't move.

From then on, I was doing the high-maintenance caregiving daily on a far more intense level than in 2016 or ever before. I arranged trips from our home in New York for her cancer treatment in Philadelphia, took care of setting up all her procedures there, and got her back and forth between the hospital and the hotel. I made whatever food she liked, and I stocked the refrigerator with her favorite juices and snacks. I was haunted daily by the lines from a Lana Del Rey song about not feeling capable, of struggling to hold the one you love in your arms without letting them fall, of hoping to become what you need to be for someone you love.

This went on until August 4th when Betsy died peacefully at home, surrounded by her family. She was smiling. The great cancer journey was over, but my own journey was just beginning.

I first became aware of the new phase two weeks after her death when I was out with my brother Jason, and he asked what I wanted to eat. I had no idea. The thought struck me as strange, but then I realized that for two years I had only eaten what Betsy wanted. When I ordered take-out, I would get what I knew she liked because she wouldn't eat it all, and I'd just finish what she left. I had no idea what kind of food I liked myself.

I realized I knew absolutely nothing about myself anymore. What kind of shows did I enjoy watching? I didn't know. What movies did I want to see? I had no idea. What sorts of places did I want to visit? Not a clue. I had dived so completely into caring for her that I forgot who I was. I have absolutely no regrets over that impulse, but it should have been tempered with a little self-restraint and a lot more self-care.

When we find ourselves in a situation like this, it's natural to move ourselves to second place. The person who needs our attention comes first. But we have to pause and realize that, if we're not taking care of ourselves, we're not going to be of much use to the one we love. I experienced eczema outbreaks, osteoarthritis flare-ups, gastrointestinal problems, chronic insomnia, anxiety attacks, and hysterical toothaches throughout the time I was caring for Betsy, and even more so afterward when my grief found its outlet through physical symptoms until therapy helped me manage it better.

I don't know if my story will have any effect on a caregiver out there going through what I did, but I hope for the best. I know, in my own case, I would not have given a second thought to this kind of advice in 2016 or 2018 because there was always so much to do, and those lists flowed relentlessly from the end of my pen every single morning. I realize now, though, I could have been better to me and, in doing so, would have been better for Betsy. I'm not saying I didn't do my best for her — I did — but I forgot to also do my best for me, which I know would have meant the world to the one I cared for.

— Joshua J. Mark —

17

Fifty and Fabulous

Good things come to those who sweat.
~Author Unknown

One night while sitting inside the 200-degree dry sauna at the local community recreation center, a masked man looked my way. I recognized him. He was a regular in the sauna, just like me. We both wore T-shirts, shorts, socks, and shoes, and sat as far apart as the space in the small sauna allowed. I wiped my face with a towel.

"Hey, I've seen you walking outside," he said.

"Yes, I have been walking outside a lot," I explained. "I need to get away from my family. We've had a little too much family togetherness since March when COVID-19 hit," I said, laughing. "Sometimes, I walk for at least an hour. It's saved my sanity."

He laughed and said he understood.

What I didn't mention is that I think the quarantine with my family saved me. Earlier in the year, I had landed in the emergency room after having chest pains. Did I have a heart attack? The doctors said no. I'm not sure what happened, but the episode scared me. I was forty-nine, taking no medication, and had no major health issues. But I was stressed, eating too many carbs, and exercising too infrequently. My scale hadn't budged in years.

It didn't help that one of my sons has severe autism, and my parents had died from cancer within nine months of each other. In addition, I had fallen passionately in love with sugar.

I needed to figure out a way to get healthier. While my three teenage sons were all home 24/7, it seemed like a good idea to change some of my habits. If we all had to be together for weeks or months, I needed to get my head in a good spot. For starters, I needed to social distance from the refrigerator.

Over the years, I had tried many ways of losing weight, but none of them seemed sustainable. I did elimination diets, which focused on being grain-free, alcohol-free, legume-free, dairy-free, sugar-free, and soy-free. Unfortunately, I also found it joy-free. Was life worth living if I couldn't enjoy a piece of bread occasionally? Or a margarita when I met a friend for dinner at a Mexican restaurant?

I had weighed myself daily for years and written down the results in a paper planner. When I looked at the weight over the years, I realized that it hadn't changed much from year to year, even if I had managed to lose ten pounds somehow during the year. The yo-yo dieting was alive and well.

One of my husband's co-workers mentioned to him that she had been successful using an app on her phone to lose weight. She said she felt amazing, changed her habits, and hadn't felt so good since she was in high school. Another friend who works in public health recommended the same program. I reached out to both and was encouraged to do a free two-week trial. I decided I had nothing to lose except time and, hopefully, a few pounds.

After two weeks, I lost five pounds. It was enough for me to decide this was it! It was a huge realization that the scale could budge again if I followed a program, ate right, and was conscious of what I consumed. One of the most important parts of the program was the exercise component, which was based on the number of steps walked. I had been walking for years but rarely went farther than two miles a day. I also never kept track of when I exercised. Was I exercising weekly? Daily? My foggy brain said I was exercising more regularly than I was.

What I have learned since starting this program is to put myself first. After nearly twenty years of being a caregiver to my three children, I've decided I need to make myself more of a priority — without feeling guilty. I spend a good deal of time daily planning my meals, cooking, walking, logging what I eat, and juggling my calories so I can still enjoy an occasional dinner out. I feel more in control than I have in years, especially of my scale. So far, I have lost twenty-four pounds. I have another fifteen pounds to go, but I'm confident I will get there eventually.

I walk every day. It has become almost a meditative experience. If I have a caregiver available for my son with autism, I can get my steps in, no problem. If I need to wait until later in the evening, I don't always get my steps completed, but I always walk at least a few miles. I was shocked one night when I realized I had missed only one day of exercise in ten weeks. Some weeks, I was walking more than twenty-four miles. No wonder I needed new tennis shoes!

Walking allows me time to clear my head, listen to podcasts, think, and keep an eye out for the beauty in the everyday scenes outside. Plus, I'm alone. Hallelujah!

I always have my phone with me, so I've been documenting beauty as I walk. I've taken pictures of a tree's shadows stretched out on the sidewalk during the evening. I've snapped pictures of old tree stumps with hundreds of concentric circles. I've documented the intricacy of a white peony, bright red maple leaves amidst a sea of green, stunning zinnias in a flower garden near the sidewalk, and brown squirrels climbing trees. I haven't been trained in photography but taking these pictures and sharing them on social media brighten my mood. I even submitted some pictures to a local organization looking for photos for next year's calendar. A girl can dream!

My son with autism has gone back to school this fall, although he only attends Thursdays and Fridays. I cherish those days when I have more free time. In prior years, I would have purchased a donut or grabbed lunch but not now. Instead, I plan my me time first, which includes getting my exercise completed while my son is at school, going to the sauna, and eating whole foods.

I realize I am a better person and mom when I can get away from my family and relieve stress. Due to COVID-19, I don't take my health for granted. I'm not perfect, that's for sure, but I'm headed in the right direction. I'm turning fifty next month. I feel fabulous. I'm proud of who I've become at this age and how — after half a century — I've decided to put myself first.

— Tyann Sheldon Rouw —

18

Shinrin-yoku Is Good for You

Fresh air is as good for the mind as for the body.
Nature always seems trying to talk to us as if she
had some great secret to tell. And so she has.
~John Lubbock

I live in Los Angeles, so you'd think I go to the beach all the time. I would if I could, but it can take an hour to get from my lovely, rent-controlled apartment to the closest beach... on a good day. Getting back home? Count on at least two. On the flip side, my place is nestled inland in Los Feliz, home to Griffith Park, which is known for its vistas and hiking and equestrian trails.

Did I take advantage of all those wonderful trails? Nope.

My friend Donna lives very close to the beach, which means that she lives far from me. We both talked about exercising more. And then talked some more. We really talked a good game, but neither of us got any closer to working out.

Being a true friend, Donna didn't point out that I had a gym in my building but failed to use it. My roommate Craig used it daily but even his shining example didn't move me. I went once when it was raining and did a few minutes on the treadmill; once when I locked myself out and needed him to lend me his key; and once when I needed him to take pictures of me (I'm an actor) using the equipment for a role as a gym rat. (That's why we call it acting.)

Donna decided to take action. She volunteered to come to my neighborhood and go for a hike with me. It is a very big deal in LA if someone offers to brave the traffic and come to your neighborhood, so this meant that I had to do it.

The day came, and she found parking easily. To any Angeleno, that is a sign. This time, instead of just talking, we talked and walked, and talked and walked, and talked and walked some more. As we climbed, we felt one with nature. We were rewarded with marvelous city views from the helipad (where they fill helicopters' water tanks during fires).

Donna joked she was probably going to wake up really sore the next day and curse me out. We laughed. The fabulous hike over, we ate fish tacos at my favorite Mexican restaurant nearby. We were proud of ourselves. We had exercised, eaten healthy and had a great time.

At the end of this wonderful afternoon, I told her that I was going to try to hike more often. "The park is so close by, and I don't use it."

"Start small," she suggested. "Try to go twice or maybe three times a week. Otherwise, if you make your goal too big, you won't achieve it and you'll feel worse, which is the exact opposite of self-care."

The next morning, I decided to go for another hike. And, again, it was lovely. Fast forward to a few months later: I now start every day with a hike. I do a small, forty-five-minute hike when my schedule is busy and a monster hike that takes about two-and-a-half hours when I have more time. I almost never bring my phone. It's like my walking meditation. I think about things I'd like to write about, learn lines and appreciate the amazing views.

I bump into many of the same people. Sometimes, I see film crews, dog walkers, families and couples. They're enjoying their day. The cyclists are amazing going up those inclines.

Now I'm truly addicted to hiking. When friends come to visit, I invite them to go with me. Many of them don't want to. I mention that no one has ever not enjoyed it, but if they still decline, I don't force the issue. Instead, I go without them. Several of my friends have even started hiking when they're back home. The frugal side of me can't help but point out that it's free.

Daily exercise improves one's life. Ask Jose. I met him hiking. He explained that he had a new workout plan to help him lose 100 pounds. I offered to send him encouraging texts. A few months later, we met for coffee. I would not have recognized him. He had lost sixty-five pounds! He said he has more energy, is more social, and now spends time exercising with his niece and nephew. What a great gift to give his loved ones.

After my monster hike today, I had the energy to sit down and write this piece. I'm calmer and can have an occasional dessert without worry. Turns out, without realizing it, I've been practicing Japanese shinrin-yoku or "forest bathing" (in the sense of soaking in the environment, not skinny-dipping), spending time in the woods, truly appreciating nature. Shinrin-yoku has been proven to have all kinds of health benefits: reducing stress, lowering heart rate and blood pressure, and boosting the immune system. In 1982, Japan even made it part of their national health plan. Because much of my hike goes through wooded areas, I truly believe my daily forest bathing, breathing in the beauty of nature, has made me more creative.

As my super-in-shape (even by L.A. standards) roommate Craig always points out, the secret is to find an activity you enjoy doing. I always thank Donna for her life-altering suggestion that we go hiking. As she listened to me rave about hiking, she vowed to take up her favorite sport again: swimming. Her exercise regimen now includes several trips to the pool every week. A simple hike between friends turned into better self-care for both of us. Who knows? Maybe I'll even start meeting Craig in the gym for a workout.

—JC Sullivan—

Not Mad, but Madly Happy

*There is no greater agony than bearing
an untold story inside you.*
~Maya Angelou

As a child, I'd spent entire afternoons creating new worlds in my mind and giving life to characters I wished could be my friends. I'd written myself into my favorite stories so I could be part of them. My mind brimmed with all the ideas I had, and I often jumped from one story to another because I wanted to tell all of them at once. Writing was a part of me; it was who I was.

However, in high school I struggled with writer's block. By the time I was in college, I'd stopped writing entirely, even though the dream remained. I wanted to publish a novel one day. It was then that I read an interview with the Belgian writer Amélie Nothomb. She said she'd go crazy if she didn't write; she needed to do it to stay sane. Her words made me feel discouraged. She was telling me that I wasn't really a writer. I had failed already because I hadn't managed to work through my writer's block. I'd always loved writing, but the past few years proved that I could live without it. I wasn't a real writer.

Or so I thought. I tried again, and it was like feeling the sun on my skin, smelling freshly cut grass, or hearing snow lightly fall. I hadn't realized it, but I hadn't really been happy until I picked up my pen again. Writing was in my blood after all.

Jotting down a few lines was enough to wake me up and show me that I hadn't been truly happy, hadn't been truly living *my* life. I'd only been half smiling and now I was beaming.

In that moment, I realized that I really am nothing like Amélie Nothomb. I don't go mad if I don't write. Writing, to me, is like the embrace of a loved one: I can live without it if I have to, but life is so much more beautiful with it.

Only a few things make me as blissfully happy as writing. It is an infallible antidote to bad humour. I can start out grumpy like a cat in the rain, but a few furiously typed lines later, I'm as happy as a puppy with a new toy. It always works, whether what I write is complete rubbish or actually resembles something worth reading.

When I felt this contentment again, I couldn't help but wonder how I had let myself stop writing. What had made me give up something that made my soul sing?

At first, I thought it was because I hadn't had a choice: My college life had been one long to-do list, and it felt like there simply hadn't been any space left on it for something like writing. I hadn't had any time for reading either, another respite for me.

But then I thought again. Even though I'd always felt there weren't enough hours in a day, I'd still managed to find thirty minutes every evening to study Finnish in preparation for my exchange semester. And after college, when I had more time, I simply filled my days with other obligations instead of carving out time for what I loved and needed. Housework suddenly took longer. In the evenings, I was often too tired to pick up my pen and come up with a story. I could have started my day with half an hour of writing, but I didn't do it. I always found an excuse.

Ultimately, it came down to one thing: Life wasn't tearing me away from doing what I loved. It was me who consistently put writing on the bottom of my to-do list. I allowed everyday life to get in the way, and I didn't even put up a fight. Really, I didn't have the right to complain.

So, I decided to put writing on the top of my list. Every day, I snuck in half an hour of writing. If that meant putting off laundry to the next day, so be it. If it meant getting to work or going to bed late, so be it. If it meant no sport for today, so be it.

At first, I was sure that I would have to pay for this indulgence one way or another. Nothing that good could be free! I was sure I would quickly exhaust myself trying to catch up with the chores I left unfinished in order to write. But, miraculously, the opposite happened: I got much more efficient and, paradoxically, had more free time than before. Why? Because as soon as I gave myself a little bit of time each day just for myself, I felt more energized and slept better. My memory improved, too, and my creativity came back.

Effortlessly, half-hours devoted to writing stretched into hours. Before, I had been frustrated all the time because I didn't advance my writing projects. Now, every day was a step forward, and I felt great about it. Before, I only dreamt about being a writer. Now, I was one.

Reading a story in the *Chicken Soup for the Soul* series one day, I was inspired to submit a few stories. I didn't do it in the hopes they would get published — I'd read enough about rejection to be realistic — but to push myself with the imposed deadlines.

And then, something amazing happened. The first story I submitted was chosen for publication! When I got the e-mail, I screamed and danced around my kitchen table. I bumped my hip, but I didn't care. I'd never been so happy in my life! Not only had I finally embraced the writer in me, but I could call myself a published author.

That moment taught me that I must keep writing — not because I'll go mad if I don't, but because I want to keep being crazily happy like that.

— Gina Gutzwiller —

Accept Help

No Superheroes Here

*You owe yourself the love that you so freely
give to other people.*
~Author Unknown

I didn't expect parenting to be hard. Oh, sure, it's difficult for other people. I heard parents complaining all the time — kids are challenging, nothing is ever clean, there's not enough time in the day to do everything.

But that was "other people," and I knew I could handle it. How complicated could it be?

I'd always dreamed of being a foster parent, and finally my dream came true one summer afternoon. Even though we had requested only one child, the caseworker asked, "Could you take a baby and his eleven-year-old brother?" Of course, we could.

Two weeks after they moved in, their two-year-old brother joined us. They had placed him in a different home from his brothers; we had room to have all three boys together. We catapulted from caring for a few pets to being the foster parents of three boys.

I spent my days rushing from task to task, cleaning and making sure they had all they needed. I constantly organized our living room, which was suddenly full of toys, and picked up the path of destruction left in the boys' wake. Cooking and cleaning after meals and snacks seemed to take half of my day. I hardly ever sat; something always needed to be done.

A month after becoming a parent for the first time, I had lost seven pounds from my already slim frame. I didn't realize it, but I was hardly taking time to eat. During meals, I was making sure that the children had full plates instead of putting food in my own mouth.

They visited their biological mom for two hours a few times a week. I filled those hours with grocery shopping, meal planning, documenting information for our caseworker and the boys' attorney, catching up on our budget, and paying bills. There was never enough time in the day.

"I think we need a date," my husband told me one evening as I was falling asleep on the couch as usual.

"Mmmmm," I mumbled.

To have a date, we had to find someone with state approval to watch the boys. We didn't know anyone who met these requirements, and the state was dragging its feet on approving several friends and family members who had applied. We'd have to send them to a stranger; the idea of it sickened me. Though we had been strangers to the children only a few short months ago, the little ones cried when they left to go to visits. Sometimes, they even cried when I tried to go to the bathroom by myself. I couldn't contemplate leaving them, even for just a few hours.

I hesitated to ask the caseworker for respite care, although I was growing more and more exhausted with each passing day. Besides meeting the physical needs of the boys, there were medical and emotional needs. Both the little ones constantly clung to me. The older child could be defiant and angry one moment but have us collapsing in laughter the next. It was never quiet in our house; as an introvert, I felt overwhelmed.

The situation grew dire. My husband was becoming resentful, and I was growing more and more agitated, snapping over little things. Physical and mental exhaustion became the norm and rolling out of bed in the morning became a task I dreaded.

One night, it came to a head as my husband said firmly that he needed a break. Whether I "needed" one or not, we were going to take one. With tears rolling down my cheeks, I nodded, knowing it was true, although I didn't want to admit my weakness.

Our caseworker matched the kids with a respite provider right away. "It's a bit of a drive, but these parents have already adopted from foster care several times. They live on a farm in a big house with plenty of room," she assured me. "How long do you want the children to stay?"

"Well, maybe just one night?"

I could hear the concern in her voice. "I think you should do two nights. You haven't used respite yet, and I know things have been hard."

I nodded, barely able to respond. I knew she was right.

We drove an hour to get to the farm. A bright yellow house perched on a hilltop, surrounded by green grass, greeted us. Children poured out of the front door; I counted five of them.

The children introduced themselves, and within a few moments our kids became lost in a sea of toys and other kids their age. "Spider-Man!" shouted our middle child. Sure enough, one over-sized bedroom with four beds had Spider-Man on every sheet and pillowcase, along with posters on the wall.

"Yes, Spider-Man! This is the room you'll stay in," the mother cheerfully announced. Enraptured, both little boys let go of my hands and reached to touch the bedspreads. Within minutes, they were opening drawers and playing with toys.

I felt a sudden wave of relief wash over me, watching them play with smiles on their faces. Even our oldest was whisked away by a boy his age to take a tour of the house and grounds.

There were no tears from me or the children as my husband and I left the farm, and the car ride home was blissfully quiet. We spent the evening relaxing and spending time together. I slept late the next morning and spent the day enjoying the sunshine as I worked in my garden. The boys had a wonderful time and were thrilled to go back and visit with their new friends a month later.

Those three little boys are now my sons, and we've added two girls and two more boys to the mix since then. Asking for help is something I must keep re-learning as time goes on, but it's getting easier.

We've moved to be closer to family; now we regularly ask our parents to watch the kids so we can take date nights or even quick trips as a couple. We implemented "quiet time" at our house each afternoon so that everyone, including me, can have some alone time to read or do something they enjoy quietly. I wake early to pray and read before the rest of the house is awake, and I make exercise a priority for my mental and physical health.

I've learned to embrace rest. I don't need to work every second of the day; things don't have to be perfect. My house is not always as clean as I would like, and sometimes we eat frozen pizza for dinner. Sometimes, the laundry piles high, and sometimes I hide in my office to wring a few extra minutes of quiet out of my day. But embracing self-care and asking for help allow each day to be filled with love and laughter instead of anxiety and frustration.

— Brynn Mahnke —

Sharing the Load

*Be strong enough to stand alone, smart enough to know
when you need help, and brave enough to ask for it.*
~Ziad K. Abdelnour

"Daddy, I used the potty three times," said Patricia. She skipped to her father. He drew her into a hug and ruffled her honey-colored curls.

"What a big girl you are," he said.

"Isn't it great?" I said. "We won't have two in diapers."

A smile lit my husband's face. "And in all that time, I never changed one."

My mouth fell open. I hadn't noticed. How was that possible? I took a deep breath and put a hand on my waist. Our baby answered with a kick. *Don't worry. Daddy will change lots of your diapers*, I thought. Another kick signaled we were in sync. I took a breath and straightened my spine. I knew what I had to do.

"I'm going to register for the classes I need to finish my master's degree," I said.

"I thought we couldn't afford it," George answered.

"We can if I'm a graduate assistant."

"How will you take care of two children, attend classes, and work at the college?"

"I'll make it work," I answered. And I did.

Five weeks later, in the middle of June, I went for an interview for the position. I walked in with confidence, even though it looked like I had a watermelon under my shirt.

The interview was very professional. The supervisor looked more uncomfortable than me. "Those are all the questions I have," she said. "Is there anything you'd like to say?"

"Yes," I said. "You may have noticed I'm pregnant."

She relaxed. Now we could talk about the subject the law prohibited her from mentioning unless I did. "When is the baby due?"

"Any day now," I answered. "The library assistantship won't start until September. Joanne, another graduate student, will stay with us during the week to eliminate her three-hour commute. She'll watch my children during the fifteen hours I work. My courses are at night. My husband will watch and bond with the children while I'm in class."

She smiled. "You've got it figured out."

"I do."

"It won't be easy."

"I know, but it's something I really want to do."

"We'll let you know tomorrow," she said.

I got the job. The call came, as promised, on Friday. Sean was born two minutes after midnight on Sunday. And so began the busiest and most rewarding year of my life.

I'm a planner. I cooked and froze meals for easy prep when I worked. I made schedules. It wasn't enough. I needed to ask for help. When I did, my husband stepped up. I'd done all the housework and childcare without thinking about it. George hadn't helped because I hadn't asked. After I asked, I wondered why I'd waited so long. Maybe it was the smug satisfaction when Patricia said, "Mommy, does Daddy know how to read?" It was so much better to share the night-time story ritual I loved. George's help changed our daughter's perception.

I'd overheard Patricia talking to her dolls. "Dads go to work. Moms cook, wash clothes, and clean the house." Her narrow views changed. I smiled when her daddy doll washed dishes, and her mommy doll kissed the baby and said, "Mommy's going to work. I'll be back in four hours."

George did more than heat up meals; he developed a few dishes of his own that he proudly served. I'm not sure either of us knows how many of Sean's diapers he changed.

Sean didn't sleep through the night for a year. I'd get up to feed him and open a textbook while he nursed. I was always on the go: family, job, classes. "I'm doing this for me," I told myself when I was exhausted. It almost always gave me the boost I needed.

"Exams are coming up. I don't know how I'm going to Christmas shop," I said.

"I've got this," George said. My family loved the sweaters he bought and wrapped, and he knew just the right things to buy for the children.

George planned special outings with the children while I studied for my exams. I'd just made spaghetti when the call came to tell me I'd passed and earned my degree. I was so excited that I poured salad dressing on my pasta. We celebrated.

George brought both children to my graduation ceremony. I was proud and wiser. My biggest lesson didn't come from class. I learned that marriage could be a true partnership, and that it was better to ask for help than pretend I could do it all.

— Judy Salcewicz —

22

Recharging Batteries

*Sometimes, asking for help is the bravest
move you can make.*
~Author Unknown

Ten minutes to go and I can lock the shop's door behind me. There are still a few customers who can't decide what to buy, who test this perfume and then that one. One lady tests all the lipsticks on the shelf. Her friend is busy with the sunglasses. They must be tourists with lots of time on their hands. I have a fake smile glued on my face as I wait behind the counter for them to make up their minds. They walk out without buying anything. Now it is ten minutes past 5:00. They have wasted my time.

Sometimes I wonder if this is really what life is about. Working from 8:00 a.m to 5:00 p.m., I catch just a glimpse of the sunrise on my way to work every morning. I wish I could stand on that hill and wait for the sun to rise. To feel that isolation and listen to the birds welcoming a new day. It feels like life is slipping through my fingers without enjoying the little things in life that would make me happy.

Going home after a day's work isn't much relief. At home, a family is waiting for my attention. While preparing dinner, I put the laundry in the washing machine and take care of the pets. After dinner, it's time to wash the dishes while the rest of the family relaxes with their own activities. I wish I could do that.

My feet are tired. My body is tired. My soul is tired. I can't go on like this. It's my own fault that I don't make time for myself. I spoiled my family over the years by doing everything by myself. No time for a walk with the dog, no time to read a book, no time to just sit on my own and stare at nothing.

Even on weekends, I get up early to clean the house properly and do the shopping, while the family sleeps in. Only on Sundays do I make time for an afternoon nap, but that is sleep, not me time. I'm not doing something interesting or enjoyable when I catch up on sleep.

Why are women like this? I am one of those women who thinks my way is the best way. If I give a family member a chore to help with, I want it done *now,* not later, so I step in and do it myself. My frustration must be a pain for everybody around me.

I need serious time for myself, time to recharge my batteries and do things that will make me a better person. I'm an outdoor person, but I spend most of my time indoors.

A family meeting is the first step. During the meeting, I explain why I am grumpy and ask them what they think would solve the problem. Everyone gets a turn to come up with ideas for how they could help me achieve my goal to have at least one hour per day to do what I like.

"Hiring someone is not an option," I tell them. I don't want a stranger to invade my privacy. The family is open to practical solutions. "What about having everyone be responsible for cleaning their own room?" I suggest. "And what about taking turns to cook, do laundry and clean up after dinner?" Their reaction is quite positive. I create a chart with the days of the week and the chores, with the name of the responsible family member each day. There are four of us and five weekdays, so I offer to do each chore twice in the five days. I don't mind. I can already see that I will get an hour to myself every day after work.

A month has passed since the new rules in the house began. The plan is working perfectly with a few hiccups now and then but nothing serious. I am impressed by how willing my family is to make life easier for me. It gives us more time to spend together, chatting and laughing. I no longer feel like I am living a rat race.

For a month now, I have been able to put on my walking shoes after work, walk the seven kilometers up the hill with my dog and watch the sunset. On weekends, I admire the sunrise and sunset. Now I have something to look forward to when I close up the shop at 5:00 p.m — or a little after. Now, I don't mind if customers are lingering in the shop when it's time to lock the door and go home. My smile is no longer fake. My boss, Gloria, noticed that I look younger and healthier and have lost that extra bit of weight that was bothering me.

My soul benefits the most during the time I can spend on my own on the hill. Later in the evening, I've got time to do some reading and, lately, try out some writing. My body is recharged from the exercise, and my mind is relaxed from the alone time. The rhythm of nature energizes me. Now I look forward to each day, knowing that I'll have the time I need to recharge my battery. All I had to do was make it a priority and ask for the help I deserved.

—Jonet Neethling—

23

An Unexpected Gift

*Occasionally it's good to pause, take a moment
and remind yourself of the things in your life
that are just fine.*
~Robert Brault, rbrault.blogspot.com

"Any polish today?"

"No, thank you," I replied.

"Only in the summer, right?" Linda asked.

"Yep. Only the summer," I said.

My monthly pedicure appointments weren't always this nonchalant and casual, at least on my end. Now, I readily accept these appointments. I look forward to them, something I never expected. And it's not because of the opportunity to have my toes painted red like Elmo or blue like Cookie Monster.

In fact, it took me a while to accept that I can't cut my toenails anymore. It took me a while to acknowledge this fact without judgment, self-criticism, or sadness.

I didn't readily admit I couldn't take care of this particular aspect of my personal hygiene. Instead, I tried different positions and seating arrangements. I sat on the top of the toilet seat. I sat on the floor, alternating between having my leg straight out in front and having my leg bent. I sat on my bed and maneuvered my leg in front of me and then to the side of me.

But I just couldn't do it.

At first, it brought tears to my eyes. One more thing I couldn't do. One more way my body had failed me. One more way I was weaker and less competent than I used to be.

I live with an autoimmune disease, an invisible disability called undifferentiated connective tissue disease. My disease has overlapping symptoms of lupus, rheumatoid arthritis, and myositis. While I look fine on the outside, inside it means that each day I live with varying levels of pain, fatigue, and weakness in my legs, with my left leg consistently worse than my right.

I've lived with this disease for ten years, and over time it has impacted all areas of my life. I had to retire from my job as an elementary-school teacher. I can't walk with my son to our neighborhood bookstore; we drive. I can no longer wear pantyhose. And now I can't cut my own toenails.

I had never been a mani/pedi type of woman. Manicures and pedicures were reserved for special occasions such as our wedding and my college graduation.

And getting a pedicure had always seemed like a waste of money. My feet are ticklish. The idea of someone rubbing the bottom of my feet with a pumice stone produced anxiety not relaxation.

At first, I saw my monthly trips to the nail salon as a chore. But then something changed. I sat there in the chair while my feet soaked in warm, soapy water, and my toenails and cuticles were cut.

I realized I was missing a valuable opportunity. My pedicure didn't need to just be about my feet. While sitting there, I had been given a valuable gift — designated reading time.

I had to re-focus my thinking. Instead of fixating on what I couldn't do, I needed to celebrate what I could do — sit and read. There was nothing else that needed to be done right then. No rugs needed vacuuming; no plants needed watering; no bills needed to be paid. In that moment, in that nail salon, I could sit and read. Uninterrupted. Unapologetically.

And that's when I realized I had given myself some valuable me time.

Reading had always been one of my favorite pastimes. As a child, a trip to the library was a good day. A visit to the bookstore was an even better day because that meant a book (or more) that I could keep.

But life gets busy, and there's a never-ending to-do list. I tried to sneak in reading time while waiting for a pot of pasta to boil, in the dentist's waiting room, and arriving at my son's school ten minutes before the dismissal bell. But that was reading in bits and pieces.

I'd read at night, curled up in bed, eyes heavy, and fall asleep while reading. The next night, I'd have to backtrack, re-reading to remind myself what I had read the night before.

But a pedicure gave me precious time to read. Time in the middle of the day when I was completely awake and aware.

Once a month, I get my pedicure and I read undisturbed.

"You're all set," Linda says.

"Thanks so much. See you next month," I reply, smiling.

— Wendy Kennar —

24

Put On Your Mask First

*Rest and self-care are so important. When you take
time to replenish your spirit, it allows you
to serve others from the overflow.
You cannot serve from an empty vessel.*

~Eleanor Brown

After suffering through a year of serious physical deterioration, my husband Mike was diagnosed with amyotrophic lateral sclerosis (ALS). At the time, the doctor said all of the typically uplifting things. But no matter how cheerful a façade he put forward, we all knew what that wretched diagnosis meant: My Michael—a loving dad, and my husband and best buddy of almost twenty years—was going to die sooner rather than later.

We left the doctor's office clinging to each other tightly. My mind whirled with dire questions: How would we financially survive? How was I going to work while caring for a terminally ill husband? Would I even be able to care for him properly? How would this diagnosis affect our nine-year-old daughter, Kendall?

Not once did I think about my own wellbeing.

The next evening, I was preparing dinner when Mike came into the kitchen, tears rolling down his cheeks. In a quivering voice that brought tears to my own eyes, he implored, "Please don't put me away."

I held his face, looked directly into his eyes and, sounding stronger than I felt, resolutely replied, "You're staying here. I will care for you as long as I'm physically and medically capable. And if the time comes when I can't, I will get in-home caregiving." While making that stubborn declaration to both Mike and the universe, I silently affirmed that life would remain as normal as humanly possible.

My own health wasn't part of the equation.

Mike's illness quickly progressed. Our marriage quietly transitioned from husband/wife to patient/caregiver. When Mike could no longer sleep in a conventional bed, a hospital bed was moved into the living room for him, and I slept on the couch nearby. Still, Kendall's schooling and activity schedule remained intact. As the now sole breadwinner, I continued to work while my mother stayed with Mike. At night, I was on duty, which meant that I never got enough sleep.

Nevertheless, to the outside world, I appeared to be managing. I'd even convinced myself that I was coping well. I was caring for Mike, keeping the household financially afloat, and seeing to it that Kendall's childhood was as normal as possible. I did notice that I was catching more colds than usual, and I was having more of my once-rare migraines. However, I pushed through those annoyances. There was no time to do otherwise.

Self-care? Me time? No chance. I couldn't even manage sleep time. There was barely enough time for me to care for my husband and child.

I soon discovered that you can fool the outside world. You might even be able to temporarily fool yourself. Despite best efforts, however, the truth will always come out, even if the bearer of truth is your own body.

I'd planned a mommy-and-me day with Kendall, a once-regular activity that had become infrequent due to the illness. Feeling ever-so-slightly under the weather and reasonably chalking it up to fatigue, I'd gone into the bedroom to dress. My mother arrived and settled in to spend the afternoon with Mike. After greeting her, Kendall burst excitedly into our bedroom.

As she hugged me, I shrieked in terrible pain. The skin on the entire left side of my body felt as though it had sustained a third-degree burn, and inside everything hurt as well. Frightened, Kendall yelled for my mother to come in while I weakly limped back to the bed. I described my symptoms to my mother, who sat on the bed, gingerly took my hand and said, "If you don't get help into this house, I will." When I feebly protested, my mother rebutted, "You know how flight attendants instruct passengers to first put on their own oxygen mask if cabin pressure is lost? Well, you've lost cabin pressure. Put on your mask."

Sensing my mother's brook-no-argument tone, I immediately called our family doctor. After instructing me to come into the office, he said, "What you are describing sounds like shingles. There are about 200 different things that trigger shingles, but I promise I know what's triggered yours." I was indeed diagnosed with shingles, the primary cause being "exceedingly high levels of stress with little to no respite."

I was thirty-nine years old at the time of my diagnosis with shingles, an illness way more common among the elderly.

I'd fooled myself into thinking I could do it all. Something had to change — quickly.

I finally realized that whenever I thought about my own care, or carving out a little me time, I thought I was being selfish. But I wasn't. Taking that time for me is an essential component of physical and mental health. And not taking it doesn't mean that I'm better at managing everything; it means I'm failing. The best caregiver builds in personal time for the caregiver.

I arranged for in-home caregiving six days a week, twelve hours a day, allowing ample time to rest. We hired a once-a-week cleaning service. I began accepting meals from friends and family, and also help with getting Kendall to her swimming lessons, Hebrew school, and other activities.

Then I created pockets of time to nourish my soul — whether it was time spent with inspirational readings in the morning, an hour at a coffeehouse in the afternoon, or an early dinner with a girlfriend. Sometimes, it was something as simple as taking myself out for a quick lunchtime chicken-avocado salad and the newspaper. Combined with getting necessary help into the house, all these periodic activities coalesced and resulted in a refreshed, renewed and revitalized wife, caregiver, mother and woman.

Since Mike's passing, I've made "me time" a permanent part of my weekly schedule. Whether it's Zumba four times a week, yoga twice a week, daily meditation, or chatting with friends, I faithfully keep my appointments with myself… and without feeling selfish or guilty.

And I'm a better "me" for taking that "time."

— Carole Brody Fleet —

25

All Things Food

Taking care of myself doesn't mean "me first."
It means "me, too."
~L.R. Knost

I was visiting my sister and watched as my fifteen-year-old nephew, Ben, emptied the trash without being asked. "You're such a great kid," I told him. "Thank you for doing that."

He smiled. "The trash is my job. I'm ATT around here."

At my confused look, my sister Mandy explained that ATT stood for All Things Trash. "Emptying the trash has always been Ben's job, and sweeping the floor is Anna's job. Whenever some of the trash would spill out onto the floor, they'd argue about whose responsibility it was to clean it up," she said. "So, we came up with the acronym ATT to solve that problem. If it has anything to do with trash, no matter where it is, it's Ben's job."

I nodded. "That makes sense. I love easy ways to solve common problems."

A few days later, I was back home with my own family. I had a deadline for a huge project at work, and I was really feeling the pressure. When I'd picked up my son from school that afternoon, I'd popped into the grocery store to buy a rotisserie chicken for dinner. I figured that would buy me an extra hour to work on my project since I wouldn't have to cook that night.

Now, it was 6:00 p.m., and I was typing away, making good

progress. My kids were downstairs watching TV. My eleven-year-old son, Nathan, came into the den and said, "Mom, I'm getting hungry. Can you warm up the chicken now?"

"In a little bit," I answered without looking up from the computer. "I'm trying to work."

Ten minutes later, my older son, Jordan, came in to tell me that he too was hungry, and I needed to warm up the chicken. "I'll do it as soon as I'm at a stopping point," I said.

Fifteen minutes after that, my eighteen-year-old daughter, Julia, made the same request.

I exploded. "Every one of you is old enough to put a rotisserie chicken in the microwave," I nearly shouted. "You guys are watching TV while I'm working on something important. I would think you would realize that I'm busy and just take some responsibility."

Twenty minutes later, a paper plate filled with chicken and macaroni and cheese appeared on the desk next to my computer. I smiled sheepishly at the kids. "Sorry I yelled at you guys. I'm just so tired of being ATF around here."

"ATF?"

"All Things Food. It's my responsibility to plan the meals, shop for the food, cook the food, and then clean up the dishes afterward. If it's food-related, it automatically falls to me. And since we eat three times a day, it's a huge job. I don't want to yell at you guys again, but I'm overwhelmed right now, and I definitely could use some help."

Julia nodded. "We understand, Mom. When's your deadline?"

"In two days, and I don't know how I'm going to finish." Tears threatened as I thought about how much work I still had to do.

Jules looked at her brothers. "For the next two days, the three of us are ATF. Let's leave Mom alone and go make a plan."

I assumed their plan would be to order pizza and get take-out until my deadline was completed, and that was fine with me. Their plan wouldn't meet the food pyramid guidelines, but I didn't have time to worry about that. For the next two days, my family was on their own. I was taking a much-needed sabbatical from my ATF duties.

The next day, when Julia came home from her job at a local grocery store, she was carrying multiple bags of food. Her brothers helped her carry in several more from her car. In the past, I'd often texted her to bring home an item or two, but this was the first time she'd ever done our full shopping.

An hour later, Nathan literally tiptoed into the den to deliver my lunch to me. As he handed me a paper plate containing a turkey sandwich, some chips and apple slices, he smiled. "I hope your work is going well," he whispered and then tiptoed back downstairs.

Just moments later, he tiptoed back with a drink. "Sorry," he whispered again. "I forgot this part on the first trip."

I laughed, took a bite, and got back to work.

That evening, after several productive hours of work, I could smell something cooking. It actually smelled good.

Nathan tiptoed into the room and whispered, "Julia sent me to find out if you want to take a break and eat at the table with us or if you're going to eat up here."

I smiled. "I've gotten a lot done today. I'll eat with you guys."

When I sat down at the table, my kids were bustling around the kitchen. My husband, Eric, came in from work, took in the scene, and smiled at me. "How was your day?" he asked. "How's your project going?"

Over a surprisingly delicious dinner, I told my family how much more I'd accomplished that day because I didn't have to take care of anything but my work project. "Thank you for handling all the food today," I said to the kids. "It was a huge help."

The next day was much the same. Nathan delivered breakfast and lunch to me at the computer. Then, to my utter delight, I typed the last words on my project at 3:00 p.m., finishing hours before I thought I would.

I went downstairs, feeling lighter than I had in weeks. "I'm done, Jules!" I said.

She congratulated me with a hug.

"Since I'm finished, I can make dinner tonight."

She shook her head. "Nope, you've earned a break. Go read or take a walk."

My mouth dropped open, but I didn't argue. I curled up in bed with a novel I'd wanted to read for months. It felt divine. Three luxurious hours later, Nathan knocked on the door. "Dinner's ready," he said.

As I enjoyed a second dinner I didn't have to cook, my kids admitted that they had no idea how much work it was to keep our family fed.

"ATF is a huge job," Jordan said. "There were three of us, and it was still a lot of work."

"Mom, we decided that no one person should be All Things Food," Julia said. "I'm going to start doing the shopping, and the boys are going to take over the dishes."

"That leaves me with the actual cooking, which is the part I like," I said.

Our new plan to divide the ATF duties is working well. While I'm not proud that I yelled at my kids, I'm glad that I finally asked for help.

I've always felt that it was my job as a mom to take care of my family, but they showed me that it's our job to take care of each other.

Sharing the load has given me more time to read and rest. And taking care of my own needs makes me a better mom.

No matter who cooks dinner.

— Diane Stark —

26

Surviving and Thriving

A thriving new beginning can be and should be a
time for amazing engagement, growth, connections,
contributions, and amazing possibilities.
~Lee M. Brower

I turned and buried my face in my husband's chest after the somber doctor told us, "Your breast biopsy showed a malignant lesion." My mind flashed to my mother, who put everyone's needs before her own, contributing to her death at age forty only thirty days before Harry and I were married. I wasn't going to make the same mistake.

I pulled myself together and wiped my tears with the neatly folded hankie Harry always carried, and we listened to the plan the doctor laid out.

For six months, my days were filled with countless medical tests and doctors' visits followed by two surgeries and thirty-three radiation treatments. Fighting for my life was a long, difficult journey, as the medications and radiation made me violently ill. When a dye the doctor injected into my tumor during surgery left my skin blue, I could only laugh. I looked like a Smurf.

In the waiting period between surgery and the beginning of radiation, I had the opportunity to travel to see our daughters. Both girls were upset they couldn't be by my side during my battle. When I returned home to start radiation, I had to grant myself permission to accept the meals and help with household chores that poured in from co-workers and even complete strangers.

My faith helped me find inner peace, a positive attitude, and the inspiration to carve out time for daily prayer. On my worst days, my beliefs kept me moving forward and focused, helping me to stay strong. My heart was touched as my name was added to dozens of prayer chains, something I had done so many times for others. Now it was my turn to receive.

It was only natural that as a woman, wife, mother and grandmother, I always made others my main concern. Reversing that role to one of care-recipient was a difficult transition. For the first time in my life, I had to make myself a priority. My survival depended on it. I went from being a strong, take-charge person to gratefully accepting the help offered by friends and family.

My self-care included splurging on weekly massages that soothed my ravaged body and helped me relax, something that would contribute to my recovery. As a bonus, my masseuse, a breast-cancer survivor herself, and I became great friends. She gave me advice on how to boost my immune system and also showed me how to massage the affected tissue to avoid the leathery skin that can result from radiation exposure.

When the radiation gave me cellulitis and I had a severe allergic reaction to the antibiotic, the members of a great cancer support group helped me sift through alternative options. These extraordinary women never missed an opportunity to share their experiences and encourage me. I had become a member of a sisterhood to which I never imagined I would belong.

Once on oral maintenance medication, my body reacted with thinning hair and unbearable aches in all my muscles and bones. My survival-sisters supported and comforted me to work through the pain and resist the urge to give up, adding a suggestion that I include water exercise in a warm therapy pool to my self-care routine. It gave me comfort when these caring women reminded me that it takes a village to combat this invader, and I was not alone.

Another wonderful thing my support group taught me was not to miss any opportunity to live life to the fullest. With that lesson firmly in mind, I planned something special to celebrate my survival. Despite being exhausted, on the day of my last radiation session, I boarded a plane for Disney World to join my daughters and grandsons. After all, it's the place where dreams come true, and I couldn't think of a better way to celebrate being declared cancer-free.

Later, while in the Magic Kingdom, I laughed and then cried as Mickey and Minnie swept my grandkids, daughters, and me into a group hug. It was as if they knew it was a new beginning for me.

I had done what I set out to do! I had taken care of myself so that I could have more years of memories with my family. Ten years later, I continue to pass on my energy and optimism while remembering to carve out me time. I count my blessings every day while I cherish the anticipation of thriving in every precious moment yet to come.

— Terry Hans —

27

The Ladies' Breakfast Club

*I don't know what I would have done so many times in
my life if I hadn't had my girlfriends.*
~Reese Witherspoon

I saunter into Cliff's Place after traveling for forty minutes to the country restaurant chosen purposely for its central location. We've designated the round table for six in the back of the dining area as ours. The waitresses have come to know us well and have no problem when we arrive at 9:00 a.m. and don't leave before the lunch crowd arrives.

Six ladies are already seated and greet me like a celebrity. Hugs are plentiful. We squeeze in until we run out of room and pull another table over to make space for all of us.

Kathie shows up with her arm in a sling. Somehow, she managed to drive herself after shoulder surgery. Barbara hobbles in with a broken foot in a boot. A couple of members are missing due to traveling.

Over eighteen years ago, my co-workers Peg and Robin started the Ladies' Breakfast Club, longing for the kinship they missed after retiring. Who would have guessed that fourteen of us women from the telephone company would still be sharing our lives today?

I still recall my friend Sylvia's profound words to me at work. She said, "We are working every day here and see more of our co-workers than our families. We work to pay mortgages on homes we don't live in."

My lighthearted response had been, "My dog lives in the house."

Spending time with these women in the office environment created a sisterhood. One by one, we retired, leaving the office where we knew each other's husbands and spent time in one another's homes. Together, we attended friends' weddings, welcomed babies into the world, supported each other during loss, and enjoyed the feelings of knowing the same women for decades.

Ranging in age from sixty-four to ninety-two, we come from different backgrounds, live in various communities, and spend free time in dissimilar activities. Our common goal is to meet for breakfast on the second Thursday of every month from September to June.

Here we find freedom to be authentic without fear of judgment. We communicate our hardships and struggles, always remembering how nice it is that we are the same people, only a bit more weathered and wiser. This morning, we take turns updating the group with our latest news. Sylvia and Robin come eager to share their children's weddings and photos with everyone.

I arrive with a heavy heart, knowing this is a place I need to be. In the group, I will find understanding friends. It won't be necessary to open up and tell of the concern I feel for a very ill family member. Intimate conversations usually take place one on one. Several might be going on at once.

I listen intently to stories of those volunteering for nonprofit organizations. Others talk about gym classes and walking. Still others tell stories of children, grandchildren and great-grandchildren's accomplishments. Family photos are passed around.

Traveling is a constant topic, with someone always going on a cruise, touring a foreign country or spending cold winter months in a warmer climate. Several members offer tips and advice.

Talents vary, too. We have blooming artists, a trainer for show dogs, and a woman trying her hand at woodworking. My writing group has published a flash fiction book. Everyone is eager to look it over, and although I am not the best salesperson, I sell thirteen copies.

As I sip my third cup of coffee, I'm brought back in time to the telephone office where it all began, where together we faced sorrow and joy. When Peggy's son David was killed, I knew her pain because we had lost our daughter, Susan. And when Donna faced her battle with lung cancer, she was surrounded by caring friends ready to help.

These women reached out to me and prayed when my husband fell ill. After his funeral, they showed up and surrounded me with words of comfort and support.

We celebrated when Mary turned ninety years old. A birthday cake awaited her after a breakfast meeting.

The kinship among us continues. We have found a way to stay close — to share our lives.

— Phyllis Cochran —

Finding Time for Me

If you feel "burnout" setting in, if you feel demoralized
and exhausted, it is best, for the sake of everyone,
to withdraw and restore yourself.
~Dalai Lama

To pass time, I stared absently out the hospital window until my thoughts were interrupted. "When are we going home?" my husband Brian asked.

"I think you will be able to go home today."

"Good. I don't like it here."

Every night, when visiting hours ended, I dreaded having to leave him and most nights ended in tears — his and mine.

Today, after two weeks, I was determined to take Brian home. The doctor had signed the release document, but I needed to meet with the Palliative Coordinator before we left. She arrived and suggested we go sit in the outdoor garden and talk. She crossed her arms over an envelope nestled in her lap. Her friendly smile and demeanor were comforting. She started our conversation by asking about Brian. I explained about his diagnosis with terminal brain cancer seven months earlier, our life before and after the diagnosis, and my fears. I told her why I wanted to take Brian home and care for him. Before I finished, my tears welled up.

"It won't be easy," she said.

"I know," I said.

As she spoke, I listened with as much attention as I could muster. She described what being a caregiver would entail in the upcoming months. She reached out and placed her hand on my shoulder, and I cried. We sat in silence until I gained control. Then she stood, handed me the envelope, and said, "Good luck." I clutched the envelope to my chest and watched her walk back through the sliding glass doors. I took a deep breath, opened the envelope, and removed a book. Tears streamed down my cheeks as I stared at the title: *A Caregiver's Guide to End-of-Life Care*

I can honestly say that I did not fully understand what being a caregiver for a palliative person would entail. All I knew was that having Brian at home would allow visitors to spend precious time with him without the confines of visiting in a care facility. And my own time with him wouldn't be limited at all.

I waited until my emotions were in check and then went back to Brian's room. Within two hours, we were home.

Before going into the hospital, Brian was able to get into a wheel-chair, but now he would remain bedridden for the remainder of his life. I was able to position his hospital bed between the kitchen and living room, near a large window so he could look out.

Now that he was home, I wondered what daily life was going to be like.

The palliative doctor visited weekly, and more than once he said to me, "Remember to take care of yourself. Sometimes, the caregiver dies before the person they are caring for because of the stress and strain."

Time ticked by ever so slowly. Days grew into weeks, and I realized how true his words were with each visit. We had no family close by to help, so I wondered how I would make time for myself. I knew I was under strain, and both my body and mind were fatigued. I tried to put on a brave face when the doctor was at the house, but in truth I was struggling.

One day, I stood at the window as Brian slept, watching as the doctor drove away. I leaned against the kitchen counter, holding myself up by my elbows. I was weary, and the weight of it was crushing me. A good night's sleep was difficult as I kept one eye open, and my ears perked for any noise from Brian. It was catching up with me.

I was startled by the feeling of a cold, wet nose on my leg as Danny nudged me. I looked down into the gentle black eyes of our Border Collie — eyes that melted my soul. I knew she felt my sadness. Those kind eyes yearned to be the centre of my attention.

How do you find time for yourself when you have a twenty-four-hours-a-day, seven-days-a-week commitment to care for a loved one? How do you put yourself first? I was scared to leave Brian's side in case something material in his medical condition changed. Most days, I was overwhelmed with decisions and the weight of the situation. I wanted my husband and my life back. I tried not to think of what the future held.

I lay awake at night with the doctor's warning to care for myself swirling in my mind. I knew it was important, but I couldn't envision how I could change my current situation. Miraculously, a solution came to me one night while I slept. In the morning, I searched several private healthcare agencies and was successful in hiring a university student to be a visitor for Brian. She was contracted to come to our home for four hours weekly, which became my salvation.

I had found a way to have free time, but what would I do? Looking at our golf clubs, I realized that golfing would allow me to be outdoors, get exercise, and let my mind relax. I knew that I had found a way to recharge my batteries!

I chose the golf course in a national park just fifteen minutes from our home. I experienced a sense of freedom every time I walked from the parking lot to the first tee box. I savoured the fresh air as I walked the fairways and enjoyed seeing the deer and rabbits that called the course home. Ducks wandered from the ponds when I approached and squawked to tell me I had broken their solitude. On lucky days, I saw herds of bison that roamed in the park. I lived in the moment and relished my surroundings. I had been given a true gift of time. I was finding strength, both physically and mentally. Each week when I returned home, I felt rejuvenated and ready to face what lay ahead.

The timeout was beneficial for both my wellbeing and Brian's.

No one knows what it is like to be a caregiver until they are faced with the situation. It is difficult when we're immersed in the situation. Many days, I felt hopeless and alone. I felt guilty about asking for help. I was fortunate to find a solution that allowed me to give back to myself. I know not all caregivers are so lucky.

When I reflect on my months caring for Brian, many things come to mind that could have made that journey easier for me. If you know someone who is a caregiver, I encourage you to reach out to them. Give them the gift of time for themselves. Offer to come and clean the house, cook a meal, do the laundry, get groceries, or offer to sit with their loved one so the caregiver can take some time out. If the caregiver has children, offer to take the children for a sleepover, out to a movie, or to the park. Young people need time away just as much as the caregiver. Be there as a shoulder to cry on or just to listen when they need to share. Be the most supportive friend you can be. I guarantee that you will feel better for it.

— Wendy Portfors —

Self-Discovery

29

Chicken Soup for the Soul

Running the Race for Me

*Respect, love, and value yourself. Always remember
to be good to yourself by taking care of yourself.*
~Stephanie Lahart

I had never been this girl. Waiting for a guy. Taking the route home from campus to pass his house. Checking his social pages to see if he had moved on. But I had not taken this break-up lightly. After a two-year relationship, I received an "It's not you, it's me" message while I was studying abroad in London.

While the official break-up was only a month fresh, we had been on and off for the past year. But I was twenty, and he was my best friend, and I had made many of the mistakes in the relationship, so I'd held on.

My friends and family were concerned about how wrapped up I was in winning him back, now. I'd become obsessed, and I stopped taking care of myself. Less exercise, more partying. They intervened, and that only served to convince me that if I worked on myself, Chad would come back.

I signed up for a half-marathon.

I had been a runner in high school — quite good, actually. But with a pushy coach and high expectations, running became unfun.

The farthest I had ever run was five or six miles, and, even then, it had been years.

Now I thought that if I trained for half a year and ran a half-marathon, I'd win back the love of my life.

After a few weeks, I noticed my energy growing and my attitude changing. The longer runs became escapes for me. I would start on Temple's campus and run over to Northern Libs and then down to Center City. My turning point was South Philly for my longer runs, which would take about an hour and a half. That time was focused on working through problems, listening to music, and seeing the city in a way one can't experience from a car.

It was a routine, and the more I focused on running and getting faster, the less I focused on Chad and winning him back.

As the fall semester began, I wanted to further my skill, so I began lifting weights. I carried three jobs going into my senior year, so it was tough scheduling time for runs and lifting, but I reminded myself how crucial this was for my growth. So, I lifted twice a week at 6:00 p.m.

To my dismay, Chad also lifted during that time.

He was hard to avoid because we were only feet from each other. I couldn't stop talking to him each time I was at the gym. It was always the same conversation on his end. "I love you, but I am not ready to get back together yet." I was a girl possessed and held onto every word, thinking it would happen any day now.

So, every time I left the gym, I was in tears. I couldn't understand how we could be so in love but still be apart.

Since I was getting distracted, I needed to recruit help. My next-door neighbor, Sam, went to the gym often. If I went with him, I would have someone to stop me from talking to Chad. So, I pitched him the idea, and he accepted.

Sam, an avid lifter and all-around athlete, promised to be the gatekeeper between Chad and me and keep me on course. Plus, I figured that if I avoided Chad, it would only confuse him.

Meanwhile, I was getting faster and I was looking forward to my daily runs. They gave me time to think, reflect and pray. In college, so many things pull you in different directions that you can feel overwhelmed. You focus on school. Then work. Then internships. Then friends. Then a social life. It never stops. But when you sign up for a race, it forces you to focus on running. And running challenges you. It's an independent sport, so you can only focus on YOU.

With the race only a month away, I decided the Homecoming 5K would be my first chance to see how far I'd come. With the Homecoming game the day before, I told myself I would hang with my friends and then get to bed early for the 7:00 a.m. race.

It was a wild day of reflecting on our final year. Honestly, I forgot about Chad. My friends, my neighbors... They were my family in college, and I felt I was ready to move on after eight months.

As I left the parking lot before the race, I ran into Chad. At first, I wanted to cry, and then suddenly I didn't care. So, I told him that I didn't want to get back together anymore, and I was okay. Sam looked on and then hugged me after Chad left.

"You've gotten stronger," he said. He was right. I was different. I found time to work on myself, and I grew in a way I never imagined. I even came in third among females in the race.

A month later, Chad was at my half-marathon. Two weeks earlier, he had asked me to get back together. But I declined. I had found something that I needed: belief in myself. Being on my own. Running a race where I'm in my own thoughts and not motivated by someone else.

Mentally, it was one of the most difficult things I had ever done (until I ran my first marathon).

You know who else was there? My now boyfriend Sam. And he was there for many more races. He did miss some races, but that was okay. I was running these races for me and no one else.

— Amber Curtis —

30

A Lost Librarian

Do not dare not to dare.
~C.S. Lewis

My simple life consisted of books, a sassy cat, and a glass of wine every evening on my patio. Occasional dinners with friends kept me from being a total shut-in.

Was this to be my entire existence? A vague sense of unease settled over me. It might be time to get out of my comfort zone or risk never truly living. My mother used to say, "You don't regret what you did but what you did not do." Honoring her philosophy, I would not let fear win.

I realized that I couldn't remember the last time I had done something just for me. I existed to help others. I volunteered at elementary schools and conducted outreach programs for the library. Previously, I had volunteered at animal shelters and senior centers. I often answered "yes" to outings with friends and family when I really wanted to stay home and relax. I worried what people thought about me. I craved constant approval.

Finally, I understood I was not responsible for everyone's happiness. I needed to set personal boundaries. "No" is just a word. It was time for me to use it.

I asked myself, "Where is the one place I would go first?"

Greece popped into my mind. I grabbed my laptop and began researching tours. A couple of keystrokes and glasses of wine later, I had booked a mainland tour. In a few months, I would fly to Greece all by myself.

The night before my big adventure, "what-ifs" crowded into my brain in the dark hours. All my friends and family were impressed with my bravado. I could not wimp out now. I had to go.

"Suck it up, buttercup!" I exclaimed to myself.

Off I went with my carry-on case. We flew across the Atlantic in the dead of night. A huge jet crammed full of vacationing families and senior citizens headed to cruise ships. This fifty-six-year-old retired librarian had actually gone through with it!

After a long, sleepless flight, I lurched off the plane into the steamy airport. Foreign languages blasted my ears as the jet lag hit me. But even that couldn't diminish my excitement. My Greek adventure beckoned.

I spotted a driver holding a sign with my name on it. I pinched myself to make sure I wasn't dreaming. I was now one of those debonair women seen in airport posters: an international world traveler.

The car sped through Athens in the blinding sunlight. Delicious smells, crowded sidewalks and colorful graffiti swirled around me. My head almost burst from sensory overload. Excitement vied with trepidation. I would meet the tour group the next night. Until then, I would be alone.

The next day, I hit Athens on foot with my cellphone and a wad of euros. This was my time. I would go where I wanted when I wanted. I would buy any and all souvenirs that called my name. I wandered the cobblestone streets without a plan. I stopped at a café for a glass of wine and an authentic Greek gyro. I window-shopped in the plaza. I had tried to learn Greek and agonized over the difficult language tapes. In the end, I only mastered about twelve words. I fretted about offending the locals with my limited knowledge and bad accent.

I meandered through a sun-dappled market where I found a stall of colorful, handmade scarves. I mumbled my new Greek phrases, worried I would offend the local women. Grateful smiles and kind encouragement met my attempts. My confidence grew as "please," "thank you," and other phrases flew from my lips at each new stop.

Taking a chance, I turned down a narrow alley lined with flower-filled window boxes. I strolled by ancient, whitewashed walls and lounging street cats. After an hour, I realized I was lost in downtown Athens. My trusty cellphone mapped my way back to the hotel. I felt empowered. I was nailing this traveling alone.

Later that evening, I rode the elevator to the hotel roof. My heart raced, and my palms sweated. I was nervous about meeting my travel companions. I had no idea what to expect. I took deep breaths and attempted to relax. Would I fit in?

I was the first to arrive at our meeting place in the open-air bar. A spectacular view of the Acropolis caught my eye. I started to breathe a little easier. Our intrepid local guide, Vassia, welcomed me with a huge smile and a friendly greeting. I settled around the table with a sigh, a glass of crisp white wine and a nighttime view of The Classic City. This was the life.

As other tour members sauntered in, a realization dawned. I was not the only solo female traveler, but I was the only American. I hadn't known the tour group was run by an Australian company. There was one cheery couple from England, but the other ten people were Aussies. Their warmth and acceptance enveloped my grateful soul.

Vassia made us each feel important and heard. This was her very first tour experience. She grew up in the Greek tourism industry and had traveled the world. A dynamo, she wrangled with city cab drivers, demanded immediate service at local tavernas, and waltzed into our accommodations with calm authority. Her organized positivity kept us moving along at a brisk pace.

I turned fifty-seven on the trip. Vassia remembered my birthday with a special Greek sweet bread. We devoured a delicious meal at a local taverna, where she and the waiter sang the Greek version of "Happy Birthday." The dynamic Aussies then sang their traditional birthday song loud and proud. I have never had a better birthday. For the first time in many years, it was all about me.

This trip was a mile marker in my life, one of spectacular vistas, incredible food, and warm people. Greece stole a piece of my heart. I felt intense gratitude for Vassia, who always made me feel safe and nurtured. The Aussies rounded out this experience with their adventurous spirit and upbeat "no worries" attitude.

Traveling alone empowered me to become a brave new woman—one who walked through fear to find a greater sense of self. I learned to focus on making time for me a priority. Now, I confidently say "no" to an event or project I don't want to handle. I no longer make excuses or feel guilty. True friends and family will love me no matter what.

I am fueled with a sense of purpose and vigor. When self-doubt creeps back in, I look back and remember that I climbed the slick marble stairs to the Acropolis. I hiked up thousands of precarious mountainside steps in the monasteries of Meteora. I got lost in Athens and found my way home.

Traveling memories have become my meditation. They help me survive the chaotic and unsure world we currently live in during the pandemic. We cannot control the future, but we can grab our laptops and a glass of wine and start planning an adventure. We can only dream them for now, but one day the world will open back up. I will be waiting.

—Lori Shepard—

31

The "Me" That I Am Left With

You find peace not by rearranging the circumstances
of your life but by realising who you are
at the deepest level.
~Eckhart Tolle

Ken and I planned to grow old together. We were a team, the two of us. Two young, gay men growing up in a small, decidedly conservative town, we had a lot in common. Plus, we had weathered storms, times when we wouldn't speak — and times when we would speak but would have been better off not doing so. We had been through a lot.

After so much, it seemed that we were finally together for the long haul. That day at the apartment, we joked about growing old together. Ken described it in great detail. "We will end up in an old folks' home, and I will still be trying to be sexy." He dramatically posed with his hand on his hip, laughing at the thought of, as he put it, "being all sags but still trying to seduce." I could see Ken doing that.

"But what about me?" I asked. "What will I be doing?" I was hesitant to ask this question. I was well aware that I didn't have Ken's good looks, and I wasn't sure if that meant I would have so interesting a future. Perhaps Ken would predict that I would, with my proven cleverness, be like a sort of mafia don on the geriatric ward. I could just picture it: "If you want that bedpan delivered PRONTO, you ask Jack to fix it for you." With this thought in mind, I looked at Ken hopefully for some such answer.

"You? Oh, you'll be feeding your lunches to the cats that gather under our room's window."

Deflated, I managed to comfort myself with the thought that, at least, I would have Ken there. If I was certain of one thing, it was that we would grow old together. The fact that he saw that future for us made me happy. I would be happy to tag along on the wild ride of life by his side.

However, only one of us is left to grow old. Ken became one of the many victims of AIDS, losing his battle with the disease just one year before the cocktail of drugs that might have saved his life became available. Ken was hardly the only person in my life lost to AIDS, but he is by far the most significant. Losing him, I found that I didn't know myself anymore.

Everything in my life was related to Ken. Everything made me think of him. If I wore a certain shirt, I remembered a time when I was wearing it and he was by my side. If I was talking with a friend, I waited to hear him interrupt and tell me that I was being snob-bish — something he often did. In everything, there was Ken. It had been "us," a team, and now I was having a hard time being a team of one. I didn't like being "me." I wasn't even sure who "me" was.

The first years after his death, I sought him out, to somehow resurrect his ghost. And that ghost haunted me in music, television, even in the soda I drank. "You know that stuff is poison. That's why you look like you just stepped out of Auschwitz." I longed for Ken's reproof, even with the attached comment about my appearance. I wanted "us" back again.

But in the end, I only went home with me and woke up with me. One day, feeling overwhelmed with loneliness for Ken, I decided that I had to do something. I was someone before I ever knew Ken. What was that person like, the "pre-Ken" me?

It certainly wasn't easy. But, like most people, I turned to my roots during such difficult days. Being Jewish wasn't really something I shared too much with Ken. He had Iberian roots that traveled deep into a glorious Castilian past. His lineage was linked with aristocracy, castles, and knights who defended Christendom for the Spanish sovereigns.

I was descended from German Jews who became, in America, part of the "Dixie Jews" of the Old South before traveling to California after the Second World War. As for me, the only "south" I knew was Southern California, and the assimilation practiced by previous generations left me aware of, but detached from, those roots. The German-Jewish ancestors who traveled the southern states, peddling their wares, were remote, but they were the only resource I had to turn to.

And to them I turned, my lifeline in time of need.

I pulled out the stored-away items that represented this past, these ancestors. Looking over the prayer book — fading, a century old, printed in Vienna — I saw the Hebrew characters with their English translation: "Form of prayer for the festival of the New Year, according to the custom of the German and Polish Jews, 5660–1900." And so, placing the worn kippah upon my rather bald head, I began where so many people who find themselves lost begin — with a head bowed in prayer.

As it happened, Rosh Hashanah would begin at sundown, the start of the days of awe, the days of repentance before Yom Kippur, the Day of Atonement. And I had much to repent for. Ken was not with me, but I owed it to him to live on as he could not. I owed it to *myself* to live on.

So, many years later, I recognize "me" once again. I try to live so as to exemplify the best in "Yiddishkeit," the quality of being a Jew. I aim to be a mensch, although I still have a long way to go. I have found my secret of joy, and it lies in the knowledge that I am one of the chosen people — not chosen for any favor, as many think the term means, but chosen for the responsibility to promote love, even if it means being the target of someone's hate.

In losing Ken, I lost a world that I will never get back. But, being left with "me," I can take all the love that I am no longer able to shower upon Ken and water the world that is still here with me. I think there is no better way to honor him and live my best life at the same time.

And somewhere in the past, I think there is an ancestor who looks very much like me, and who, with head bowed in prayer, asks to be remembered. Looking in the mirror, I catch a glimpse of him and thank him for the lifeline given in my time of need. I thank him for being part of me.

—Jack Byron—

32

What Do You Need, Son?

In suffering, we find our truest selves.
~Jessie Burton

"What do you need?" My dad always asked me this question when I was sick or feeling down. He would sit next to me, put his hand on my head, listen to my request, and then do his best to provide what I needed. I never responded with a grandiose request. Most of the time, I needed more quiet space, some hot soup or an extra blanket. What gave me most warmth, however, was that someone had taken the time to listen to me.

Even when he moved overseas, he was still able to enquire compassionately about my health and well-being via a phone call. My dad always wanted our family to enjoy ourselves and be well taken care of. He had had a troubled upbringing, and his family hadn't provided that support to him, so he was determined to offer this caring attitude to us.

I spoke to him one day as he told me about his plans to visit Japan. He was like a little boy who was excited to go on another adventure. He wanted me to come, and I could not help but get caught up in his exuberance.

The next day, I received a phone call from my mum at the hospital. Time stood still as I listened to her words. Two days later, he was gone.

The following year was a blur. Christmas was tough. His birthday was tough. All of it was tough. I found it hard to accept the reality of his loss, which led to a maelstrom of emotions that overwhelmed and drained me. I felt sad, lonely and adrift.

A simple phone call from him would have encouraged me to take better care of myself. Why could the person who would have helped me the most, whom I really needed, not be here for me?

Others tried their best to support me, but they could only offer unsolicited advice: "You need to take better care of yourself, and this is how you do it," "Don't feel like that; feel like this." "This is what you need." Why could no one ask me how I felt or what I needed?

If there was no one to help me, maybe I could do my utmost to help others. I decided to throw myself into work that had real purpose. I volunteered, took training courses, and spent every waking hour helping those with chronic health conditions, anxiety and grief.

But this work took a toll on me. I was exhausted, both by the emotional turmoil of my dad's passing and the physical demands of helping so many others. I felt like I had no time to breathe.

One excruciatingly painful and tiring day, I collapsed onto my couch and lay there almost comatose, zoning out to the trees swaying in the breeze. That's when I heard it, almost imperceptible at first, but then quite clearly, "What do you need, Son?"

"I need you, Dad," I replied.

There was no answer.

I continued to lie there, tears in my eyes, looking out at the blustery autumnal day, when again I heard that same voice, carried by the wind. "What do you need, Son?"

I stopped and took a deep breath.

What did I need?

I realized that whenever my dad would ask me what I needed, what he really offered was the space that allowed me to answer him. He was not here anymore, but I could still respond to his question.

I told him that this upcoming winter, I needed some time for myself, away from everyone. A time to reflect, write and be quiet. I wished he could have organised it and put together a box of all my favorite things to give me comfort on this retreat of mine, but he was not here to do so.

It was enough. This pain was enough. This tiredness was enough.

I summoned up some strength and scoured the Internet, eventually finding a cabin in the forest that I could rent for a week. Then I started to fill a box with some of my favorite books, mementos and comfort foods. I filled another box with memories of my dad, such as his old sweater and some letters I had written him. He would be coming on this self-care retreat with me.

And that winter, that's exactly what I did.

I spent my days in solitude, receiving the quiet I needed, looking out into nature, writing, reflecting, eating nourishing foods and finding the comfort I had so yearned for.

It was what I had so desperately needed.

I had been able to nurture myself, while being mindful of my grief and loss.

On the final day of my retreat, I sat looking out at the moss-covered trees and the falling rain. Their presence brought me comfort. Once again, I heard an echo on the wind. "What do you need, Son? What do you need?"

"It's okay, Dad," I replied. "I got this."

— Ankit Raghuvir Rao —

33

Letting Go of the Reins

The only journey is the one within.
~Rainer Maria Rilka

I clutched the seat under me as the ATV lurched to life, bouncing me into the air. There were no doors, rails, or seatbelt — nothing to keep me from flying off the roaring machine. I'm sure my knuckles were white, but my hands were tucked into gloves to keep them from getting frostbite.

A bookish Manhattanite, I'd traveled solo north of the Arctic Circle to the Swedish Lapland. I was there ostensibly to connect with my heritage, but more so because I didn't want to look back on my fortieth birthday as the day I attended another vendor meeting in the office. I needed to break free from my careful life — to be pushed out of my comfort zone. I felt an urgency to live life to the fullest, and so I answered the call of the wild.

Apprehensive yet eager to take the reins in life, I booked a Husky sledding tour. When I arrived at the dog compound, the pack of wolf-like creatures licked their lips from inside their massive chain-link cages. Their long tongues rolled out like a red carpet from a curtain of pointy teeth. Their piercing eyes seemed to see all, even anticipating movements. They were intelligent dogs, happy yet fierce. Their handlers, all men, seized them by their collars, directing them to one long metal chain that lay on the ground. The dogs and I sized each other up.

I'd spent weeks agonizing over selecting the "perfect" Husky sled-ding tour, trying to convince myself that I wouldn't injure myself or the dogs on the journey. I hadn't driven a car since moving to New York City more than a decade earlier, hadn't ridden a bike since I was a teenager, and doubted my ability to steer a pack of energetic creatures over the frozen Torne River as the website had described. What if I steered them into a tree? What if they stopped in the middle of the river and the ice began to crack under us?

I considered sticking to a tour of the Icehotel. I considered playing it safe. Then I remembered the promise I'd made to myself to take more risks and chase my dreams in the year leading up to my milestone birthday. I decided to book the dogsled tour. When I landed in Kiruna, though, I got a call that there wasn't enough snow for the sleds. We'd have to take the dogs out on something called an ATV instead.

The fluffy chain gang now waited as I struggled into multiple layers of clothing and then maneuvered my way onto what looked like a mini monster truck. At least I'd have a lot of extra padding if I fell off this open vehicle.

The pack of Huskies erupted in a cacophony of barks and howls as we took off, curving out of the driveway of the dog compound and hitting the open road. I tried to appear nonchalant as I bounced out of my seat when we hit a pothole. I plied my guide with questions. His American accent giving him away, he was clearly not one of the indigenous Sami people. How had he ended up north of the Arctic Circle on a Husky compound? He intimated he was in it for the thrill, and even as the wind whipped my face, I sensed he was holding back for my benefit. His ease at the wheel and frenetic energy suggested that he liked to race, to push the yapping dogs to their highest speed. I craved that audacity to chase adventure, but only had the bravery to do it in the form of a neatly curated vacation.

We sped down a long, straight road, the meager snow crunching under our tires. I was vigilant, looking for turns and hazards so I could prepare. We came upon a tiny bridge. It felt less like a connector and more like a dividing line. I was the reluctant heroine clinging to safety, but my driver plowed over the bridge, crossed the threshold, and we embarked on our journey into the unknown.

The dog compound was no longer in view. Where would this road take us? My question wasn't just about the jolting ride. I pondered my career, my relationship, my life. A vast stretch of wild opened before us. Tall conifers created a tunnel of trees. My faux-fur hat slipped low on my head from all the jostling, and I pushed it up out of my eyes to search past the thicket of trees where hay-colored grass fought through the patchy snow in the near-barren flat land. Between the tree branches, nature lay bare. Exposed.

I yearned to catch a glimpse of the native wildlife — the serene moose, the sly arctic fox, the magical reindeer. These creatures seemed straight from a storybook, but the landscape was brutally quiet. I was searching. I was becoming more like the Huskies, all senses alert, eager for adventure.

I strained my eyes as far as they could see so I would know what the future held. The vantage point between road and sky merged and became one. Snowy street met milky-white sky. Perhaps the earth and the heavens were one. Perhaps life wasn't so much about tightening the reins but letting go and trusting the adventure. Perhaps we even need a little inclement weather, the cold, the slippery snow, to experience the joy of soaring. I was ready for more.

— Stephanie Nikolopoulos —

34

Alone at the Kabuki Baths

*Spending time alone in your own company reinforces
your self-worth and is often the number-one way
to replenish your resilience reserves.*
~Sam Owen, Resilient Me: How to Worry Less
and Achieve More

A visit to the Kabuki baths in San Francisco's Japantown is one of my favorite ways to unwind. I go with one or more of my friends — Pat, Diane, and Sally — for a soothing soak in the hot tub followed by a dry sauna, steam room, and salt rub. We whisper inside and then have a long chatty visit over a meal afterward. We go on women-only Wednesdays, Fridays, or Sundays, usually in the evening. To me, it's the perfect ladies' night out.

One Wednesday in May, Pat and I agreed to meet at the Kabuki at 6:00 p.m. I arrived early and parked near the entrance, just as Pat, sounding stressed, called to cancel. Her son was sick.

I was disappointed. I'd arrived anticipating relaxation and social interaction. Suddenly, I faced an evening alone. I considered doing something else instead — maybe dinner or a film. But the thought of a solitary meal or movie didn't appeal to me. I called another friend, but she was unavailable. In the end, I decided since I was already there, I might as well make the best of it and go in.

I opened the wood-framed doors to the Kabuki Springs & Spa and stepped inside. It felt odd checking in alone — walking the softly lit, carpeted hallway with its display of fragrant bath and hair-care products, turning right at the statue of Buddha, and then entering the locker room. There I undressed, secured my possessions in a locker, slipped on acupressure sandals, wrapped myself in a fluffy white towel, and entered the main bathing room heading for the showers… in silence. In fact, the only words I spoke to anyone during my three hours at the spa were "Thank you" when I received my locker key and when an attendant brought fresh tea.

I began by showering in a Western-style stall, helping myself to cucumber bath gel, and rosemary shampoo and conditioner from dispensers on the wall. When I stepped, towel-wrapped, from the shower, I stood a minute looking around.

It was early evening. The bathing room, an oasis of rest and relaxation, was half-empty at dinner hour. Nearby, women sat on traditional wooden bathing stools, lazily soaping themselves and rinsing with flexible handheld hoses. Across the room to my left was the dry sauna, with the steam room to its right. A handful of women soaked in the spacious, tiled hot tub beside me, conversing in whispers. Others rested, eyes closed, on teakwood benches.

Lulled by the sound of water — bubbling, dribbling, splashing, flowing — I began to relax and enjoy myself. Since I was alone, there was no need for whispered consultations. Without the distraction of being social, time slowed down.

In the dry sauna, my breathing slowed as my stress and tension drained away. When I left the sauna, the air in the main room felt cool against my skin. I submerged myself to my shoulders in the one-hundred-four-degree hot tub, half-floating, letting the heat permeate. Later, I sipped jasmine tea and then rested on a bench with cucumber slices on my eyes.

I worked my way to the steam room. The hissing steam was as thick as coastal fog, and the 120-degree heat so intense I could hardly breathe. Almost immediately, sweat poured down my face and stung my eyes. I stuck it out for several minutes — long enough to scrub my skin with salt before rushing from the room to the cold plunge where I submerged myself to my chin. Then I alternated between steam and cold until my blood rushed to the surface, and every inch of my skin tingled.

When I finished bathing, I stood squarely on my feet, arms stretched high over my head, raising my rib cage, straightening my spine. Lowering my arms to my sides, I breathed slowly and deeply. My shoulders relaxed. I felt calm.

Dressing to leave, I felt so clean, almost sterilized. My skin was infant-smooth, every pore clean and tight. I sighed with pure satisfaction. My entire body felt vibrant and alive.

At 9:00 p.m., I turned in my key at the front desk and left the Kabuki baths. When I stepped outside, the wind had died down, and the mild evening air felt deliciously cool against my skin. Bathed in moonlight, I was so relaxed that I practically floated as I walked up the street to my car. I had worried that my evening would be ruined, but going alone made it a whole new experience.

— Lynn Sunday —

35

A Case of Shaken Identity

Who in the world am I? Ah, that's the great puzzle.
~Lewis Carroll, Alice in Wonderland

I'd always known I was the daughter of an Italian American father and a mother descended from British, French, German, Irish, and Native American ancestors. A truly American blend. But curiosity about that last ancestor led to my undoing when I discovered that I am not who I thought I was.

As my sixty-eighth birthday approached, my husband asked what he could give me. I have all the "things" I've ever wanted, so it's hard to come up with a new gift idea. Then we saw two TV commercials: In the first, a man exclaimed, "I traded in my lederhosen for a kilt." In the second, a woman, surrounded by pottery, said, "I never knew I was part Native American." Something clicked! Wouldn't it be fun to find out how much of my DNA was contributed by my mother's Native American grandmother? So, I said, "How about getting one of those DNA kits?"

The box arrived, and I registered my account online. I filled the tube with saliva, shook it, sealed it and sent it off. Weeks passed.

April 7, 2017 was an ordinary day. It followed my birthday and was wedged between April Fool's Day and Tax Day, so I didn't expect any surprises. I turned on the computer and opened my e-mail account: "Your DNA results are ready to view." *Okay,* I thought, *I'll take a quick look and then read my other messages.*

No surprises on my mother's side. My Native American great-grandmother was accurately represented in my DNA. But when I looked for Italian ancestry on my father's side, instead of finding 50 percent, the results reported 0 percent. Zero! No Italian ancestry at all! What? I knew my grandfather, my father's father. And I knew my father's sister and brother: Aunt Anna and Uncle Charlie. They were Italian. They spoke Italian. Grandpa spoke only Italian — my father had to translate for my mother and me. How could I be 0 percent? And if I wasn't half Italian, then what was I?

The report answered: "Ashkenazi Jew." I thought, *This must be a mistake. They must have mixed up my sample with someone else's.* So, I asked. And they answered. And I asked again — four times during the next week. Finally satisfied with their quality control, I asked myself, "What do I do now?"

Then I discovered genealogy. And along with genealogy, I found an online community of Jewish people who greeted me, saying: "Welcome to the Tribe." It's a really big tribe, but not the one I expected! I wanted to know where I fit in, but I didn't have a name to trace. So, I began my search.

At first, I suspected that my paternal grandparents might have been Italian Jews who changed their identity when they immigrated. Over the next few months, I contacted professors and authors in the United States, as well as historians and genealogists in Italy. It wasn't so.

I have no siblings, so I reached out to my only cousin on my father's side — Aunt Anna's daughter. She is eighteen years older than me and lives on the other side of the continent, so we don't have a close relationship. However, intrigued by my story, she agreed to take a DNA test. If our parents were siblings, then either she is half Jewish too, or she and I are not biologically related. The results revealed that her mother — my father's sister — was not Italian. She wasn't Jewish, either! We are not cousins. We conclude that our parents had been adopted.

| *Self-Discovery*

So, who were my father's biological parents? I tried to find birth and adoption records — a challenge because he was born one hundred and fourteen years earlier. Both of his biological parents had to have been Jewish, but without knowing his birth mother's name, finding these records is an impossible task.

The only tool on which I could rely now was DNA matching. My online community taught me how to use statistical DNA comparisons to find relatives. But no one matched me more recently than four generations ago — too great a distance in time to help find living relatives today. I submitted my DNA to six other matching organizations to increase my chances of finding a living biological relative on my Jewish side. None. At this point, all I could do was wait until someone more closely related to me submitted DNA for analysis.

At first, I checked my accounts every day, excitedly anticipating a match. Then every other day. Then twice a week. Then, at random intervals. It was like checking to see if you have the winning ticket in a lottery, never expecting it to happen. I accepted that I would live my remaining years never knowing if there was a family tree somewhere on which my name belonged.

Eleven months passed from the day my identity was shaken. And then it happened: A woman matched me! She's a first cousin once removed. That makes her the daughter of a first cousin whom I've never known! Within a month, six more cousins matched me.

I contacted my first match, a helpful young woman who sent a copy of her family tree to me. We identified a couple who were most likely my grandparents — her great-grandparents. If these people were my grandparents, then they would have been my father's parents. Right?

Well, some things didn't quite add up. Those grandparents had not yet immigrated to the United States when my father was born. They hadn't even met each other yet — they were living with their parents in different countries at that time: he in Russia, and she in Austria. And, to complicate matters even more, they were too young to have been anyone's parents when my father was born!

So, by the way in which the dates and DNA matches made sense, it became clear that the man I knew as my father could not have come from this family — my family. At this moment, I realized that the father I knew, and grew up with, was not my biological father, and he may have never known that. Furthermore, anyone who might have known the story of my origin is gone.

I now know my Jewish family name, and I know where I belong on the family tree. I'm spending my golden years trying to get to know new-to-me relatives. It's like being "born" into a family, but at the age of a grandmother!

The path to learning my true identity leads to this advice: If you're a senior, like me, before you get your DNA analyzed, get your heart checked!

The truth is out there.

— Marilyn Haight —

36

Deep Breath In, Deep Breath Out

Self-worth is so vital to your happiness.
If you don't feel good about you,
it's hard to feel good about anything else.
~Sandy Hale

"Deep breath in." *Did I answer that client's e-mail before I left work?*

"Deep breath out." *Why did I eat all those French fries? Is this why I'm still fat?*

"Check to make sure your mind isn't wandering. Bring it back to the breath." *Dang it. Busted.*

Nithya, the leader of the weekend's self-care retreat, softly rang the Tibetan singing bowl, calling us back to consciousness — a consciousness I had never quite figured out how to leave.

It was day one of my weekend at a self-care retreat, the first self-care retreat I had ever attended. I like to think I typically take care of myself, but after a particularly stressful week, the retreat could not have come at a more opportune time.

At the beginning of the retreat, Nithya asked us our intention for the retreat — why we were there and what we were hoping to get out of it. I made up a fluff answer, something about aligning my aspirations with my current trajectory in life. But if I were really honest, I knew that wasn't my intention at all. I wasn't there to force my aspirations to fit with my life trajectory; I needed a new life trajectory that would fit with my long-ignored aspirations.

I felt stuck, helplessly watching everyone else's life move forward while mine seemed to be on pause. I always thought that, after college, I'd be traveling around the world or falling deeply in love with some handsome stranger. Instead, I graduated from college and moved back to the same town I grew up in, with the same friends, same local haunts, and same exact life.

After work, I would often wind up scrolling through Instagram, liking photos of friends trekking across the globe and living in far-off countries and places. I couldn't help but wonder if I had settled into the working world too soon. I felt like I was missing the grand-adventure narrative that supposedly happens in our twenties. Instead of globetrotting, the most recent adventure I went on was a thrilling trip to the grocery store for stockings.

As the self-care retreat progressed to day two, I continued to sit near the flickering fire in the corner of the room and practice my breathing.

"Deep breath in." *I wonder if I would be happier if I was in Bali right now.*

"Deep breath out." *Am I going to die alone?*

Nithya rang the Tibetan singing bowl once again as we launched into our next session. "We seek happiness in the peak experiences, forgetting that there is so much cost to get to the top. True happiness," Nithya carefully rearranged the blanket on his lap, "is not in the peak experiences, but rather in the valley — the moments that are always there."

I nodded, furiously jotting Nithya's sage words into my journal.

"Anything you can gain, you can lose. Everything in this world can be debated and questioned. The only thing you cannot debate or lose is 'I am.' And that 'I am' is where you find peace."

I underlined "I am" in my journal, starring it three times for emphasis.

Later that evening, while reflecting on the day I came back to those two words in my plethora of notes. I looked at their shape, their form, their essence, and then felt them in my breath and lungs.

"I am…"

Content in who I am.

"I am…"

Grateful for my life and my opportunities.

"I am…"

Enough.

For the next several minutes, I repeated those words like a liturgy or mantra, feeling their truth sink into my bones.

On the third and last day of the self-care retreat, Nithya rang the Tibetan singing bowl once again, bringing us into a state of breathing. And this time, as I breathed in, my mind no longer wandered toward the laundry list of responsibilities, the places I wanted to see or the life I wanted to live. Instead, I focused on the here and now. The self. The I am.

"Deep breath in."

I am.

"Deep breath out."

I am.

I meditated on those two words for the rest of the retreat and into the next several weeks, before I once again got caught in the hamster wheel of life and jealousy.

A visit from one of my best friends in college led me to a particular roller coaster of emotions, as I transitioned from the joy of seeing her to the sadness of knowing that it would be months before I would or could see her again.

The night she left, I sat on my bed feeling numb and morose, once again wishing I wasn't stuck so far away from those whom I cared for so deeply. But as I dwelled on my external sadness, I heard Nithya's calming voice in my head, drawing me back to the center of myself.

Deep breath in.

"I am," I whispered into the silence of my room.

Deep breath out.

"I am." This time, I whispered the two words slightly louder, feeling the power of those two simple words.

I continued to breathe in and out and repeat that phrase until I felt my muscles relax. Several minutes later, I reopened my eyes and gazed around with a newfound sense of peace and serenity because I knew Nithya was right. Though life changes, though we gain and lose opportunities, though we move far from friends and family whom we love, one thing remains that can never be lost or debated.

In "I am," I found peace.

And, although there are still moments of sadness and grief, that peace, I've found, is enough.

— Dana Drosdick —

37

Learning to Take Care of Me

Owning our story and loving ourselves through that
process is the bravest thing that we'll ever do.
~Brené Brown

bout a decade ago, my world was shifted right off its axis.
I was a thirty-six-year-old mother of two. I was happily
married with a great career (albeit challenging at times).
My husband and I had an amazing group of friends, many
of them living within walking distance of our suburban home. We
spent Friday nights at the local VFW playing co-ed kickball and
Saturday nights at the neighbor's house, chatting around the bonfire
or playing family games. My family was healthy, material goods were
plentiful, and love surrounded us in all forms. My life, for the most
part, was happy, healthy, beautiful and fulfilled.

Then the phone rang one Monday morning, and life would never
be the same. I was at my desk preparing for a business trip, and my
husband called. In a strange and shaky voice, he told me that I needed
to meet him at his doctor's office immediately. I honestly didn't take
it seriously; I didn't think anything could be that urgent. I spent too
much time tidying up my desk before I left for the half-hour drive to
the doctor's office. I didn't stop to consider that my husband might
be sitting there waiting for me anxiously and on the verge of tears.

When I arrived at the doctor's office, they led me into the room where my husband was, and the doctor immediately came in and told me that he was sorry we had to meet under these circumstances. That was when I understood that life was about to change drastically. My husband's complexion was yellow and pale. He looked terrified. The doctor explained that he had found a tumor on my husband's pancreas, and we needed to get to a hospital right away. He was positive my husband had a very advanced stage of pancreatic cancer.

Six months later, I found myself a widow with two daughters, ages thirteen and two, and very little idea of what on earth I was supposed to do next.

I was numb, in shock, and terrified. Everyone had advice for me, and the one thing I was told over and over — like a chant from the bleachers of a high-school football game — was, "Make sure you take care of yourself. Those girls need you!" While I appreciated the love and thought behind that statement, I honestly had no idea how to do that. Every time I heard it, it stressed me out.

For a good chunk of time, I just cried. Whenever life felt overwhelming, I cried. When the kids were sad, mad or sassy, I cried. When the dog wanted to go outside but I didn't want to get out of bed, I cried. I literally cried at the drop of a hat for the entire first year after he passed away. I didn't know if letting all those emotions out was "taking care of myself," but it was what my body and heart demanded, so I did it wherever and whenever I needed to. Eventually, I found a great support network of people who had experienced similar things, and my tears didn't come quite as often.

I found ways to take care of myself. I drank wine, which probably wasn't the healthiest habit, but it did help me sleep. I gardened, which was wonderfully therapeutic until I ended up on the surgeon's table with a blown disk in my spine. I did artwork because that has always made me feel good. I also wrote long, depressing stories (on a quickly created blog) about how much grief hurts and how faith, family, and friends can get you through. All of these felt like self-care at the time, although if I attempted to do them now, the result wouldn't be as therapeutic.

Over the next decade, I experienced changes and obstacles like I never experienced before. My older daughter struggled deeply with depression, and I learned the sheer desperation of parenting a child who needed healing that I couldn't provide on my own. I re-entered an old relationship and battled the guilt and shame of finding love again after the death of my spouse. I had enormous financial struggles and ended up selling my family home.

I moved hours away from everyone and everything I loved and started a new life, establishing myself in a new community. I gave birth to my third child, a little boy who is gentle, kind and joyful. I also went back to school and started the process of creating a new purpose for my life. I have yet to really nail down what that purpose will be, but it will have something to do with art and healing. Through all these changes, joys and roadblocks, I continually looked for the best way to take care of myself so I could stay positive, support my children, and move forward in life.

People kept asking if I was taking care of myself. I never really had a good response. Eventually, I discovered there is no one solution for taking care of yourself, and it's okay not to have a perfect answer when someone asks that question. Today, I might need to get out in the fresh air and silently thank Mother Nature for the miracle of life. Tomorrow, I may need to sit in my pajamas on the couch and eat a pint of mint chocolate-chip ice cream. This Sunday, I may need to go to church to feel fulfilled and calm, but next Sunday I may need to soak in a bath all day, away from any other human contact. On Wednesday, I may need to join a group of girlfriends at dinner to share laughter and love, and on Thursday I may need to spend the day connecting with my children instead.

I can't make a schedule or checklist that will allow me to keep track of whether I am taking care of myself or not. Self-care is fluid and evolving. What I need in the middle of a crisis will be vastly different from what I need during a joyful period of life.

Taking care of yourself means listening, and then reacting, to the voice in your head that is guiding you through each day. It means not resisting the urge to sit down and play a song at the piano even though you have a million things to get done. It means feeling comfortable sitting down and hugging your child for a moment or two when you can feel that you both need just that. It simply means listening and responding to your voice and heart.

Now that I have learned this lesson, I no longer stress over the question, "Are you taking care of yourself?" I simply respond, "Yes." In a million different ways each day, I am listening to my mind, body, and spirit, and responding as necessary. And each day, that looks and feels different. But I can tell by the calm in my spirit that it's working.

— C. Ede —

38

Slow Cooking, Slow Living

If you neglect to recharge a battery, it dies.
And if you run full speed ahead without stopping for water,
you lose momentum to finish the race.
~Oprah Winfrey

I dropped a Crock-Pot on my bare feet. More accurately, I slipped down the back steps of our house on a rainy night in November while carrying the ceramic insert for a Crock-Pot. In the nanoseconds that followed, I tossed the cookware into the air and grabbed for the railing so I wouldn't tumble like a ragdoll down the stairs. I could picture the headline: "Mother Dies Doing Dishes After Dinner."

I managed to stay upright and landed on my backside with my feet in front of me, which was a victory except that the Crock-Pot also landed upright—and on my feet, where it cracked in two. The juices I was trying to dispose of in the outdoor trash flew in the air, defied gravity until I landed on the bottom step, and then rained down upon me.

At that precise moment, our dog saw the back door wide open and took the opportunity to escape into the unfenced yard. He flew past me and into the rain. But when he caught the scent of the juices, he stopped in his tracks. He ran back to the stairs, sat down next to me on the bottom step, and began licking the juices off my arms and face. By the time I was able to stand up and hobble inside, both the dog and I were soaking wet.

If you ever drop a Crock-Pot on your feet (which I do not recommend), let me offer some advice: Walk on your heels to lessen the pain in your toes. This act would be difficult for me in a normal situation because I have the dexterity of a sloth, but it is even harder when you are trying to chase down a wet dog who wants to spread his smelly odor by rolling around on every piece of furniture in the house. One hour and several towels later, both the dog and I were dry but exhausted.

In the following days, I faced two challenges as a result of my tumble down the stairs.

Problem #1: shoes. I couldn't wear traditional footwear because when the Crock-Pot cracked, the shards created two big gashes on my toes and feet. Solution: slip-on house shoes.

Problem #2: wardrobe. My fall down the steps left monolithic bruises on my buttocks, arms, legs, and back, making every stitch of clothing uncomfortable. Solution: yoga pants.

These fashion choices are fine if you spend your days as a hermit, but they are not so stylish if you go out in public, especially in the South where a trip to the grocery store merits full make-up and a cute outfit. So, I had two choices: 1) Stay at home for a week while the cuts and bruises healed; or 2) Suck it up. I chose the latter. Life goes on even if you drop a Crock-Pot on your foot.

However, my daily routine slowed to a crawl because I had to walk at a snail's pace. And I had to cancel non-essential outings and appointments. (Who wants to hang out with a girl wearing slippers in public?) At first, I resented the interruption in my plans, but I soon realized my injuries had given me a gift: spare time. I rediscovered long-forgotten joys I'd tossed aside because I was too busy for such "luxuries." I read a book for pleasure, not for its educational value or career tips. I caught up with friends and family members in e-mails and texts. I spent time in meditation and silence. I experimented with my watercolor set. And my spirit came alive again.

I had been living at such a frenzied pace for so long that it had become my daily routine: Get up early, bury myself in my tasks at work, run errands on the way home, help my daughter with homework, cook supper, clean up, do housework, and collapse in the evening with no recollection of what I had actually done in the past twelve hours. When I was forced to slow down, I realized how unhealthy my lifestyle had become — not just physically, but emotionally and spiritually as well. Something had to change, or I would suffer the consequences.

Finding a healthier balance has been an ongoing process, but I have been able to see some improvement. I have stopped cramming my schedule with back-to-back meetings and obligations. I try to leave some margin in my time so I can breathe, think and pray. I pay attention to my emotions, especially those that tell me I "should" do something. That's a red flag telling me I'm living for others' expectations and not my own. And, above all, I make time for the activities and practices that bring me joy, like going for walks or enjoying a meal with good friends.

Not that I'm a pro at this self-care stuff. Sometimes, I take on too much. I worry about what others think when I say "no." I don't always pay attention to my emotions, and I don't always make time for myself. But I am learning… And sometimes, by the grace of God, I manage to get it right.

Just a few minutes ago, my daughter plopped down beside me on the couch and put her head in my lap, which was occupied by my laptop. I took the hint and closed my computer so I could focus on her. She didn't share any earth-shattering news or need advice. She wanted to know what was for dinner (of course), and she told me what she wanted for Christmas — a list that changes daily. Then she lay in silence while I played with her hair. For two whole minutes, we connected, and then she was off to conquer a game on her phone.

That encounter reinforced the importance of self-care. If I hadn't been learning to take care of myself, if I were overloaded and over-whelmed, if I were trying to do too much, I might have missed that moment. I might have sacrificed my relationship with her for the expediency of my work or other priorities. But I am grateful that, for those few minutes, I chose wisely, and we both benefited. There will be instances when my needs trump hers, and I will need to tell her to wait. And that's okay. I'm modeling self-care for her.

Every time I cook in our new Crock-Pot, I remember the importance of slowing down and living with purpose and intentionality. I make sure my schedule isn't overloaded. I remember to ask for help when I need it. I try to pick up my paintbrushes more often and sneak away to used bookstores to find hidden gems.

And I never, ever walk down wet stairs with a Crock-Pot in my hands.

—Pam Gibbs—

39

Trail of Hope

The story ends up being a journey of self-discovery.
~Elijah Wood

My future glistened in the distance like a desert oasis. After twenty-two years raising three children, I was about to be introduced to an unfamiliar concept: the empty nest. Apparently, this was now my time. My time to dive into new experiences, develop new hobbies, and explore the world. It was time to reconnect with my husband and give my writing career a fresh jolt of energy. Why, then, was I not excited?

My oldest child had just begun life on her own; the other two were attending college 1,100 miles away. I missed them all terribly. My husband and I had sold our home and moved to a neighboring state for a job opportunity. Since we were living in temporary housing, I hadn't yet met neighbors or made new friends, and most of my colleagues were only accessible through an Internet connection. I began to feel isolated. I wasn't quite sure how to move forward.

"Why don't we go for a walk?" my husband suggested.

When I discovered a trail only a short drive from our apartment, I was thrilled. My husband and I began to use it regularly.

The paved trail meandered along a river lined with shrubs and towering trees. Mallard ducks lazed on the riverbanks. Robins perched in the treetops. Canada geese flew overhead. Often, a blue heron stood motionless on a rock in the center of the river. At dusk, small rabbits hopped across the pathway, then skittered into the brush.

One evening, a beaver diligently collected sticks, then disappeared with them downstream. These small snippets of nature provided me with a peaceful distraction, but only slightly lifted me out of my malaise.

Still, I continued to walk the path.

The trail was filled with fellow walkers, joggers, and bikers at all times of day.

"On your left," the bikers would shout as they zipped by us and continued up the trail. Some were single riders. Some rode in groups. Some toted children in attached seats or hauled them behind in trailers. They were young and old. They were thin and not so thin. On every walk, I spotted something new: unicycles, tandem bicycles, adult-sized tricycles.

One Saturday, I was astonished to see a homemade, automated race car speeding down the trail, and on another, a man with a prosthetic right leg sailing by me effortlessly.

I'd come home after a walk feeling vaguely different than when I left. Was it simply the fresh air and bright sunshine? Or was it the heart-pumping, endorphin-releasing exercise? I had a hunch it was something else entirely. But I didn't know what.

I began to take a longer look at my fellow trail users. A dad and two sons riding their scooters. A young husband and wife teaching their daughter how to ride her first two-wheeler. Couples, young and old, holding hands, chatting as they walked. Generations of families taking evening strolls together. Joggers, huffing and panting, as they raced toward that sixth, seventh, eighth mile. A woman doing Tai Chi on a platform next to the water. Not to mention the dogs. A plethora of breeds, sizes, and temperaments all took advantage of the trail.

These were just ordinary people doing the same thing I was doing: exercising and spending time with loved ones. That's what I thought. But I'd return home with a smile on my face, my excursion replenishing something I seemed to have lost. How could something so simple, so uncomplicated, alter my outlook on life?

I couldn't seem to get enough, so I returned to the trail again and again. Sometimes with my husband; sometimes alone.

As I walked, I'd peer into faces and listen for snippets of conversation, my eyes hidden behind my sunglasses. These people spoke French, Russian, Hindi, and numerous other languages I couldn't understand. They represented all races and cultures, and I became fascinated with the lives of these strangers: who they were, where they lived, how they were related. Most of all, I thought about their stories. Surely they had stories. What challenges did they face? Did any of them feel lost and empty? How were they moving forward?

One cloudy morning, I hiked up the trail, determined to find answers, or at the very least, inspiration. After thirty minutes, I turned to head back the way I had come, slightly disappointed that the trail held very little for me that day. Until I saw her. An elderly, gray-haired woman clasping the handles of her walker. She sprinted by me in the opposite direction like a marathon runner. I turned around to catch another glimpse of this one-woman wonder. She was definitely moving forward. She wasn't letting anything hold her back. Certainly not her age.

That's when it hit me. Nobody was.

Not the man with the prosthetic leg. Not the toddler taking his first steps. Not the two young boys casting their fishing lines into the river after the sun had already disappeared. Not even the group of four new mothers, tired though they may have been, standing in front of their strollers, counting aloud to their babies' delight. Everyone seemed to be rushing headlong into life. Rushing with optimism, clarity, and determinedness.

My fellow trail users were pushing past whatever challenges they were experiencing. Why, then, was I not doing the same? My nest may have been empty, but it didn't have to be joyless.

As I walked toward the car, remembering the elderly woman's energy and enthusiasm, I made a decision. I would rush home and fill my empty nest with abundance. Like the strangers-turned-allies on the trail, I wouldn't let anything hold me back. I was ready for the glittery future that stretched before me.

—Annette Gulati—

Self-Care Isn't Selfish

40

Somewhere In-Between

Self-care is how you take your power back.
~Lalah Delia

The house was quiet. My husband was asleep with our sweet, little Maltese curled up at his feet. Even though I was exhausted, and it was 3:00 a.m., I couldn't sleep. I sat outside on the deck, in the still, silent darkness. My heart was pounding in my chest; I was on the verge of panic. How did I get here... yet again? I felt off-track, off-balance, like my life was not my own. I closed my eyes and tried to breathe deeply.

My husband and I were into our forty-fifth year of marriage. Several months into 2020, he began spending more and more time at home. I put aside my work to assist him with tasks relating to his committee work, a home-based business, and his late mom's estate.

My elderly dad, recently widowed when my mom passed away, had some critical health issues. I also undertook management of his health care — keeping track of and taking him to all his medical appointments and tests. Twice hospitalized since COVID-19 struck, my dad had been put through the ringer and was needing more and more of my time.

I grew increasingly frustrated with all these demands on my time. My life wasn't my own. I had dreams and fantasies about living alone in a brand-new condominium — so clean, decorated in all-white, with a studio just for me.

As a result, I sat outside on my deck at 3:00 a.m. Unsettled, confused and oh-so-weary, I grabbed my iPad and began desperate, random Googling. I searched things like: Why am I so exhausted (but can't sleep)? How can I get my life back on track? How can I reclaim my life? Each search led me to a response about "self-care." Self-care? That was not at all what I had anticipated! I was expecting something medicinal.

Diving deeper into the subject, I stumbled upon a book called *Self-Care for Empaths: 100 Activities to Help You Relax, Recharge, and Rebalance Your Life,* by Tanya Carroll Richardson. Having no idea what an empath was or even if that term applied to me, I ordered the book.

It arrived two days later. As I thumbed through the first few pages, my pink highlighter started working overtime. So much of what I read struck a chord. I learned that my very nature is easily overwhelmed by the emotions and energies of others. I learned that although I felt the emotions of others so deeply, I wasn't responsible for their emotions. I learned that I needed to spend time identifying and tending to my own emotional needs. But, most important, I came to understand and appreciate that if I wanted a life that was on track, in balance and truly my own, self-care was not a want for me; it was a *need*. Translation: My self-care meant spending mandated time alone.

I had a chat with my husband about my revelations. Looking a tad bemused, he said, "I know… You want your privacy."

"But it's so much more than that," I said. "It's not just about privacy. It's about taking care of myself, figuring out what I need to live a happy and balanced life. My soul craves some peace and quiet."

He looked skeptical but cooperated nonetheless.

Since my dad was doing surprisingly well and my husband was on board, I packed up the car and headed for the lake. Alone. It had been months since I'd last been there. Throughout the three-hour drive, I joyfully sang aloud to every tune on my playlist.

At the lake, I stayed up late and slept in. I wrote and journalled at the dining-room table in my PJs until late in the day. I watched my beloved Toronto Blue Jays play baseball on TV. I sat on the shores of the lake, literally lapping up its fresh, transformative energy. I sat on a bench under my favourite tree, not worrying about anything. I took dozens of photos of God's natural handiwork: the Purcell Mountains, clear emerald lakes, and the forests and trees. It was just the tonic I craved. I felt more like myself again.

I wasn't anxious to leave, but it was time to go home. The three-hour drive gave me some forced thinking time. I realized the last thing I wanted was to neglect or abandon my family responsibilities. My husband is my best friend; my true soulmate. I don't want to live alone. But I do want to steer my own ship, satisfy my own emotional needs, and live a life that feels balanced.

Now, I schedule me time; it's on the calendar. It doesn't always have to involve a trip to the lake. It can be as simple as a solitary walk in nature, making sure I fit in my yoga class, or enjoying every moment in my empty home when my husband has gone fishing. I'm taking the time to learn more about myself. I've discovered it's not all or nothing, but somewhere in-between.

— Kim Hanson —

41

Permission to Joyride

Listen, are you breathing a little and calling it a life?
~Mary Oliver

ith my head against the glass of our fifth-story hospital window, my gaze lingered on the row of red rental bikes across the street at our Ronald McDonald House. Once again we were sequestered post-operatively with our daughter at a children's hospital a thousand miles from home. And by day eight of our stay, my bike-riding daydreams were quite vivid.

As the parents of a child with complex medical needs, this life wasn't new to us. Our little patient had endured a complex, eight-hour, multi-surgeon operation. We'd been working through recovery with a pain pump, follow-up therapies, and an endless flow of medical professionals through our tiny fifth-floor room. The hardest challenge? She was under NPO (nil per os) orders: nothing by mouth — no food and no drinks. It had not been easy for her or me, her caretaker.

Then came a Sunday afternoon when the doctors had completed their rounds, our girl was finally comfortable and happy, and my mom was with us. It was a calm day of rest. So, as we clicked on *Frozen* for our eleventh viewing, I looked longingly again at those rental bikes shining in the summer sun. I'd left our daughter's bedside many times for naps or laundry, but could I leave her for a joyride?

As I wondered if it might finally be possible to slip away, my familiar doubts arose. What if the surgeon came back? What if a nurse needed me? What if my daughter cried? What if they forgot to give her pain meds?

"Go," urged my mom.

"Go," urged everything in me.

So, I pushed aside those noisy doubts and my guilty-mom feelings. I walked through the hospital doors into the open air, bound for that row of bikes.

As I swiped my credit card and the bike unlocked, something in me unlocked as well. For two freeing hours, I pumped the pedals fast, and then I meandered slowly. My hair blew, and my heart pumped. My soul responded with a flood of emotions from elation to buried, angry tears, then back to grateful joy. I even stopped to take a few photos of a flower garden.

When I returned and locked my bike back into its spot, my ride was over, but new breath filled my lungs.

Back on the other side of the hospital glass, my girl smiled wide when I re-entered, happy to see me. And instead of clicking onto yet another movie, I decided it would be better to pull out our unused paints and turn on some music. Soul care was long overdue for her, too.

That joyride shifted my thinking. Yes, my priority is my family. Yes, life is hard, full, and even scary, but I'd gotten a good taste of the value of attending to the soul.

The reality is, I am a medical mom of four children. So, unfortunately, my "me time" has limited parameters. We've got long to-do lists and a full schedule. There are multiplication tables to memorize, dishes to scrub, book reports to complete, and Cub Scout meetings to attend.

But now I have a changed perspective and a tea towel in my kitchen that reminds me: "Do something each day that brings you joy."

When I care for my soul and take a little me time, it might feel unproductive, but it's also a gift to my whole family. A happy momma often results in a happy family. And, while I want my kids to know how to subtract and make a bed, I also want them to discover what makes them come alive. I want to help them increase their capacities to survive and thrive. If they see me take joyrides, maybe they will, too.

I wrote myself a permission slip to seize a little slice of joy that day in the pediatric hospital, and it has made all the difference.

After that Sunday bike ride, Monday inevitably came. The new day brought my girl discomfort and agitation. For hours, I tried to no avail to do everything I could think of, from holding her to distracting her with Snapchat filters.

Then I remembered my joyride. So, I dimmed the lights, pulled a chair and tray table close to her bed, and dumped out a 100-piece puzzle. I hummed as I sorted through the pieces. She was annoyed at first, but I kept humming and sorting. Then slowly, as I settled, so did she. I moved the tray closer, and her little hands went to work, helping me find all the blue-sky pieces.

As it turns out, when I took the time to attend to my soul, it helped my daughter settle hers as well.

— Rebecca Radicchi —

42

Farmer's Hours

It's not selfish to love yourself, take care of yourself,
and to make your happiness a priority. It's necessary.
~Mandy Hale

"I just finished *The Girl on the Train*," Melissa said during our warm-up.

"Oh, I've read that!" Carla said. "What did you think?"

"I liked it," Melissa said. "It's intense, but I liked the psychology in it."

Kristen chimed in, "I haven't read that one yet."

"Oh, I've seen the movie preview," I said. "Not sure it's my genre."

It was a little after 5:00 in the morning, and we were warming up for our CrossFit workout. The 5:15 class has a small but dedicated group of regulars, and these women have become good friends over the years. We discuss books, work, spouses, and kids, along with how sore we are, how much we hate the assault bike, and how yesterday's workout went. We've become a tight-knit group and banter on a group text when outside the gym (including Caley, who's been out with a shoulder injury for several months).

I set my alarm for 4:40 a.m. every weekday so I can go. As a stay-at-home mom to five-and-a-half-year-old twins, a four-year-old and a two-year-old, my me time happens before dawn, before they're awake, before I'm fully awake. And it's wonderful.

On my twenty-minute drive, I listen to music without interruption, questions or requests. I contemplate the day ahead. Once there,

I get to interact with adults! We joke around and laugh a lot. I have fun! That kind of time is precious and invigorating. Almost as much as the workout.

When COVID-19 hit our state, our gym shut down for nearly five months, but we continued to work out on Zoom together. It did wonders for my mental and physical health.

I started these early morning workouts before having kids and intended to keep it up after having them, so I had to make it a priority. During the newborn/early-morning-feeding phases, that sometimes meant waking up at 4:00 a.m. and then staying up to go to the gym. Sometimes, I'd dash out after having heard a child wake up. But I left without guilt, knowing said child would crawl into bed with my husband and fall back to sleep. Occasionally, I would have to remind myself that I am a mother, not a martyr.

I knew I had to continue taking care of myself. And I wanted to. I'd seen the toll that not taking care of yourself takes on a person. Growing up, I saw my mother put everyone else in our house — me, my two brothers, my dad, her elderly mother, our dogs — ahead of herself. She did not complain, but it clearly took a toll on her. My mom, still young, would have trouble sleeping. She often got migraines that, ironically, necessitated she take a break and lie down. But I didn't want to have to reach a breaking point before taking a break. I had to change my mindset and realize self-care is not selfish.

That regular quiet and thoughtful time to myself is key to my wellbeing and ability to take care of my family. I will sacrifice a few hours of sleep for this alone time because I am more alert, perky, and happy having done so.

— Kristiana Pastir —

43

One Day

*Taking time to rest, renew, and refresh yourself isn't
wasted time. Recharge. Choose what energizes you.*
~Melody Beattie, Journey to the Heart

When my husband asked me what I wanted for Mother's Day, I said sheepishly, "A night away. By myself. Oh, and I'll take the dog."

I felt guilty asking for a night away. After all, I was a new mom, blessed with a beautiful daughter, then five months old. I loved her to the moon and back. But I was tired, exhausted. I wanted to drive somewhere and spend the night, read and sleep with no interruptions.

My husband looked a bit surprised, but he assured me it would be okay. Even with his encouragement, I felt a pang of guilt when I looked into my baby's eyes. What had I heard about mothers and guilt? It comes to new mothers along with all the other gifts, wrapped in a pretty bow... the gift that keeps on giving.

To save money, I would be staying in a friend's cabin at a local ski resort. Beverly said it would be quiet since it was May, with no snow or skiers. That suited me just fine. Quiet. Peaceful. Bliss.

The next day, I packed and kissed my daughter and husband goodbye. My Golden Retriever, Kia, eagerly jumped into the hatchback.

"Bye," I said, waving. I pulled out of the driveway, trying not to look back at my daughter, who was starting to cry, holding out her arms to me. *Should I go back? No, keep going. She'll be fine for one night.*

She'll be fine.

The day was overcast and hazy. As I drove, I yawned, willing myself to stay awake. Houses and neighborhoods yielded to evergreens and snow-capped mountains. The newly budded deciduous trees, a light green curtain, waved in the breeze.

At the resort, cabins on stilts looked strange without the snow. Beverly's cabin was not the quaint retreat I had imagined. In fact, it was old and needed a heavy dose of TLC. The paint was faded and peeling, and the stairs looked rickety, as if they might give way at any moment.

A musty smell greeted me as I entered, but everything looked clean. I put a sandwich (my dinner) in the fridge. I thought of taking a hot shower but found there was none, just an old bathtub with rust spots.

The cabin was dark, and the lighting was minimal. I hated when people used low-watt bulbs. Don't people read anymore? I noticed an axe propped in the corner, like something from a horror film. *They probably need it to chop firewood,* I thought, although I didn't see any wood. I made some hot cocoa, which smelled heavenly. As I turned to get my book, a mouse scurried across the floor.

I shrieked and jumped. *Oh, my gosh!* My heart was beating fast. I took a deep breath. I would tell Beverly she had a squatter.

"You stay away from us, Mr. Mouse, and we'll stay away from you." I looked at Kia. "Maybe we should go back home."

She barked. "What's that?" I asked. "Just deal with it?" She barked again.

"Okay, okay."

I fed Kia and ate my sandwich. Birds chirped outside the kitchen window. I started feeling better. Nature and a quiet place, no interruptions. I sat in a big chair and started reading but soon nodded off. I woke with a start. It wasn't that late, but I decided to go to bed.

I eyed that axe again. I picked it up and took it into the bedroom. I'd feel better knowing it was nearby.

Kia followed me and curled up next to the bed. I liked to sleep with two pillows. There was only a skimpy one on my bed, and I didn't see another pillow on the bed across from me. I changed into pajamas and found some towels to put under the pillow. Not great, but it would do for one night. The bed was lumpy, and I could feel springs poking my body. *Where did she get this thing?* Despite the bed and pillow, I fell asleep.

I dreamed about floating on a cloud that cradled and rocked me. Then I heard something strange. I opened my eyes. I sat up. *What in the world?* I heard what sounded like hundreds of mice running through the walls and in the attic. I jumped up. My foot caught in the blanket, and I fell. Kia pounced and barked.

I imagined mice crawling all over me. *Oh. Oh. Oh!* I made it up and turned on the light. I didn't see any mice in the room but still heard them moving wildly in the walls and attic. It was just a matter of time before they decided to invade the bedroom. *Hundreds of rodents... too much!*

"C'mon, Kia," I said. "We're getting out of here." I dressed as fast as I could and threw my things together.

Once I was on the highway, tears clouded my vision. *What a disaster. I can't even get one night away to myself. I might as well admit defeat and go home.*

Then, up ahead, I saw a hotel with a Vacancy sign lit up like a beacon. I hadn't wanted to spend money on a hotel, but it was just for one night... The car seemed to turn into the parking lot on its own.

Fortunately, the man at the hotel desk said they had pet-friendly rooms.

"And there's a complimentary breakfast buffet in the morning," he said.

"Breakfast buffet? What's in it?" I asked.

"Bacon and eggs, toast, hash browns..."

"What else?"

"French toast, waffles, pancakes, oatmeal, Danish, donuts, muffins, juices, coffee..."

As he rambled on, a smorgasbord danced in my head.

I went to my room. Spacious and nice. Big, comfy, king-sized bed, no lumps. Plenty of fluffy pillows. The sheets were pulled down, and two mints perched on the pillow. The bathroom was modern, with a large shower. I would get a good night's sleep, shower in the morning, and eat as much as I wanted for breakfast. No cooking. No cleaning up. Sweet. I deserved this one night. For sure. I turned off the light, and the guilt.

—Wendy Hairfield—

44

Grace over Guilt

If your compassion does not include yourself,
it is incomplete.
~Jack Kornfield

I n late August, I opened an e-mail from one of my favorite authors, Jon Acuff. Jon writes about productivity and time management in a fun, entertaining way. His e-mails always made me laugh and often inspired me to make a change in my life.

In this e-mail, Jon wrote about his September–January challenge. He said that September, like January, is the perfect month for a re-do. Since it's the start of a new school year, it often feels like a fresh start in life, too. He said it's the right time to implement a new habit that can bring positive changes into our lives. His e-mail included an attached calendar for the month. He encouraged readers to print one out, choose a new habit they want to see in their lives, and then color in a square for each day they follow through on their intentions.

It sounded like a great idea to me. I thought about the habits I'd like to adopt in my own life. Walk five miles every day. Drink a gallon of water daily. Spend an hour each day organizing closets, junk drawers, and other areas of my home that I usually ignored when I was cleaning. Write 2,000 words every day. Do something special for a family member each day.

All these habits seemed like worthy ones to adopt. How could I choose just one? And why would I only change one thing about myself if I could re-vamp my whole life in a single month?

I didn't choose. I printed out five calendars and labeled each one with one of the habits I wanted to add into my already busy life. September was going to be a big month for me.

Bright and early on September first, I filled my gallon jug with water. I downed it until I felt like I would float away and then set off on my five-mile walk. About a mile in, I realized that the water hadn't been the best idea. I rushed back home to use the bathroom. I'd planned to go back out to finish my walk, but my son, Nathan, was up earlier than usual and needed my help with his at-home learning. (Did I forget to mention that I decided to re-vamp my life during a global pandemic?)

The rest of my walk would have to wait until later.

As we worked through his schoolwork, I chugged my water and thought about which cleaning project I wanted to tackle that day.

Three hours later, when his e-learning was finally done, I went upstairs to work on re-organizing my walk-in closet. It had become a dumping ground for everything in the house that didn't have a place somewhere else. It was an eyesore, and I knew that working on it for only an hour would hardly make a dent in the mess.

I decided to double my goal for the day and clean for two hours. Of course, I didn't get as much done as I would've liked because I had to take so many bathroom breaks because of my water drinking.

At 2:00 p.m., I realized that I still needed to walk three more miles and write 2,000 words, plus do something special for a family member. And my water was only half finished.

I sat down at the computer and worked on a story I'd been wanting to write for weeks. I'd written only 500 words when I realized it was time to drive Nathan to his tennis practice. Ugh. I hadn't actually accomplished a single one of my goals for the day.

An hour later, I was back home, and it was time to start dinner. I decided to make my husband's favorite meal and count that as my "something special" for the day. At least I'll be able to check off one thing.

As I cooked, I continued to chug my water. No matter how much

I drank, the gallon didn't seem to be emptying.

My husband was grateful for the delicious dinner. At 7:00 p.m., I was finally able to color in the first of my calendar squares for the day.

After dinner, I went back to the computer and wrote another 500 words. Then it was time to tuck Nathan into bed. As I read to him, my body began to relax, and I realized that I was exhausted.

I had to accept that I wasn't going to complete Day One of my life re-vamp. But because I'm stubborn, I did choke down the rest of the water and then proudly colored in my second square for the day.

The next morning, I felt terrible. I knew it was because I'd been up multiple times in the night to use the bathroom and had hardly slept — an obvious result of drinking a half-gallon of water at 9:00 p.m.

I sat at the kitchen table with my coffee and my five September calendar pages, beating myself up for the failure of my first day.

My seventeen-year-old daughter, Julia, sat down. "What's wrong with you?"

I explained about the September challenge and how I'd done with it the day before.

"Did the author tell you to print out five calendars and adopt five new habits all in the same month? All while homeschooling during a pandemic?"

"Umm, no. I think he intended for people to just do one."

Julia arched her eyebrows. "Then why did you choose five?"

"If one is good, then five is better, right?"

She shook her head. "Mom, you're feeling guilty — and, I'm sorry, but you're looking awful — all because you took on five times as much as you were supposed to. You need to give yourself some grace, not guilt, when making changes in your life."

I nodded. "Grace over guilt. I like that."

Julia picked up the calendar pages. "Which one of these do you want? Because I'm throwing the rest away."

I didn't have to think about it. "I'm going to keep the Do Something Special goal. I'll try to build the other habits down the road." I smiled. "But one at a time, so I don't get so stressed out."

Julia grinned back. "Giving yourself grace instead of guilt is the next habit you need to work on."

I knew she was right. I needed to kick perfectionism and guilt out of my life. I needed to be more forgiving of my own flaws and less critical of myself. In short, I needed to give myself the same amount of grace I extended to those I love.

I looked at my one remaining calendar page — the one with the goal to do something special for a family member each day.

I thought of the novel that sat on my nightstand, the one I'd wanted to read for months. Today I would be the family member for whom I would do something special.

Reading — and a second cup of coffee — were the perfect way to give myself some much-needed grace.

— Diane Stark —

45

Finding My Footing

Self-care is giving the world the best of you instead of
what's left of you.
~Author Unknown

I hung up the phone, put my face in my hands, and burst into tears. My husband, Richard, got up from the sofa to bring me some tissues and rub my back.

Since my father's death the previous month, this scene had become commonplace. I hadn't cried much when I knew he was in the hospital except for when I said my last goodbye, the nurse holding the phone to his ear, his breathing raspy and uneasy. I'd accepted that I couldn't go home to the U.S. for his funeral — a travel ban because of the pandemic left me stuck at our home in Japan — and I attended a visitation via video call with my mother, and my brother Bob and his family.

This time, though, the tears were for something completely different. My sister-in-law, Jenny, was rushed to the hospital the morning of my father's funeral. Always in fragile health due to her long-running battle with alcoholism, her heart finally gave out. My middle brother, Edward, barely arrived at the hospital in time to say goodbye. A recovering alcoholic himself, the double-whammy of our father's and his wife's death pushed him over the edge. He started drinking again.

My mother, stoic about my father's death, now sounded tired and exhausted when I spoke to her on the phone. My oldest brother and Edward hadn't spoken in more than ten years.

That left me calling everyone. I worked with Edward's neighbor and sister-in-law to try and sort out help for him, make arrangements for the funeral, and try to persuade Edward to enter a recovery program. It seemed clear that I had to return home. This time, the mess was too big, and I feared my mother would be drawn in despite the danger of the pandemic and the unpredictability of Edward's mental state. However, if I went back, I wouldn't be able to re-enter Japan.

"I want to go home," I sobbed, "but I'm risking everything: my career, our marriage, our income."

"We can handle it," my husband soothed. "We'll be fine.

I appreciated his words, but I didn't buy them. Yes, we were fine financially, and our marriage was solid, but the future was far too unclear. If I left Japan and then was banned from re-entering from the U.S., I could end up unemployed, uninsured, and indefinitely separated from my husband.

"I'll think about it," I said, taking a deep breath. "I need to make another call."

This one was to my best friend, Kris. We had talked almost daily starting just before my father died, when the assorted meanings and implications of his death had been the sole items running through my head. Now, it was fear as well as anger at Edward and this disease, along with worry about the impact on my mother.

"Can I tell you what my mother heart says?" Kris asked after I spewed all of this, my voice cracking with emotion by the end.

"Sure," I said, reaching for a tissue.

Then, her voice low and steady, she made her case. By staying in Japan, I put myself in a better place, financially as well as emotionally, to support Edward and, in turn, my mother, as this long, slow crisis took its course.

We sat silently for a moment. Outside, I could hear the wind in the camellia bushes. I heard Richard making breakfast in the kitchen. Her advice felt wrong, but I promised to think over what she had said. Kris and I talked a bit longer and then signed off so she could go to bed and I could start my day.

I realized, as I sipped my coffee and mulled over her words, that I hadn't exercised for over two weeks and had stopped meditating. My daily journaling focused only on this crisis. I was distracted and grumpy, falling behind on work. I was giving everything to this crisis, forgetting about what I needed to get through it.

After breakfast, I disconnected all my devices from the Internet and sat down to meditate. My mind jumped hither and yon as my breath came in rapid bursts, but I stayed put. Then, I set out for a long hike into the nearby foothills, eventually settling on a bench near a small temple, gazing out over the plain below to the sea. Overhead, birds chattered lazily in the trees. At my feet, an iridescent salamander sunbathed. Giant black butterflies, Alpine black swallowtails, floated past, and the old gray-and-white tomcat who lives on the mountain dozed on a picnic table. When the light waned, I headed down the trail to home. There was work to be done.

I established a schedule for calls and e-mails — nothing before 7:00 a.m. and nothing after 9:00 p.m. — unless it was an emergency or scheduled meeting. I resumed my daily meditation practice, and Richard and I took long walks together, pointedly not discussing my family unless absolutely necessary. I took on new writing assignments with an eye on income and keeping busy but also not overextending myself. I contacted a counselor. I did a lot of weeding in the garden, and when the gym opened again, I started swimming three times a week.

I still spent plenty of time on the phone and e-mailing with family, social workers, nurses, and doctors, as well as with Edward's neighbor and sister-in-law as we all tried to keep him safe until he might agree to enter a recovery program. Slowly, though, I felt myself steadying and my vision clearing. As the days turned to weeks and then months, smaller crises flared up, but I felt more able to meet them. Even now, there are still moments where I weep with my head in my hands, but when they pass, I find myself on increasingly solid ground. Firm-footed once more, I reach out to do what I can from where I am.

— Joan Bailey —

Self-Care Isn't Selfish

46

Better Reader, Better Mother, Better Me

*Many people, myself among them, feel better at the
mere sight of a book.*
~Jane Smiley

I was thrilled when I found out I was pregnant for the first time. When I started telling family and friends, they were thrilled, too. But I quickly learned that the hardest part of pregnancy wasn't fatigue, nausea, or swelling. The hardest part, for me, was listening to person after person tell me that once the baby was born, I would never read a book again. They said it in that tone of gleeful foreboding people often use with parents-to-be, and I'm sure none of them grasped how much their dire predictions upset me.

Books are the backbone of my life. I have degrees in English and library science. I am a writer. But before any of that, I'm a reader. Being a reader has remained the most consistent part of my identity throughout my life, the practice that makes me feel most like myself. I can always tell when I'm not reading enough because I get cranky and anxious. Books are my anchor; without them I feel adrift and unsettled. No matter how my day has gone, I can find a few minutes of peace in the book on my bedside table. There are many things I can cheerfully sacrifice for the privilege of motherhood, but reading isn't one of them.

My pregnancy became marked by worry as many people predicted I'd never finish a book again. I was surprised by the apparent joy people who cared about me took in what I saw as my impending doom. I could forgive them only by telling myself they couldn't possibly understand how important reading is to my well-being. I knew if I had to stop reading, I wouldn't be the best me, and I wouldn't be the best mother for my baby.

My husband did his best to comfort me. "People do what they want to do," he said. "The people who quit reading after they had kids never made reading a top priority in the first place."

In time, I discovered that he was right. I thought of my fellow avid readers who were already moms. I knew they were still reading because we talked about our reading lives all the time. I thought of all the people with other hobbies who remained devoted practitioners after becoming parents. Maybe they participated in their chosen activities a little less for a while, but they never walked away completely. A few internet searches even yielded a number of articles written by other literary moms who had heard the exact same warnings I had and wanted to reassure other women that one can be both a reader and a mother.

Of course, my newborn required constant attention. She wouldn't sleep unless she was held, and she wanted to nurse all the time. But there's a great benefit in rocking a baby who's nursing or napping in your arms; it gives you lots of time to read. I had resisted using my e-reader until then, but it became my best friend as I discovered that I could hold it with one hand and download library books when I was stuck in the house. I read over one hundred books in my daughter's first year, far surpassing my own record. I have never read so many books at one time as I did when my daughter was an infant, and I credit reading with getting me through those difficult early months. When everything in my life seemed topsy-turvy, books remained my constant friends.

I get the same benefit from an hour with a book and a cup of tea that some people get from an hour at the spa. I feel renewed, refreshed, and better able to face whatever the day throws at me. I no longer have the same long hours to read that I had when I was immobilized under a sleeping baby, but I still spend time with a book every day, as I have since I first learned to read. I know when I'm not plugged into a book because something feels off with my brain and my mood, and that sense that something's wrong corrects itself as soon as I jump into a new story.

Reading isn't a luxury for me. It's essential to my mental health. I have discovered that this is also true for my daughter. We're through the turbulent toddler years now, but when she was in the midst of a tantrum, I would pick her up, carry her to the reading chair, and open a book. It soothed her. As we settled into the chair, she often said, "Mama, please read me a story. It's the only way I can calm down." How insightful of her to know so early how to care for herself.

I'm a better person and a better mother when I'm reading every day. Should my daughter one day choose to have a child herself, I will not tell her that she'll never read again. And if anyone else dares to say that, I'll remind her that people do what they want to do, and good moms take care of themselves — even if they have to read one hundred books to do it.

— Courtney McKinney-Whitaker —

47

Refilling the Bucket

I have come to believe that caring for myself is not self-indulgent.
Caring for myself is an act of survival.
~Audre Lorde

nce a nurse, always a nurse. Even in retirement, I continue to find my greatest joy in caring for people. I take care of others. It's what I do — who I am. Caregiving provides my identity.

However, caring too much and too often come at a high cost. Intermittently, throughout my career, I have found myself experiencing compassion fatigue, unable to understand how I could love my career so much and yet feel so discouraged and depressed. Constantly giving depletes the reservoir. The compassion and care I provide to myself directly affects my ability to serve others.

Unfortunately, somewhere along the way I developed a misguided concept — making myself a priority equaled a self-centered attitude. Whenever I did something for myself, I felt guilty.

Initially, the COVID-19 virus served me well. It forced me to take a much-needed break from my over-scheduled, crazy life. I quarantined, attacked neglected projects, and sincerely enjoyed my home. I immersed myself in Bible study, books, movies, and far too much television.

As the isolation dragged on, I missed my normal schedule and found myself sitting too much and accomplishing little. Although my five-year gratitude journal helped me focus on blessing instead of stressing, discouragement and boredom threatened my mental, emotional, and spiritual well-being.

As if the pandemic weren't enough, the first day I ventured out to resume exercising, I returned to find my husband sitting on the ground. Missing the last step on the ladder resulted in a fractured femur and an entirely new caregiving challenge.

He calmly greeted me with a list. "I need you to do a few things for me. Gather my tools and remnants of this unfinished project. Take them and the ladder into the garage. Get my cigarettes and don't give me any grief."

I bit my tongue to avoid chastising him and quietly completed his list while we waited for the ambulance to arrive.

He commented contritely, "I know you've heard this before, but I'm never getting on another ladder." Yes, I had heard that before. It was not our first rodeo with ladders. But I breathed deeply and remained calm. He was really hurt and there would be time for me to fall apart later.

Over our fifty-year marriage, we had faced multiple health and injury crises. However, watching the EMTs load my husband into the ambulance shook me. The medication eased his pain and rendered him unresponsive. Distraught by his pallor and fixed gaze, I focused on Kerry's chest to assure myself he was alive and breathing.

I arrived at the emergency room only to be denied entry due to the pandemic. Sitting in the parking lot, I realized my inability to control this situation. Word travels quickly in small towns and our pastor joined me in the car where we prayed for my husband and the medical team who cared for him. Then, a bit more at peace, I drove home and waited for telephone updates.

The following weeks led us down an uncharted path. The hospital allowed me to visit during the two days post-op. Then a move to an inpatient rehab facility gave us a taste of real isolation. For nine days, we saw each other only through the window of his room. Fortunately,

Kerry responded quickly, and he returned home to recuperate.

The previous isolation of COVID-19 made adaptation to the physical restrictions of rehabilitation easier. Assisting with personal care and assuming responsibility for all household chores gave me a new appreciation for my husband's contributions to our smoothly running home. Under my husband's expert tutelage, I attempted maintenance tasks and emerged with newfound confidence.

The counterintuitive nature of self-care is not my go-to response and requires a shift in my mindset. I have to force myself to accept that my bucket needs to be refilled regularly. So I make quiet time a priority. This time encompasses scripture reading, prayer and meditation, maintaining a gratitude journal, and also my personal journal. A variety of hobbies feed mind, body and spirit. Attending Weight Watchers, consuming healthy foods, and exercising help me maintain good overall health. Those are the components of my "me time" now. I might choose to do something different in the future.

Though I need my alone time, I also crave socialization, which requires creativity during a pandemic. My social activities often combine with exercise or groups who share my passion for Bible study, reading or writing. Staying connected remains a challenge. Technology provides valuable tools, which even senior adults can master.

Prior to the pandemic, I spoke with and saw my two sisters regularly. COVID-19 isolation encourages us to find new ways to connect. Our Wednesday evening Zoom meetings provide an unanticipated blessing. While it may not be the same as a hug or personal visit, it allows the three of us to connect.

I value the insights gained from COVID-19, my husband's accident and the resulting isolation. I realize that participation in every group or activity is not required. I get to choose those things that recharge and refresh my spirit.

As an oncology nurse, I counseled caregivers to also care for themselves, frequently posing a thought-provoking question, "What happens to your loved one if you get sick?"

Too often, I failed to heed my own advice. I cannot share water from an empty container. Taking care of myself does not equal selfishness. It is a gift I give to those for whom I care and who care for me. When I do so, I give back the best version of myself.

— Wanda Strange —

The Day I Saved Myself

An empty lantern provides no light. Self-care is the fuel
that allows your light to shine brightly.
~Author Unknown

I t had been weeks of the most extreme stress — pre-term labor, an emergency C-section, troubled twins in the NICU. I couldn't remember the last time I ate, showered, or looked in a mirror. I felt at my breaking point as I sat and watched in terror as doctors suddenly streamed into the hospital room, working swiftly at my son's incubator.

It took less than an hour before their exams were completed, and we had a diagnosis: necrotizing enterocolitis. *Necrotizing. Doesn't that mean the death of cells? That can't be what he just said,* I thought to myself.

The doctor continued, and I felt heat behind my eyes as I tried to concentrate on his every word. I captured only fragments: X-rays every six hours; possible intestinal removal; if he doesn't degrade further in forty-eight hours, he will likely survive; there is no cure; he must fight. Tears finally overpowered my ability to restrain them, and a gurgling sob escaped my mouth. The gentle doctor put his hand on my shoulder. "Go home. Call us in six hours and come back in the morning."

My husband braced my arm as we said goodbye to our infant sons and staggered out of the NICU. The pain was unlike anything

I'd ever experienced. It reached so deep inside that it felt like I was being ripped in pieces.

In six hours, we called. No change in his status. The next morning, my son Hayden looked so fragile. I feared holding him, as if moving his little body would spread the death that lurked inside him. The day passed in a blur of exams and worry. I felt inhuman, a ghost, and a failure as a mother. He was only eleven days old and I could not protect him.

My ability to function dwindled as we waited — for hope, for sorrow, for a judgment to be handed down. The next day, at lunchtime, with his status still unchanged but my mental state continuing to degrade, my husband packed me in his truck and dropped me off a mile away from the hospital at a long-forgotten hair appointment. I despairingly asked how I could possibly get my hair colored while my son lay fighting for his life. He squeezed my hand. "You must fight, too. You have two sons and a daughter. We need you to function. Go and forget everything for one hour. You will feel better able to handle all this."

The extreme weight of guilt hung on my shoulders as I stepped into the little hair studio. My usual colorist was out on maternity leave, but her replacement, April, was all smiles. She looked ravishing in all black. I wore yoga pants and yesterday's dirty shirt. My eyes were red with dark circles underneath, and my hair was matted.

When I sat in her chair and viewed my reflection in the mirror, I gasped. There had to be a human inside of me, but I didn't see her. I tried to apologize for my appearance, but I couldn't get the words out. Instead, I bawled. And then I exploded with words; I unleashed on this poor woman all my terror for my son.

April smiled gently and listened without judgment. Every so often, she'd ask a question, which I took as permission to continue rambling. When I finished, there was a moment's pause. Then she calmly told me she was experiencing her own tragedy at that exact moment — a miscarriage, her fifth to be precise. For the first time, I looked into her eyes.

We were a pair of total strangers being knocked down by the cruelties of life. Yet, in her eyes, I saw unbridled hope. Her story, while similar to my own, had one key difference: She knew that everything would work out. She believed. She never doubted that her dream of having a child would come true, even after so much heartbreak.

For an hour, we talked. The mind, she believed, powered life—her life, my life, even my son's life. Our minds function when we function, and that can only occur when we take care of ourselves.

When the appointment was over, I hugged her tight, not wanting to let her go. Then I wiped my tears, and I knew that my mind was stronger. I knew I could fight beside my son. I thanked my husband for driving me to the appointment and told him, "Hayden will survive. We will fight, and he will live."

From that fortuitous moment on, I let go of the guilt. After that appointment, I never doubted. I leaned in on my positive thoughts. I felt strong, and I gave that strength to my son. I knew he would make it.

Six months later, as I waited in the lobby of that hair studio, I saw her—the woman who had given me permission to care for myself. As she turned to wave, I noticed she had a distinct round bump.

She had done it. We had done it.

We had envisioned our best lives. We had cared for ourselves in the face of our worst fears, and our dreams had come true. We believed. We pushed doubt out. We made our minds strong. And today we have the most beautiful babies, who remind us every day that strength comes from both the body and the mind.

— Kristin Baldwin Homsi —

Declutter, Detox, Defend

49

Giving Thanks by Letting Go

You've got to make a conscious choice every day
to shed the old—whatever "the old" means for you.
~Sarah Ban Breathnach

I sneak away to my bedroom to make the phone call. I ease the door closed using both hands, being careful not to let the handle click. The house is full of the smell of roasting turkey. The table is set for nine with the inherited white china and my autumn-themed tablecloth and napkins.

Setting the table for special occasions is one of my favorite tasks. The silverware is polished and placed perfectly on either side of the plates. My grandma passed her silverware on to me, and my mother-in-law has added some of her pieces. I don't care that they don't match; I love that they come together in random order, just as families merge over time. Every time I pull them out, I think of holidays around Grandma's long table so many years ago.

My kids are home for the Thanksgiving weekend, and the usual quiet order of the house has given way to lively conversation and lots of extra work like loads of laundry. We are also hosting my son's girlfriend and her family in addition to my mother-in-law. It's our first time having our son's girlfriend for a holiday, and I'm excited. I can see our families merging in the future, which makes me happy. My mother-in-law is the only grandparent my kids really know; I'm happy she's here, too. My mom, however, is not invited to this Thanksgiving gathering. There have been too many holidays ruined by her drinking.

I've decided to call her today to ease my guilt, to tell myself, "See, I am a good daughter. At least I call my mom on Thanksgiving, even though I can't invite her to my home." I'm hoping she'll tell me that she is spending the day with my sister's family or maybe with her husband's kids. This will also help ease my guilt. I check the bedside clock: 11:45. I'm barely in time for my self-imposed noon deadline. After 12:00, Mom will usually have begun drinking.

My heart pounds fast. I take a deep breath. I know I should not make this phone call. The risk is high. My husband has cautioned me many times, after soothing away another set of tears. But I am drawn to do it anyway, just like a moth that is attracted to the light and his eventual demise.

I'm using the landline and have to look up her number. I think it's odd that I don't know my mother's phone number by heart. My hands shake as I punch in the digits.

"Hello?" Mom answers. My heart beats faster.

"Hi, Mom. I just wanted to say, 'Happy Thanksgiving.'" I can picture her sitting at her kitchen table, cigarette in one hand, pencil in the other. She's probably working on the last few clues of the morning crossword puzzle. Mom still has a thin but sturdy frame, but the years of drinking have given her a big belly. Her gray hair, which she refuses to color anymore, hangs down in long waves, framing her weathered face. She looks older than her seventy-one years, a life of sun, physical labor and smoking having taken their toll.

"Thank you. Happy Thanksgiving to you, too." Her voice is calm, maybe a little surprised to hear from me.

"So, what are your plans today?" I close my eyes, pushing my hope for good news into the universe.

"Not much. Just cooking a turkey for me and Richie."

"Oh. That sounds nice. Is anyone else coming over?" I ask cheerfully.

"No, just the two of us." First pangs of guilt.

"So, what else are you cooking?" I need to change the direction of this conversation.

"Oh, I'll make all the trimmings, too. You know how I like to cook."

"Yes. I'm sure it'll be delicious." She is a great cook.

"Are the kids home?" she asks.

"Yes, they're both home for the long weekend."

"Oh, that's nice to have your kids home with you." The guilt stabs me again.

"Yes, it's so great to have them home." Is she going to ask how they are, what they are up to these days?

"Well, I'll let you go now." She says "let you go now" as if she is the one who called, as if we've been talking for half an hour when it's only been three minutes.

I feel sad about her being home on Thanksgiving with only her husband to keep her company. I know that she will have a hard day taking orders and insults from him and wondering what all her kids are doing. Instead of easing my guilt, this call has only heightened it. I shouldn't be surprised.

I blurt out, "I love you, Mom." I have no idea where that came from. We don't say that or haven't in as long as I can remember.

"Okay," she responds. "Bye." Click.

"Okay? Okay? Who says 'okay' when their daughter says, 'I love you'?" I say to the empty room. "Who does that?"

I look out the window to the back yard. The lawn is damp with last night's rain, but the sun shines brightly. Yellow, orange, red, and brown leaves stick to the wet patio. A slight breeze picks up outside, and more leaves free themselves from the branches and drift down. How easily a tree rids itself of the things that it no longer needs. Without a thought, it discards the leaves that held a purpose all spring and summer but won't be needed for the winter while the tree rests and prepares for spring. It must do this in order to be strong enough to generate new growth.

I pace around my bedroom and ask myself, "Why have I done this to myself again? Why do I keep trying to get her to love me?"

But this time I do not cry. I think of the voices I hear in the kitchen: my husband and my two wonderful kids. They are laughing about something. I think about the phone calls I have with them, each one ending with "I love you" and a reciprocal "I love you, too." I think about the new lives they are both forging with their significant others and the "new" families we will add to our own; new branches to our family tree, new growth. I think about the day ahead and all the fun, warmth and laughter that we will enjoy.

I have more than I ever could have dreamed possible. The futility of my struggle with my mom hits me like a fierce autumn wind. I shake my head. It is finally as clear to me as the blue sky above: I will never get what I want from my mother, but I am finally okay with that. Just like those trees outside, I too must shed what I no longer need and prepare for the new season to come. I head back to the smell of roasting turkey, laughter, and hugs. I have so much to be thankful for on this day.

— Maggie John —

50

The Day I Banished Busy-ness

Half of the troubles of this life can be traced to saying
yes too quickly and not saying no soon enough.
~Josh Billings

I will never forget the moment I banished my busy-ness. We were living in Sydney, Australia, at the time. It was a difficult place to live on just my husband's income, so I was working almost full-time at a location that took one agonizing hour to reach during rush hour.

My husband often traveled for work. Our two children were at school, and our daughter had a number of after-school activities throughout the week. The household chores were a constant demand on my time, and I had decided that my identity was not going to be limited by the roles of mother, wife and housekeeper. Therefore, I played several sports, sang in a choir and attended a weekly theater class. I was also producing a television pilot and hosting the occasional speaking gig about well-being.

Life was full. Life was fast. And, supposedly, life was fulfilling.

The idea of taking a vacation emerged slowly. I was often too busy to pay full attention to my thoughts, and deep reflection was reserved for my random, hurried meditations. So, it was some weeks before I realized that a simple yearning had crept into my awareness, which came in the form of one static image: the view of my own toes, sprinkled with sand, raised to a vertical position with a peaceful ocean view beyond them.

Eventually, the yearning transformed into action, and a family vacation was booked: five days and nights on Green Island, in the tropical waters of the Great Barrier Reef. Green Island is tiny. It boasts a dash of native forest, a handful of resort chalets, a crocodile park, stunning snorkeling spots just off the beach, hundreds of sea turtles and free sunset cocktails on the sand every evening. And for five glorious days, it hosted my toes — often in a very grateful, vertical position.

What the island doesn't have is crowds, cellphone coverage or Internet connection… and I must admit that the fear of being bored flashed across my mind when we arrived. When you're used to living life at breakneck speed, rest doesn't always feel like relief. Sometimes, it feels like a torturous nothingness.

Strangely, I didn't feel the change happening. I knew I was slower; I knew I was enjoying having nowhere to be. And I was surprised at how little I yearned for the quick-fire stimulation of my phone and the Internet. But, when we left the island at the conclusion of our stay, I didn't truly realize all the things I wasn't.

I wasn't running logistical algorithms though my mind, mentally juggling people, locations and activities at warp speed. I wasn't stiff in my shoulders or feeling vice-like tension in my neck. I wasn't breathing in quick, shallow gulps; the gripping pressure of stress in my chest had disappeared. I wasn't desperate to get online and check the news, flick through Facebook, check the latest listings… anything, anything, to feed the constant, frantic pace of my mind. I wasn't snappy or impatient, snarling at others (internally or verbally) to hurry up, get out of my way and, for goodness' sake, DO. NOT. SLOW. ME. DOWN!

I didn't notice these things had gone, but as we boarded the plane to return to Sydney, I noticed them returning. Steadily. Insidiously. Emphatically.

As we flew farther south, I became increasingly aware of what needed to happen in the week ahead. My husband was flying to the U.S. the next day. I had the usual activities to coordinate — my daughter's and mine — plus a speaking gig booked for that week. I would have to arrange a babysitter and make sure that I had two nights' worth of dinner prepared. I would have to cook those meals somewhere between my sports and my son's dentist appointment because there was no way I could get that done between my daughter's activities and mine. My husband's best shirts were in the ironing pile; I would find them as soon as we got home, after I had taken out the garbage. He would have to iron them himself when he arrived at his hotel.

As my mind flew into its familiar frenzy, my body began to tense up again. In less than an hour, the stillness and relaxation of five days were rendered completely useless. It was then, suddenly and sincerely, that a powerful intention rushed through my body: STOP! NO! I WILL NOT DO THIS TO MYSELF!

A few hours prior, I had been relaxing, toes vertical, in the warm sands of Green Island… and my body remembered what that felt like. I wanted it back badly. And I didn't believe that I should have to live in this horrible, overwhelming, exhausting, adrenaline-fueled state of mania anymore.

The changes started as soon as we got home. I cancelled my speaking gig. "So sorry, but this week is not the best timing for me." I gave my daughter the chance to choose the one activity she loved the most, and I wrote an e-mail removing her from the others. Then, I did the same for me. I looked up a sports team that played weekends and I dropped my weekday events. At my first day of work, I approached my boss to discuss how I could work friendlier hours, both to free some time and miss a lot of the rush-hour traffic.

I began to say "no." A lot. I began to notice the state of my body, and to pay attention to tension and unease. I started stopping off at a small forest near our home, just for five minutes every day on the way home from work. Five minutes where I would just sit, breathe, and acknowledge that the world could function without me for those few brief moments.

I learned how to turn my commute — those long minutes in stalled traffic — into a celebration of solitude. That's when I would sing my favorite songs, shed any private tears, ponder unsolved challenges, or work through any unprocessed emotions.

I learned that doing something for me, as an intelligent and empowered woman, can be as simple as paying attention to my truest needs. I learned to prioritize what was most important to me and vital to the well-being of my family. And I decided not to stress over what we could be missing out on if we didn't follow through on an activity or opportunity. I learned how to lovingly offend people, on occasion, if a scheduled event was looming large and causing me, or my family, stress about how to make it happen.

There would still be those times that were too busy. I figured out how to get through those, too. After my husband's longer work trips, school holiday madness, or our relocation back to Singapore, I made sure I had time to unwind, refresh and drain the stress from my body. Now I give myself a gift whenever my body tells me it's necessary — the chance to view my toes, weary and grateful, in some secluded hideaway, and in a definitively vertical position.

— Kim Forrester —

51

A Working Man's Chuck-It List

The first step in crafting the life you want is to get rid
of everything you don't.
~Joshua Becker

bucket list is all about those ambitious tasks and exciting dreams you've been putting off until retirement. The list often includes goals you hope to accomplish and dreams you believe will complete your life. What would you like to do before you die? Attend Burning Man? Drive across the country? Ride a camel in the desert? Tackle a snowman? Play a zombie in a major movie? Hunt for buried treasure in Timbuktu? Crawl through hallways of lasers like a spy? Live in a van down by the river?

I'm a working man entering the later years of my seventh decade. My needs and requirements are small. I would like to rescue a kitten stuck in a tree and die a hero. That's about it. I'm not wealthy or ambitious enough for a bucket list, so I've developed a "chuck-it list" that contains objectives I'm willing and able to let go of. By this I mean anything that drags me down or holds me back from living a happy and comfortable life.

I've spent the last several months putting together my chuck-it list. I've thought about people I never want to meet (Madonna, Freddy Krueger, the inventor of My Pillow), activities I detest most (opera, golf, yoga), and places I wouldn't visit if you paid me (Iraq, Afghanistan, and Disneyland). There are many exotic places and unique experiences that I could care less about. When I wrote them down, a few really pegged my Ick-O-Meter. I'm certain that if I can cross some of this stuff off my list, I will be blissful and fulfilled. Here are a few things I'm giving the old heave-ho:

It's time to say chuck-it to wealth, materialism, and consumerism. I'm not interested in owning the latest iPhone or electronic gadget; I wouldn't use half their features anyway and I don't need to appear trendy. I drive a pickup made of rust and base my fashion taste on what doesn't itch or make me sweat. I don't care about "looking good for my age." Those who have seen me walking around the house in my underwear and sporting a three-day beard can attest to that. Most of the time, I resemble a guy who should be deep-frying butterballs at the county fair. I'm all for feeling energetic and vibrant. (Good health is important, right?) But as far as turning myself into sixty-nine-year-old eye candy, forget about it. A salad can only stay fresh for so long, if you catch my drift.

Higher education has to go. I'm chucking my degree in Philosophy from Humboldt State. What has it gotten me? My small life isn't really progressing toward anything. I haven't amassed a fortune or even risen above the day-to-day muck of a foot soldier. I've also become a little "squirrely" in my senior years. I hear voices and talk to myself a lot. Sometimes, I get into heated internal debates and don't always win. I wear a Bluetooth headset so I don't look completely crazy when I'm talking to no one.

How have I kept from being committed to a home for the mentally disturbed? It has to be a miracle. That's the only explanation.

Another item I'm chucking is "exotic" foods, starting with sushi. I once ate a ball of wasabi thinking it was avocado that had fallen out of my California roll. Gizzards are equally disgusting. I'll never eat them again. Kidneys are just as bad. They taste like pee. I'm chucking candy, too. Well, at least Reese's Pieces. I was recently eating a handful and thought I had dropped one on the carpet. I'm all about the five-second rule so I ate it, but immediately wondered what I had just eaten, as it made a rather sickening crunch between my teeth.

I think you get the point. I've only touched the surface of my chuck-it items. Chances are my list will continue to grow, and as it does, I will congratulate myself on all the adventures and experiences I get to avoid. That's me time at its finest.

— Timothy Martin —

A Little
Housekeeping

Real friends are those who, when you've made a fool of yourself,
don't feel that you've done a permanent job.
~Erwin T. Randall

"You're just a number, and it's just a job for them," announced my best friend. "My advice to you is to keep quiet and smile."

"What?" I asked. "Are you telling me this to make me feel better or worse?"

My friend, Linda, had come all the way from California to take care of our little family in Lancaster, Pennsylvania, while I underwent radiation treatment for breast cancer. I appreciated her help — especially with our boys (ages nine and fourteen) — but some of the things she said absolutely unnerved me.

I had radiation treatments five days a week, and Linda accompanied me every day. That Friday, the "light bulb" went out in the radiation machine. It would take a week for a new bulb to arrive, which would put me back a week and a half on scheduled treatments because of the Memorial Day weekend. I made it known to the receptionist that it simply wasn't acceptable. "Don't you keep extra 'light bulbs' around just in case one goes out?" I asked, rather annoyed.

The receptionist informed me that it wasn't any ordinary "light bulb," and it cost a lot of money. They were doing their best to get one to the radiation center as soon as possible, but I needed to be patient.

It was cloudy outside and threatening to rain. My gloomy mood spilled over to all the staff and my best friend, who kept informing me how out of line I was.

As I sat on the sofa surrounded by travel magazines, I let my friend undo the damage I had caused with my not-so-polite behavior. I was within earshot of everything Linda said as she scheduled my next appointment, including the fact that I was "emotionally unstable."

Linda and I had been best friends since fourth grade, and we had weathered a lot of storms together, but cancer was putting our friendship to the test. Something about facing your own mortality makes you question a lot of things — including the friends you have in your life. For the most part, Linda was a stormy kind of person. She had a way of putting me in my place and treating me as if I were a child. The "hurricane force winds" that blew inside the house even had my husband and boys wondering if it was a good idea to have Linda around.

Normally, I was the stable one and hardly ever made a fuss, even when Linda was at her worst. She was, for the most part, the drama queen. She was also homecoming queen in high school and could talk me into almost anything — including trying out for sign carrier in the band (next to the majorettes). I learned my routine, put Vaseline on my teeth to keep my smile shining, and outperformed even my own expectations during tryouts. I made the cut, but I didn't like being in the limelight. It was Linda who enjoyed that.

I was working full-time and radiating on my lunch break (except on Fridays when I finished work at noon). On the one day I thought we could have a semi-normal day, it was ruined by my outburst at the treatment center. Would our relationship ever be the same? Worse yet, even though she'd been right in her assessment of my behavior, did I want Linda in my life? As we drove home from radiation oncology, I had a heart-to-heart with Linda. "This isn't easy, but I feel like I have to say something," I said tentatively. "Breast cancer at forty has taken me by storm. I'm vulnerable right now, and you can't blurt out everything that's on your mind."

Linda stared at me and replied, "You are so ungrateful. I gave up my life for a week to take care of your family, and this is the thanks I get?"

I pulled off to the side of the road and explained, "My life has been turned upside down, and I'm re-evaluating everything — my job, my friends, and what I want to do with the rest of my life."

It was a quiet ride back to the house after that. It had rained, but now the sun was out and we saw a beautiful rainbow; normally, I'd have stopped to take a picture, but I didn't have the strength.

Linda was leaving the next day, and I had hoped for a better ending, but she went up to the guest room, and I ended up fixing dinner. I tapped lightly on the bedroom door and whispered, "Dinner is ready. Would you like some?"

I got the silent treatment, so I let her be. The next day, as I drove Linda to the airport I apologized and let her know how much I appreciated her help during my final week of radiation.

In typical Linda fashion, she gathered up her things while I parked curbside under the departure sign. She didn't say a word, got out, and slammed the car door behind her. That was the last time I saw Linda.

It's been almost twenty-four years since that spring day in 1996, and I've learned a lot about myself through cancer. It changes you. You figure out what's important in your life and what's not. You set boundaries, and you protect your heart from unhealthy relationships. I had to let go of all the "Lindas" in my life.

Little did I know that my "friendship housekeeping" would come in handy for my second breast-cancer diagnosis three years ago. I was older, wiser, and much more prepared than I was the first time. I learned the secret: Always stay close to people who make you feel like sunshine, and you'll weather any storm that life brings your way.

— Connie K. Pombo —

53

No Service Means No Worries

Being connected to everything has disconnected us from
ourselves and the preciousness of this present moment.
~L.M. Browning, Vagabonds and Sundries

A couple of months before I started high school, my parents gave me the greatest gift any teenage boy could ask for: a cellphone. I lived on that phone all summer with my face buried in its screen. I held multi-day marathon texts with every friend who was lucky enough to have a texting plan. I talked to my girlfriend every night. I ignored my family, my surroundings and, on one unfortunate afternoon, a closed door that seemed to appear out of nowhere. What I was doing was secondary to what everyone else was doing. Being connected was more important than being present.

So, you can imagine my displeasure when I learned what my dad had planned for our family vacation that year. Not the Disneyland trip that I had been hoping for. No beach vacation. "This year," my dad said in the voice of a parent who knows he'll be met with attitude but is soldiering on nonetheless, "we'll be doing something special, something I used to do with my dad when I was a kid. We're going camping!"

His excitement was met with a disappointed sigh, which was my signature communication style at that age, but he was unfazed.

And for the most part, so was I. It wasn't my dream vacation, but it was still a vacation. I remained unbothered throughout the packing, planning and, of course, the instructions that went in one ear and out the other. My mind was on my phone, and the texts were flying back and forth. I was so engrossed in the screen in my hand, in fact, that the first time I can remember truly looking up was when we drove across a bridge en route to our campsite.

I stared out the window in a daze and saw redwoods towering above us, their branches threatening to pierce the blue sky. I saw a roaring river, with slivers of silky black water appearing between crashing white rapids. The air blowing into the car from the open windows was hot and smelled of pine. But none of that mattered to me. The reason I had looked up was for something far more serious. More shocking. My phone no longer had service.

The last hour of the drive was increasingly tense. My dad disclosed that he had chosen a campsite that had no cell service, and my phone — my lifeline — would be useless until we returned home. I would be trapped in the forest for four days with no way to contact the outside world. I went through the full cycle of teenage emotions during the first day of the trip. I raged. I bargained. I pleaded. I flip-flopped from a depressive state to anger and back. None of it mattered. None of it would add bars to my cell service.

I went to bed angry that night. But when I awoke in the morning, something had changed. Instead of lifting my head from the pillow and immediately burying it in my phone, I focused on something else: my surroundings. I let the noise of the wilderness wash over me, animals and bugs creating a ruckus that was both loud and serene at the same time. As my dad and I walked the trails, I felt the rocky earth below me, each step grounding me. Each minute I sank deeper into a peaceful world. We reached a vista, and as I strained my eyes to view the vast expanse that unfolded below me, I felt the weight of a thousand stressors I didn't know I had melt from my shoulders.

The more I let myself become a passive part of nature, the more I focused on myself. I let my mind speak to me. I listened to what I was feeling. I realized I had been so focused on doing, speaking, and staying connected that I hadn't been hearing my own thoughts. I had been neglecting myself.

Those four days passed in a flash. I hiked. I swam. I fished. I learned fishing is boring, even in my newly enlightened state. I spoke less than usual, and I listened more than I had before. My dad and I learned how to start a fire together, after several false starts and some borrowed lighter fluid. He told me stories of his life. Stories I had never heard. Or perhaps I hadn't been listening. I saw the brightest stars I had ever seen, smelled the freshest air I had ever smelled, and ate the sweetest marshmallows I had ever tasted. And when the weekend came to an end, I realized I hadn't thought of my phone once. I hadn't felt the need to be connected to anywhere else. Why would I? What could be better than the moments I was sharing with just my father and nature?

That was nearly fifteen years ago, and I carry that lesson to this day. Especially now. The day I received my first work e-mail, I understood the reason my dad chose a campsite with no access to technology. In a world that asks for more and more connectivity, the need to unplug becomes stronger and stronger. Having me time is nearly impossible when I can be reached at any time of day or night. So, I need to work harder at it.

Whenever I feel like my inner self is slipping, like I'm ignoring the little voice in my head that needs a break, I take a page out of my dad's guide. I pack up the tent and drive until my phone shows those two magic words: "No service."

— Noam Paoletti —

54

Forever Changed

We live in a wonderful world that is full of beauty,
charm and adventure. There is no end to the
adventures we can have if only we seek them
with our eyes open.
~Jawaharial Nehru

Resting on my swing, rocking back and forth, I close my eyes and enjoy the sounds of autumn — the cool wind, the leaves rustling as they fall to the forest's floor. The caw of a crow, the coo of some doves, and the rat-a-tat-tat of a woodpecker add to the sensory experience.

Several years ago, I retired after more than three decades in a stressful and exhausting job in a city of millions of people. Back then, if I closed my eyes, I would hear the racket of traffic, sirens and the chatter of people around me all the time.

I was a shift manager in passenger service for an enormous airline in the busiest terminal in one of the largest airports in the world. And if that wasn't rough enough, I was the guy everyone called to deal with the loudest passengers with the biggest problems. I wore stress like a suit and then internalized it into an ever-churning stomachache. Oh, I got good at handling it, but I was tired and longed for escape.

So, I left and moved from a tiny apartment at the bottom of a stack of other tiny apartments. Everyone told me I wouldn't leave the big city, or I wouldn't last long before coming back.

They were wrong. I now live in a house in the middle of a forest.

My closest neighbor is over half a mile away. I live five miles from a small town and thirty miles from a small city. When I close my eyes now, there are no bustling people, cars clanking or any of the manmade noises that polluted my existence.

I'm home, where after basking in the surrounding sounds, I can open my eyes and spot a spectacular cardinal in a tree forty feet away or watch a bunny nibbling grass under a gardenia bush a few steps beyond my patio's edge.

Several times a day, I go outside to immerse myself in the great outdoors, with my dogs Thunder and Trixie accompanying me. With me on my swing and my dogs on their cots, we marvel at the grand performance of Mother Nature.

Seasons change, temperatures rise and fall, and witnessing it fulfills my love of the phenomena of our natural world. Every hour of every day is a wondrous adventure when spent amongst this scenery within my reach.

To spy a little green lizard change his colors as he halts his scurry, pauses on a different colored surface and then blends his hue is amazing. To see my dogs go crazy at the sight of a wild turkey — one who's unconcerned about their excited barking behind our fence — fulfills me.

Sometimes, the slightest hint of skunk swirls in the air as he hides just beyond the forest's boundary. Recently, I witnessed a possum trot out of the woods' undergrowth a few feet into view and then head back to cover. After a few seconds, a second possum followed the exact track of the first.

My house sits on a hill with a pond at the bottom of a slope. It's a whole different ecosystem from my forest but just as relaxing and fascinating to observe. Clinging willows and silver maples satisfy their thirst, cattails sprout right out of the water, and prairie cordgrass stabilizes the wet bank. An abundance of critters also depends on the giving waters of the pond. Gray and white cranes frequent the spot as they fish for their lunch. Deer stop by for a drink. Ducks visit every year as they pass through, escaping the harsh winter of the North and then returning for spring's awakening.

Focusing on the pond and its surroundings allays my tension and deepens my understanding that man's touch need not be on everything. Since moving to my forest, my blood pressure has stabilized in a healthy range. I've lost weight, and I am no longer subject to an addictive personality and immediate gratification. Spiritually, the woods have found me, and I breathe in a life of calm and satisfaction.

I've never slept better or felt more rested. I focus on what's in front of me with little interest in the distractions that kept me off balance in the past.

Thoreau's quest in living next to Walden Pond was to live deliberately and simplify his life. Living in the forest, my goal was to escape the rat race. But a funny thing happened on this journey: I found a beautiful world of unspoiled landscape, and I am forever changed by it.

— Jonney Scoggin —

55

The Cleanup

*Having a simplified, uncluttered home
is a form of self-care.*
~Emma Scheib

I used to make the same New Year's resolution every year — to simplify my life and make time for me — but I was always too busy to stick with it for very long. Change is not easy for me. I liked helping people and hated to say "no" when I was asked for help. I was so overcommitted that it felt like I was dragging an anchor around all the time. I didn't have time to write, quilt, or just sit and read a book.

I often jumped in the car, backed out of the driveway and forgot where I was going. I once forgot my son! I had dropped him off for his swimming lesson and then gone on to do errands. When I got home, I thought, *Where's Darren?* Then I remembered where I had left him. I screeched into the parking lot, and he was sitting on the curb crying. I felt terrible, and I was cured… for a while.

I soon went back to overcommitting but became an avid list maker. That kept me a little better organized. If I did something that was not on the list, I would write it down just so I could cross it off! It made me feel more productive when I could see all the things I had accomplished at the end of the day.

I thought the lists would help me accomplish things more effectively so I would have time for myself each day. Instead, I felt tired all the time, and it was hard to fall asleep as I mentally went over my to-do list for the next day. I was stressed and miserable.

I was always doing five things at once but never felt like I was doing a good job at anything. Once, while hosting a meeting for my Girl Scouts' parents, I heard a little snicker or two every time I turned around to write something on the board. Later when I got home and changed my clothes, I found that when I rushed to get my pants out of the dryer, an extra pair of underwear had clung to the inside and hung over right in the back. I was mortified!

As I ran from task to task, I could never outrun the feeling that something was missing; that was real happiness, which seemed just out of reach. I felt like I was missing a key piece of the instructions on how to put my life together.

My real awakening came about in a strange way a few years ago. We were having the inside of our house painted and so we had to move all the knickknacks, curtains and accessories out of the painters' way as they moved from room to room. We put most of these items in the garage. We lived a simpler life — without stacks of magazines, photos and "treasures" — while our house was transformed with new, restful colors.

Somehow, we got along quite well without all the items we had collected over the years. We decided to think hard about what we would put back. Layers of lace curtains were replaced with simple, sheer curtains in the living room. Across the back of the house, we left the windows with just the lovely, wooden blinds that had been overshadowed by curtains before. My husband painted the old, crazed chandeliers black and they looked brand-new!

And so it went from room to room. We eliminated many decorations that friends and family had thoughtfully given us, because they made the rooms feel small and cluttered. Even though I hadn't wanted to hurt anyone's feelings, it was liberating to put back only the things we really wanted. The house felt so much more open, peaceful and beautiful.

When I started to hang our calendar back up, I noticed how full each day was. Every square was filled in. I decided to continue my decluttering with the calendar.

It was near the end of July, so I started "clearing" August and September. I kept doctors' appointments, family events and commitments to church. But I removed extra tasks I had taken on that left me very little time to relax, read or spend time with family.

At first, people were surprised when I told them in the most loving way I could that I wouldn't be able to help them. Over time, I got used to saying it and they got used to hearing it. Now, I think carefully before I take on anything new.

I am more relaxed, and I have found ways to help in advisory capacities instead. I also review projects via e-mail rather than committing to weekly or monthly meetings. The funny thing is that stepping back has allowed other people to step forward and realize their potential.

I still make lists to keep myself organized, but I am down to one page. I feel like I have blessed others by donating our unused items to charity. But, most of all, I schedule time for me each day — to do what I want. The uncluttered beauty of our home and schedule gives me great peace and joy.

— Judee Stapp —

56

Learning to Read Again

Reading is essential for those who seek
to rise above the ordinary.
~Jim Rohn

"I noticed something," my friend Ashley said. "Your bookshelf is empty."

I nodded absently, listening to the various park sounds around us. Kids were running and laughing, the wind was blowing, and the sun was keeping a warm day bright. I could feel the sun on my face just as much as I could feel my best friend staring at me with concern.

"I'm looking at your online bookshelf right now. It's clear of books this year. Why?" she asked.

"I wish I could read, but I just don't have enough time," I replied, thinking about the many hours I'd spent, in the past month alone, helping someone with their computer or browsing online news articles instead of reading novels.

"But, like, who's going to recommend fun books to me?" Ashley asked, sounding shocked. "You always were my book buddy. What happened?"

"I don't know," I said. As if to reveal all my secrets, my iPhone emitted a high-pitched ding and then started reading off my next calendar event.

"Help Tom with his computer. Two hours."

"Well, there's your problem!" Ashley said excitedly. "Try to slot in some reading time."

When I got home that day, I deleted a calendar event that was supposed to happen at 9:00 that night and typed into the description box, "Read a novel."

When the event arrived, I felt so guilty that I hesitated to turn on the audiobook. With resolve, though, I pressed Play and sank into a cozy young-adult novel. I soon relaxed and noticed that I was genuinely enjoying myself.

The next morning, I woke up a lot happier than usual. I usually woke up feeling like I didn't get enough sleep, like I'd *never* get enough sleep. That morning was different. My movements felt a lot smoother. I caught myself smiling as I ate cereal. I realized I was eager to get back into the story I was reading the night before.

I had forgotten the excitement I used to have when I read on a regular basis. Throughout that day, a feeling of happiness came over me. I wanted to experience this feeling again in the future, so I called Tom at lunch.

"Hey, Tom," I said. "I know I'm supposed to come over today, but I wanna stay home and read tonight. Is that okay?"

"Of course," Tom replied. "Have a good time tonight."

"You, too," I said.

I spent the rest of the day doing something I hadn't done in years: clear my calendar for myself. Each time I put "personal time" in my calendar, I felt really happy.

When it came time to read for the second night in a row, it was easier than the previous night. I even turned off my phone and sank into bed with headphones on.

Then I turned my phone back on and called Ashley to tell her that I had canceled a lot of upcoming appointments. She was excited. "That's really great. My bookshelf is dwindling. I'm glad to have my book buddy back."

"I'm glad to be back," I said. "Now I have to go. I need to finish this chapter."

—Robert Kingett—

57

Me First Beats Martyrdom

As you grow older, you will discover that you have two hands,
one for helping yourself, the other for helping others.
~Maya Angelou

We all hear, all the time, that we need to take care of ourselves first — because that's how you're the most helpful to everyone else in your life, namely your children, aging parents, neighbors, or any loved one nearby. Yet, how often does that me-first mandate translate to everyday life?

For me, it's not often, and I suspect I am the norm, not the exception. For some reason, we women are wired differently. I can barely recall an incident where my own needs trumped someone else's. Even as a child, I can remember not wanting my little brother or sister to do without, hence I did. Whether it was a Christmas celebration where the children outnumbered the gifts, a birthday party where the take-home prizes fell one short, or a family dessert where there were two cupcakes for three children, I was always the one who did without while smiling.

Such behavior followed me to the workplace. I found myself assuming similar roles: the big sister, the peacemaker, the appeaser. A pressing Friday deadline? No worries, I'll stay late. No coffee in the office kitchen? No problem, I'll make a Starbucks run. An unexpected Sunday meeting? No big deal, I'll cover it. And that routine continued for years — until the day that it didn't.

Looking back, I am at a loss to identify what significant event triggered such a change. Truth be told, I don't think there was a single event. Rather, it was a years-in-the-making build-up. But I do recall the day I just said, "No!" My boss at the time was packing up early on a summer Friday afternoon, expecting me to cover an unexpected deadline. I recall marching into his office and simply stating that I had to leave by 5:00 p.m. He hadn't asked me to stay late. Rather, he just assumed that I would and, with all due respect, had no reason to think that I would not since I had stayed late for years without being asked.

Truth be told, I guess he must have been a bit surprised — incredulous perhaps — but I did not linger to discuss it. I merely returned to my cubicle, feeling rather giddy, and packed up my things by 4:55 p.m. I was prepared to enjoy a summer weekend.

That day marked a turning point in my life and a new chapter in self-care. I wish I could say that the change was dramatic, but it was not. That self-care muscle had to be developed and then exercised regularly. That summer weekend did turn a new page, but it would take years for that book to be finished.

My journey to self-care started with leaving my job on time. Well, almost on time — old habits die hard. And some days, I was still there after 5:00. But most days, I arrived home when there was still daylight. That was a new phenomenon, and my first reaction was guilt. *The sun is just setting… I should be at work,* I told myself.

Years ago, I learned that the quickest way to silence that nagging voice in my head was exercise. So, I laced up my sneakers and started to walk every evening upon arriving home. A creature of habit, those twilight walks became a ritual, and I looked forward to the alone time these walks provided. Before long, I was completing three miles within an hour.

One good habit seemed to beget another, and soon I was sleeping better and eating healthier. My energy level was at an all-time high. Feeling so much better about myself, I visited a new hair salon and had my "crowning glory" cut, re-styled, and highlighted. That week, I received so many compliments on my appearance that I decided to incorporate a weekly visit to the salon into my budget.

Ironically, every employee received a cost-of-living increase the following week, and mine was exactly the cost of a salon visit. For someone who had religiously banked every increase, I felt almost giddy earmarking the money for a weekly indulgence. But I also felt that the Universe was applauding me. Phrases like "Yes, you are worth it!" suddenly started to challenge that nagging voice.

While routine visits to the local hair and nail salon can be outward signs of self-care, I also felt an internal, seismic shift within myself. Ironically, while I now had more me time and downtime, I found myself becoming more possessive of that time. It was difficult to articulate, but I didn't want to just "fill time."

Perhaps I sensed somehow that time is a limited and precious commodity. While I may have had more hours each day, I knew that there were symbolically more grains of sand in the bottom of the hourglass than were at the top. And what a wake-up call that realization proved to be.

In the coming weeks, I thought a lot about what makes me happy, gives me pleasure, and provides me with purpose. I started spending more time in nature, treasuring conversations with friends and loved ones, and enjoying cultural pursuits.

An avid reader my entire life, I made a pact with myself concerning all the time I devoted to reading. If I didn't thoroughly enjoy a book by the third chapter, I stopped reading it. That may sound like a minor tweaking to most, but for someone like me, who on occasion portrays some OCD traits, it felt like freedom. A self-confessed people pleaser, I then promised myself that if certain friendships had run their course, I didn't have to continue to nurture them. And while I continued to eat healthy, I gave myself a lifetime pass to never eat turnips, Brussels sprouts, or broccoli again!

It's been close to ten years now since I began my self-care regimen. Looking back, I cringe when I think about how negligent I was in regard to caring for my younger self. Back then, I measured my worth by how much I gave, how much I sacrificed, or even how much I had suffered for some greater good, which I still have trouble defining. Truth be told, by taking better care of myself, I find that I have become a better, more accepting and authentic person than the martyr I had been so proud to emulate in my misguided youth.

— Barbara Davey —

58

Out of Breath

Yoga is the ultimate practice. It simultaneously
stimulates our inner light and quiets our overactive
minds. It is both energy and rest. Yin and Yang.
We feel the burn and find our bliss.
~Elise Joan

I t felt like someone had clenched their fist around the center of my chest and wouldn't let go. The tension was from the stuff of everyday life: raising kids, working, keeping the house, and worry, worry, worry.

I worried about my kids while they slept, listening for their soft breathing long after they'd advanced from cribs to toddler beds to bunk beds. I worried about hurts, real and imagined. I worried about sicknesses, minor and non-existent. About potty training, first days of school, and sleepovers at friends' houses.

I fretted about finances. Would there be enough to pay the bills? Could we afford our mortgage? What if something went wrong?

I stressed about things I'd done and things I wished I'd done, what I'd said and how I imagined others heard what I'd said.

I took work home in my head.

I worried I was in the wrong marriage.

And I was a hypochondriac. A flutter in the chest must be a heart attack; a headache meant I had a brain tumour.

There was so much to worry about. I let things that were completely out of my control spin through my head day and night.

I couldn't breathe.

So, I signed up for a yoga class. I loved the stretching; it felt so good to stretch. I was proud of myself for being able to manage some of the poses, but while it offered a brief pause from the chaos of life, I couldn't figure out how to carry it through my day. And what the heck was the instructor talking about when she said I should breathe from my belly anyway? My breath went as far as my upper ribcage, and that was about it. As far as I was concerned, breathing from the belly was anatomically impossible.

I finished the eight-week class and went back to worrying.

I became overwhelmed at work, cranky with the kids, unhappy with my husband, and tired all the time.

And the tightness in my chest stayed through it all. The more I worried, the tighter it got. The tighter it got, the more I worried.

I had to do something.

I decided to go back to yoga. I'd loved it, even if I hadn't exactly retained what I learned.

This time, it changed my life.

The tension wasn't just in my chest; it had radiated into my joints. One knee wouldn't go down when I sat cross-legged; it seemed my hip had seized. My shoulders were so tight that I could barely hold a plank position. My sensitive back went into shock, and I nearly couldn't get up off my mat.

Something kept calling me back, though, and I returned again and again. With persistence, I became more fit and flexible. I languished in child's pose, held warrior strong, and balanced in tree.

And this time I learned how to breathe.

With each pose, the reminder: inhale, exhale. Gradually, my breaths got deeper, but I would still become frustrated when I tried to picture my breath flowing into my abdomen, beyond the length of my lungs.

Until this: With one hand on my heart and the other on my belly, I followed my breath as it flowed through my nose, my throat, my hand moving upward as it reached my chest. This time, I didn't stop. This time, I kept breathing, deeper and deeper, until I felt my belly rise. And there it was: the elusive breath. I had breathed through the blockage. I finally understood.

With each successive inhalation and long, slow exhalation, something unexpected happened: I loosened the grip, repeatedly, until it let go completely.

I could breathe.

The physical release was palpable. I felt freed from the knot I had carried for so long. I might have expected it had I known I could breathe past it, but I wouldn't have anticipated the power that came from learning how to control my breath. Suddenly, I had this ability to intercept the tension at its source.

It's helped me to realize that while I can't control the universe, I can control my breath. I learned that breath is not limited to my lungs. My breath is no longer trapped in the upper recesses of my ribcage; I can breathe beyond my chest. I can breathe into the length of my legs, into the tips of my fingers, up to the top of my head.

Life has happened since then, good things and bad. And the reel of worries hasn't prevented or produced a single event. Ironically, in learning how to control my breath, I learned how to let go of control.

Now, when the worries start creeping in, I just breathe.

—Dawn Marie Mann—

59

The Six Months Test

Your purpose should dictate how you spend your time.
~Brenda Johnson Padgitt

I stare out the window at the first roses of the season. Even their exquisite beauty doesn't register with me. Self-diagnosis reveals that I have a huge case of the "overwhelms."

Since I've retired, I've taken on too many activities to fill my so-called discretionary time. The result is that I have no time for myself—to finish reading the novel I started two months ago, go to lunch with a friend, or sometimes even return phone calls. My mild depression is certainly not life-threatening, but I can see no change for my schedule in the foreseeable future!

Where does my time go? At the end of the day, can I even account for my activities?

I somehow find the common sense to deal with this. I decide to evaluate what I would do if I only had six months to live. It's The Six Months Test. I make a list of all my activities other than those that involve my husband and home. It's a hodge-podge:

Tutoring
Babysit grandchildren

Church choir
Testing for a commercial college
Bible study
Sunday school helper
Writing
Writers' critique groups

Then I analyze it. What makes my heart sing? Where is my unique competence? What am I particularly suited for? Why am I doing some things and not doing others?

My determined focus is kids, and more specifically, writing for kids. With that in mind I put a "K" by all items that have to do with kids in my life, and an "A" by all activities that have to do primarily with adults. That helps me see if my activities are really in line with my stated focus.

There are other things to consider, too. Do I need income from any of my activities? Is the remuneration I receive from an activity enough to warrant my involvement? As a writer, I find that some projects take an enormous amount of my time and the pay isn't commensurate with the effort. So unless I write fast, ten cents a word will not make me rich.

Will an activity keep me in touch with the significant people in my life or will it hinder quality relationships? Will I still have time to do the things that keep love alive in my marriage?

Does an activity harmonize with my current interests or will it take me in an entirely unrelated direction? For example, I have been asked to collect donations in my neighborhood, and to help with costumes for the church play. Are these really things I would do if I had six months to live?

Probably the most important question I ask is, "Which of my commitments could others carry out if necessary? Which can only I meet?"

If I learned I had only six months to live, here's what I decided to keep on my list:

1. I would babysit. These are my grandchildren. We've mixed cookies together sitting on a beach towel on the kitchen

floor. We make Play-Doh food to use in the playhouse, we rake leaf-houses together, and carve roads in the dirt. We have a mutual love affair going.

2. I would tutor. My remedial students have begun to like reading. Often, I am their number one fan. Of course, someone else could teach them, but no one can give them exactly what I do. Our interaction is unique, so I'd keep them as long as I could.

3. I would continue attending my Bible study class. I can study alone. I do, and I find it rewarding, but I would need the prayer support of the class members during my final six months.

4. I'd write because I must. God called me to take my life-long love of Bible stories and write them in simple and exciting ways for little children. It is my passion in life.

So, I have four things that passed The Six Months Test. Interestingly, these are identical to those I perceived as mine alone to do.

I put down my pen and slowly rock in my chair, processing my next steps. Because my mind has shifted off my pressure pile and onto my priorities and passions, this was time well spent. I can now grant myself permission, with certainty, to cut some activities at their logical termination points, and sever the cord immediately on others.

That simple test was just the attitude adjustment I needed. Now I can step outside into the sunshine and begin enjoying those first roses of the season.

— Pauline Youd —

Giving Your Time with Joy

60

Patched-Together Positives

The true meaning of life is to plant trees,
under whose shade you do not expect to sit.
~Nelson Henderson

"How many blankets do you have ready?" my husband asked that crisp February morning as we finished breakfast. A semi-retired teacher, he didn't have a substitute teaching job for the day. The highways were clear of the most recent snow, and he had cabin fever. The "cure" was a road trip that offered sightings of deer and bald eagles.

Blankets? He also saw the day's open slate as an opportunity to drive to a hospital in an impoverished area about seventy miles away where I'd regularly donated baby blankets for families in need.

"Twelve," I replied.

"How soon can you hit the road?"

About two hours later, I walked into the obstetrics wing and handed the bags of blankets to an astonished charge nurse.

"I was down to my last blanket," she said, "and I didn't know how I would get more." Then she and the other nurse opened the bags and admired every blanket.

Afterward, as my husband and I shared a big bowl of chicken soup in the hospital cafeteria, we expressed awe over this trip's timing.

A decade earlier, I'd started donating home-sewn baby blankets as part of my church's one-day community volunteer emphasis. Worship services were canceled, and we were to fan out and bless our town. Public places got weeded, graffiti was painted over, the elderly or shut-ins were helped with repairs or yard work, and the cars of single mothers were serviced.

My asthma meant bypassing the dirty or outdoor jobs. I'm clumsy with a hammer and useless around car repairs. But I can sew, and I had learned that our local hospital could use about a dozen baby blankets a month to give to needy families. That fit the weekend's "serving" emphasis. A dozen would stretch my sewing skills, but I could assemble them over several days.

When I delivered the completed blankets to the grateful nurses, something clicked inside. I enjoyed doing this. I could do more.

I never imagined that I'd sew and donate 175 blankets over that first year. Or that a decade later, I would have delivered more than 1,200 blankets to several local hospitals and ministries. Creating something pretty and being in touch with appreciative people also became "good medicine" at a time when life events made me feel emotionally depleted.

Friends and strangers began sharing from their sewing supplies, and I shopped thrift stores and yard sales for fabric and batting. At one yard sale, when I told the seller what I would do with her fabric, she replied, "Give me your phone number. I have more." Within a week, she delivered a heaping box of juvenile fabrics from her quilter's stash. When I asked how much I owed her, she said, "Nothing. I know you'll put it to good use." That yielded twenty-six blankets.

At another yard sale, the seller had more scrap fabric but needed time to gather it up. When she called a week later, I expected just a small trash bag of scraps. Instead, she hauled out several bulging garbage bags of big flannel scraps from her business of sewing pajama pants. She seemed unwell, and something told me to sew these as quickly as possible. Within a few weeks, I sent her a thank-you note with a photo of fifteen baby blankets made from her scraps. A few months later, I saw her obituary in the paper. She'd died of cancer — perhaps aware when we met that she wouldn't live long.

One day, a woman came to buy a used bike from us. Learning she worked at the hospital where I donated blankets, I invited her to come in and see the blanket I was currently finishing. She not only bought the bike but came back with a sack of fabric scraps for future blankets!

One creative friend, planning a surprise party for my sixty-fifth birthday, turned it into a "future blankets event." She asked guests to bring baby-appropriate fabric or fabric-store gift cards as my gifts!

Before long, I started donating to other hospitals in adjacent counties that also had significant "needy" populations.

Confidentiality rules meant I never knew who got the blankets, but I heard a few stories. One blanket became the "comfort quilt" for a very sick little boy taken by ambulance to a larger hospital 150 miles away. The blankets also went with newborns discharged to foster homes — some awaiting adoption, others "drug babies" needing special care.

One friend, an obstetrics nurse, shared in general terms about a woman who showed up at the hospital alone to deliver her fifth child. With no family member or friend to support her, and hampered by a language barrier, the woman cried throughout labor and delivery. "I felt she needed special encouragement," my friend said, "so I gave her one of your blankets."

My blankets weren't fancy, just colorful and fun: forty-nine five-inch squares, arranged seven-by-seven, thin batting for the "sandwich," and backed by flannel or a similar soft fabric. Each blanket took about two hours to make. Sometimes, while sewing, I thought back to this project's genesis with my faith community and how they symbolized Isaiah 61:1, which says God can "bind up the brokenhearted." That was my hope: that these blankets, created by "binding up" scraps of fabric, would end up in homes of personal, social or financial brokenness — with people who needed a caring touch.

Eventually, arthritis in my hands slowed the sewing pace, but the blankets accomplished another purpose beyond wrapping somebody's baby. They helped affirm that I am a valued person, and that what I do with my free time matters in a positive way.

— Jeanne Zornes —

61

The Cheerleader

Be kinder to yourself. And then let your kindness
flood the world.
~Pema Chodron

I opened my car window and called out, "Ma'am! Ma'am!" The only lady in the parking lot looked around until she saw me. "I just wanted to tell you how nice you look today," I said. "The colors you have on are beautiful on you."

Her face registered surprise for a second, and then she smiled. "Thank you!" she called back.

Her final steps to her car seemed lighter, and I smiled to myself.

I have made it a point in recent years to compliment people, especially women and girls. Instead of just thinking that someone looks nice or did a great job, I say it out loud.

It doesn't take long, and it's easy. So, I wonder, why don't more people do this?

It's like having a cheerleader in my head. When I see someone who deserves a compliment or a kind word, the cheerleader jumps up and down and throws her pompoms in the air.

I grew up with very few cheerleaders in my own life. It wasn't until the last five or ten years that people have come forward to compliment me on my artwork. I have never been assertive and not having any cheerleaders on my team hindered my self-growth.

In 2006, my counseling book entitled *Jellybean Jamboree* was published. It was the first time I felt really good about myself. My mother embraced the book, showing it to everyone within a fifty-mile radius who couldn't run away fast enough. She became my cheerleader.

But I was in the middle of fighting a battle for my life. I had been diagnosed with clinical depression, along with anxiety and panic attacks. In those days, it was frowned upon to talk about mental illnesses in public. Now, with all the celebrities going public about their illnesses, it feels like it's become almost prestigious to have a mental illness in Hollywood.

It has taken many years and more effort and determination than I thought I was capable of to conquer this illness. With no cheerleaders in my court, I fought this battle alone. I am proud of the progress I have made thus far.

There are times when I thought, *If only I had someone to hold me and say, "Susan, I believe in you. You can do this, and I'll be there every step of the way."* I wonder how much sooner I would have recovered. I'll never know.

As women, we have learned from our role models to be quiet. We downplay our own achievements even when we do receive a rare compliment.

Now, when I compliment someone and she starts the game of denial, I say to her, "Just say thank you." Most women are relieved that they don't have to deny the compliment; they can accept the praise without guilt.

Recently, I met a cheerleader. He told me to quit making excuses and putting myself down. He told me I wasn't a victim of anything except my own thinking. He and I talked about the brick wall I had built around me. I hung up the phone after a conversation and felt my shoulders straighten.

Yesterday, I stopped at the Dairy Queen after a very difficult morning. The young girl at the drive-through window was stunning.

"Oh, my gosh!" I gushed. "Your eyes are beautiful! You are so beautiful!"

The girl reacted like every other female that I have complimented out of the blue. Then she smiled. I added on: "You have dimples! You are so beautiful!"

She gave me my meal, and I drove off smiling. My morning was completely forgotten. I only saw the beautiful face of someone whose day I had made.

It made my day, too. It feels good to be a cheerleader.

Cheerleading doesn't require any skills. It only takes a few seconds, although you do have to remind yourself to do it. Eventually, it becomes a habit.

— Susan Jelleberg —

62

Self-Care Found in a Library Basement

The world was hers for the reading.
~Betty Smith

For the better part of the last decade, I've been a housewife. A mommy. An aspiring chef. A homeschooling teacher. A student. A founder of an organization for grieving parents. A querying novelist who usually wakes up to rejection notices.

I'm exhausted.

This year, I decided to make things easier. I got on a cleaning schedule so I wouldn't always feel behind. I gave myself time in the morning to brush my hair, shower, brush teeth, and get out of sweats or pajamas. Moisturize my face. Perhaps even paint my nails.

It worked great. For a week. Maybe two.

Then I realized that doing those things weren't my version of self-care. They were just personal chores to feel presentable. Picking out clothes, brushing hair, and moisturizing my face weren't calming. It was physical self-care, but I needed more. I needed mental and emotional self-care, too.

I started reading at night. It was my personal time to forget everything but the fictional world I was sinking into. But I was so exhausted from the day that I'd read two pages and fall asleep. If I managed longer, a dog would bark for attention. A cat would scratch at the door until I let it in. A kid would wake up and need to go potty. Relaxing? Not quite. Each time I brought a mug of chamomile tea to bed, it always went cold before I could enjoy it.

With kids home all day, being a one-car family, and working at home, I couldn't find anywhere that made me feel relaxed. My anxiety levels rose. Stress dreams caused me to grit my teeth, make my jaw sore, and tear up my mouth. I never felt rested when I woke. Even with a schedule, there were always more things I didn't do that weighed heavily on me. Should I have read the kids one more story when they begged for it? Did I have enough patience? Did I slow down and stop the endless chores to give them enough attention today? Did I remember to enjoy them enough, as time is so fleeting?

Then one of my personal favorite days of the year arrived — my library's giant book sale, where I usually come home with no less than a hundred books. I never missed the event — not for pouring rain, lack of vehicle, or a babysitter who calls last minute to say she can't make it. No matter what, I found a way to get there and be first in line. This year, miraculously, there was nothing standing in my way.

My husband and I were first in line with an hour to wait as the workers chatted in front of us. Then they said this was the last year. After more than twenty-five years, the people who ran it would be retiring. No one had stepped up to take their place. Certain that I had heard wrong, I glanced at the flyer, but there it was — where the announcement for next year's book sale date was, I saw a blank spot.

"This can't be the last year," I said to my husband. "I've been coming here for more than half my life!"

"You should do it," my husband said, pushing me forward with his elbow.

The idea instantly made me excited. Working at the library had been a lifelong dream. But instead of signing up, I laughed. "I can't do that," I said, rolling my eyes. "What about the kids? I'm already too busy. I can't stretch myself any further than I already am. This is a huge job, especially for one person."

"We could figure something out. You'd be perfect for this."

One of the leaders of the book sale walked over to check the long line. It was nearly time to let everyone in. I looked over my shoulder. So much of the community had turned out for this event.

"My wife is interested in volunteering to run the book sale," I heard my husband say.

I sent daggers at him with my eyes. As an introverted, shy person, I hated the attention I suddenly had when everyone surrounded me.

"You would?" one exclaimed. "Come with me. I'll introduce you to everyone before the sale starts."

I hadn't said a word yet, but my hand was being pulled, and I was being introduced to the team.

"Could you start on Thursday? We'll get you down to the basement where we keep all the books, and you can start sorting. We'll teach you how to do it. You could come down maybe two or three times a week to do it."

Two or three times a week? But the idea of seeing the library's basement, going into a place that was always locked, intrigued me too much to back out. One meeting couldn't hurt anyway, right? I'd give it a go.

The excitement of the book sale dimmed as this new prospect invaded my mind. I could finally work for the library. I could touch all the books. I'd be the one to choose which books went into the book sale. The event that I loved dearly would be mine to run.

Suddenly, I couldn't wait. The nervous part of my mind quieted as the eager part took over. For the next several days, it was all I could think about.

On Thursday, when I met the team, the nervous part vanished. I loved my role. I loved the team of library volunteers. I loved the basement that made my nose runny and needed a constant loud dehumidifier, with frequently damp floors from excess rain. I loved every single part of it.

I had been scared that it would be too much and take away time for the self-care that I desperately needed.

Instead, it became my mental self-care. Three times a week, first thing in the morning, I do my physical self-care chores. I get dressed, brush my hair and teeth, and put on my shoes. I say goodbye to my family and walk three and a half blocks to the library, where I say hello to the librarian and unlock the basement door. Once there, I get an hour or two all to myself. No one is there, just me and books. I spend the time in solitude around some of my favorite things in the world. I sort the books into boxes, looking through them and removing cute bookmarks to take home.

Getting alone time out of the house, in the place I've loved since I was eleven years old, and handling hundreds of books at a time, has become the perfect self-care I never knew I needed. By taking on the library job, I get a peaceful start to my day. Relaxed. Excited. On the days I don't go, I'm eager to wake up the next day and think about what amazing books are waiting for me.

I always heard that self-care looks different for everyone. Mine just happens to look like a hundred-year-old, dingy library basement covered in books.

— Jill Keller —

63

Redefining Doing It All

*Practice self-rescue first before you "help"
someone else.*
~Maureen Joyce Connolly

"I have no idea how you do it all," a friend remarked after I had a speaking engagement in Cleveland. Before I even thought about answering her with some witty remark, I was thinking about what "doing it all" entailed.

Two days earlier, I had stumbled into my closet at 5:15 a.m. to put on yoga pants and swap out the brightly colored dresses I had originally packed in my suitcase for ones with muted colors. I gulped down a yogurt and banana. I forgot to make the bed and take out the trash. Then, on the flight I was too excited to sleep. I was answering e-mails from my full-time job after checking into my hotel. The conference I was speaking at had an afternoon reception. I made a point to change out of my yoga pants and into my most sensible heels and a black dress with little pink flowers on it.

After dinner in downtown Cleveland that night, I worried about how I would make it to the convention center by 7:30 the next morning. Would I even be able to deliver an hour-long keynote presentation and two other presentations that day? I'm a confident public speaker, but I was worried about looking presentable, conveying my enthusiasm

(I'm not a morning person), and using my voice constantly throughout the day.

The speaking went off without a hitch (other than having no voice by the end of the day and drinking excessive amounts of water in hopes of recovering). I miraculously boarded my 5:55 a.m. flight back to Miami the next morning.

I wear a lot of different hats. I'm twenty-five years old and employed as an attorney. I also do a lot of other things, and my life seems to be one long "mad dash."

A few months before the Cleveland trip, I went viral for becoming Florida's first openly autistic attorney. It's a title I both cherish and question, because I know I'm not the only attorney out there on the autism spectrum. Nevertheless, I feel unbelievably blessed to have a bigger platform to spread the acceptance, inclusion, and further understanding I'd already been advocating for the past twelve years of my life. I'm considered a public figure in the autism community, so I connect with fans and followers through social media and e-mail.

I run all my social media accounts. I manage my calendar and accept or turn down my media and interview requests. I travel for speaking engagements to talk about autism and related disabilities at least once a month. I run the business aspect of public speaking, so I plan content for my sessions and work closely with host organizations to make sure their events are successful.

I serve on several nonprofit boards and volunteer whatever time I can to help others in the disability community. I co-host a podcast each week. I write books and articles when I have time. At the time of the Cleveland trip, I was also the subject of a documentary and had a filmmaker shadowing me with her camera. If everything I mentioned sounds like a lot, keep in mind I practice law full-time and do my best to be in the office forty hours per week.

When I make a list of things I do, it does sound like I "do it all," as my friend said. But when I look inward, I see the cost of that. I consider the pain in my shoulders, the fatigue in my body, and the dark circles under my eyes that I actively cover with concealer. I have too many unanswered text messages from friends, and I don't call my mom enough. I'm also sad that I haven't been drawing and painting as much as I would like.

I feel like I'm running my engine on all cylinders and could use about a hundred years' worth of sleep. I'm really good at being an advocate for other people, but I'm terrible at taking care of myself.

I've started to learn, though. I originally booked that 5:55 a.m. flight out of Cleveland so I'd make it to my lawyer job that same morning and put in a full day. Yet when I touched down in Miami with my body begging for rest, I decided to listen. I walked into my messy apartment that morning, set down my luggage in the kitchen, and crawled into the unmade bed I had left behind. By the time I woke up, it was dark outside. I ignored all my missed e-mails and text messages, ordered delivery for dinner, and put on a movie instead. I felt rejuvenated.

A month later, I gave myself permission to take a mental-health day during the workweek. I said "no" to tasks competing for my attention. Instead, I went to a Pilates class, got a massage to relieve the tension in my shoulders, and took a long nap. When I woke up, I made it a point to draw a picture and color it with my markers.

Now I try to plan at least one day each month for self-care. For me, self-care doesn't only look like bubble baths and a glass of wine after watching a movie on my couch. It also looks like more sleep, ways to make my body ache less, drawing and painting, and feeling in touch with my physical and emotional wellbeing.

Every day now, no matter how much I have to do, I do a "body scan." I ask myself, "How am I feeling?" Then, I let my brain register if my eyes feel heavy or if I feel tense. I give myself an hour each day to do something for me, whether it is drawing, writing a poem, Pilates or other exercise, sleeping in a little later, going to bed a little earlier, taking a nap, eating a snack, taking a bubble bath, or staying in comfy clothes. If I am lucky and feel up to it, my daily self-care hour combines activities. Sometimes, my best answer is a full mental-health day. That's okay, too.

"I have no idea how you do it all," my friend repeated that day after my whirlwind Cleveland trip, afraid her compliment didn't register with me. I replied, "I don't do it all because I neglect myself in the process, and that needs to change. That means I'm not actually doing it all."

Now I understand that doing it all means adding self-care to my to-do list. After all, if I can't take care of myself, how can I take care of the change I want to make in this world?

— Haley Moss —

64

Being Intentional about Self-Care

*I always try to remember that I'll be the best me I can
be if I prioritize myself.*
~Michelle Obama

I n late 2011, my father was hospitalized in Kaufman,
Texas. I was living 250 miles away in Houston, driving
on weekends to be with him. He had been living with
Alzheimer's for more than twelve years. My mom, who
was much younger than my father, had resigned from her job to care
for him full-time.

The doctor was making his morning rounds when I came around
the corner. After listening to my dad's heart and his breathing, the
doctor lingered in the room. The pause was long enough to become
awkward. After glancing at the worried look on my mother's face, the
doctor asked if I minded stepping outside with him to discuss a few
things. I guess he thought I would be better able to handle what he
was going to say.

He reviewed my dad's vitals and shared the results from a few
tests they had run. I remember hearing the doctor say, "Unfortunately,
Mr. Louis's health is beginning to decline rapidly. He could pass away
at any time. It could be a week or a few months." Tears began to run
down my face. My head immediately started throbbing, and I felt like

someone had just placed fifty pounds of concrete on my shoulders.

I thanked the doctor for his great care and bedside manner, and then I burst into uncontrollable tears. The poor man couldn't leave. I remember thinking, *Why are you being so dramatic right now, LaQuita?* Then I thought, *When will I have time to plan a funeral? My plate is already beyond full right now.*

I managed to regain my composure and stuck my head back into the room to reassure my mother that everything was okay, and I would be back shortly after taking a work call. I felt as though I was about to have a panic attack. My heart was pounding, I could barely breathe, and my hands were trembling. I found the sign in the hallway pointing toward the chapel. I needed a quiet place to meditate, reflect, and gather my thoughts. It was obvious that I was hopelessly overwhelmed.

When I walked into the small, intimate room, I felt immediate peace. It became evident that I had allowed work-related stress, church ministries, marriage expectations, volunteer commitments, and family obligations to overwhelm me. I had become too busy to be still. I began praying and crying profusely at this self-discovery. I had simply failed to care for my own personal needs.

I asked God to give my family and me more time with my father to get things in order, both for myself and the needs of the family. Truth be told, my father had lived this long, in part, because of how he had taken care of himself. Even being over eighty years of age, the muscles in his arms and legs were still defined. He rarely ever raised his voice or showed any visible stress, and he always found time to read his Bible and say his prayers on his knees every night.

My father passed away four months later. Shortly after my father's burial, I began practicing daily downtime. My activities vary: fifteen to thirty minutes of journaling, prayer, quiet meditation, reviewing Sunday school lessons, or yoga flow movements. When I first started this process, I had to set the alarm on my cellphone to ensure I maintained a minimum of ten minutes because my natural response was to get back to being busy.

Five years ago, during one of my self-care sessions, God put it on my heart to start a nonprofit, Angels with a Mission, to provide hope and support to homeless and foster children. I was not sure how it was all going to come together, but I knew that I had to listen to the guidance I had received. I had always been an avid volunteer in the community, but starting my own nonprofit was a bit adventurous and sounded like a lot of work. I recalled that, as a little girl, I had watched my father grow vegetables year after year to pass out to the elderly citizens in the community. Aha! My dad had engaged in what he enjoyed doing — gardening — and was able to take the benefits from his hobby to bless those around him.

As a result of learning to be intentional about taking care of me, during my closet prayer time, the Lord reveals things for me to do. For instance, He places individuals upon my heart whom I might pray for or reach out to via a card or phone call. In the past, I would have been running around like a chicken with my head cut off trying to save the world. Now I know that if I will just take the time to be still, my heavenly Father will reveal specifics to me. He literally takes the footwork out of "finding my purpose" and delivers a clear roadmap for me to follow.

Maya Angelou once said, "If I am not good to myself, how can I expect anyone else to be good to me?" This is so true. I have learned to never get too busy to take care of myself.

— LaQuita Jean Starr —

65

Counsel Walking

Walking is man's best medicine.
~Hippocrates

I turned off the classroom light, only to find a tearful Laura outside the door. "Sister Jo, can I talk to you? Like… do you have time?"

Flicking the light on again, I smiled. "I always have time for you, hon." But inwardly, I sighed. I loved Laura, but I needed A WALK.

I had been lamenting, "I never have time for *me*. I love teaching but correcting essays and writing lesson plans take most of my day."

Ah, but today would be different! After teaching high school for seven hours, I had promised myself a brisk hike in the fresh air. All day, the blue sky and vibrant autumn leaves had beckoned from my four wide classroom windows.

An avid walker, I had lately developed the bad habit of staying after school to grade tests and prepare new lessons. Today, I gave myself a scolding: "You're missing autumn! Go outside! Get the chalk dust out of your lungs. You can do schoolwork at night." So, I had vowed, "TODAY, I SHALL WALK!"

But Laura's troubled face left me no choice. We sat in the empty classroom as she described the havoc her dad's alcoholism was wreaking. I listened, handing her tissues, trying not to glance out the window where the janitor was mowing the lawn. I tried to focus on Laura, not on the fragrance of freshly cut grass.

After a half-hour, she sighed. "I know you can't do anything about it, Sister, but thanks for listening. My mom cries when she talks about it. She keeps saying, 'He's sick! Alcoholism is a disease!'" I promised to pray for her family and gave her a hug.

I got to the convent chapel just in time for 5:00 p.m. vespers. I knew I had done the right thing, but my feet didn't. They tapped with pent-up energy. Then it hit me! Why hadn't I taken Laura out walking with me?

The next day was just as lovely. "TODAY, I will walk!" I vowed. But at 3:00 p.m., Brian was at the door. "Hi, can I talk to you?"

"Sure," I answered. "But it's such perfect weather. Can we go for a walk?"

We circled the small lake near our school and talked about helping emotionally disturbed kids, his goal after college. After twenty minutes, we headed back to school.

On Laura's next visit, she eagerly accepted my invitation to walk. I had a surprise for her. Classmate Tom had given me brochures from Alateen, a support group for teens with alcoholic parents. "Someone in your class said his dad has the same problem," I told Laura. "If I may share your story, he'll drive you to Alateen meetings — with your mom's permission, of course."

Laura was enlightened by the coping techniques in the leaflets. "Okay, you can tell that guy about me. My mom will let me ride with him, if you say he's okay." Laura left, consoled that she wasn't the only teen with an alcoholic parent. Plus, she had gotten fresh air and exercise. "I really feel better, Sister. Thank you!"

And so, it became a pattern. Whoever came to chat after school was invited to walk. One drizzly day, Dennis appeared after scripture class, asking to discuss questions he had about the Bible. No, he didn't mind walking. As we hiked briskly around the lake, I marveled at this young man's insight into the spiritual world. Our walk ended with hot chocolate in the convent kitchen.

True, not every after-school chat calls for a walk. I don't do blizzards or tornado watches. And when a tearful kid needs to spill her guts in private, we use my quiet classroom, with tissue box at hand.

But whenever we can, we walk! In the steady stride, inhale-and-exhale rhythm, with fresh oxygen flowing to the brain, these kids find relief from the pressures and frustrations they face.

And I've lost ten pounds!

— Sister Josephine Palmeri —

66

Reaching Out

Friendship is born at that moment when one person
says to another, "What! You, too?
I thought I was the only one."
~C.S. Lewis

I found myself having yet another heated argument with one of my three teenage daughters. I left the house crying and went for a walk. I really wanted to talk to another mom, not only for possible suggestions but also hoping to hear that my struggles were common to moms of teenagers. I realized with sadness that for the past several years, I had been so focused on taking care of my new husband and three girls that I had neglected to develop deep friendships for myself in the new city I had moved to after remarrying.

During my crying-walk, I texted a lady I knew in my neighborhood. Even though we had barely seen each other in the past two years, she said to come on over. We then walked together and talked, sharing our hearts with each other. This made me realize that, especially since my girls are now older and more independent, I needed to start cultivating deep friendships of my own. My best friend lives in a different state, and I had no women in my new neighborhood whom I ever just met for lunch, a movie, or called to catch up.

After my walk with my neighbor, I felt called to start a neighborhood women's friendship group. As it was almost summer, I decided to start the group in September, after the start of the new school year.

As September approached, I felt more and more anxious. What if no one came? What if people thought it was a stupid idea? I e-mailed my pastor's wife with my idea, asking for her input and freely admitting that I was apprehensive about the whole thing. She graciously met with me, gave me some great ideas, helped me clarify what the group could be, and prayed with me about it.

When the time came, I invited all the women in my neighborhood whom I already knew (not many!) and posted an invitation to the approximately 350 women in our online neighborhood community, which is mainly used for sharing information about babysitters, handymen, etc.

At the first meeting, six women showed up — three whom I already knew and three who saw the invitation online. We had a wonderful time just talking and getting to know each other. Every woman thanked me for starting the group, and several even expressed that, like me, they had been feeling isolated and lonely. We started meeting every two weeks and developed some truly beautiful friendships, spanning multiple ethnicities, religions, and ages.

Soon, other women saw my recurring online post and joined us. At Christmastime, we had a lovely progressive lunch, going from house to house of anyone who wanted to host, admiring the different holiday decorations and enjoying a special food and/or drink at each house. As an extra blessing, I have gotten together several times with one of the women I had invited to the group but who was not able to make it because of a previous commitment. My husband and daughters are all awesome, but I can't relate to them in the same way that I can my women friends.

On a humorous note, a lady from church said to me once, "Hey, our daughters had such a great time at the nail salon today. You and I should go sometime." I responded, "The nail salon is not really my thing, but thanks for the invite." As I thought about it while driving home, I realized that the invitation was probably not about nails. When I got home, I texted her, "Sorry I am such an idiot! The nail salon is not somewhere I enjoy, but let's get together for lunch, a movie, or to see some live theater," interests I knew we both shared.

I got a response back quickly, "Absolutely! Love to!" I've taken personality tests that say I'm more introverted than extroverted, but I managed to make the effort to find new friendships, and what a life-changing gift I gave myself. In reaching out, I discovered that almost everyone is looking for deeper connections. That's the kind of me time and self-care we all need.

— Margaret Lea —

67

Finding My Way Back

*Self-care is never a selfish act — it is simply good
stewardship of the only gift I have, the gift I was
put on earth to offer to others.*
~Parker Palmer

I had just finished giving my mother a bath, which can be physically and emotionally challenging for me. But knowing that it relaxes and rejuvenates her makes it completely worthwhile. Her radiant smile confirmed it.

It has been twelve years since the stroke took away Mom's independence, and perhaps mine as well. As soon as she was released from the hospital, I moved into my mother's house to care for her.

Nearly all my attention has been focused on giving her the best possible care. Believing I was invincible, I disregarded the warnings from doctors, nurses and other professionals concerning my own health.

Mom has thrived under my care, but as the years have progressed, so have the demands. Neither of us is getting any younger — Mom is now ninety-nine. She is no longer able to get around without me supporting her entire weight, even with the aid of her walker. She hasn't been able to talk for years, but when dementia crept in, she started a routine of yelling for hours, usually beginning in the early evening. There is no apparent reason other than the dementia.

For years, every day has begun with getting my mother out of bed in the morning and has ended with putting her to bed at night, leaving very little time for myself. In no way is any of this Mom's fault, and the last thing she'd ever want is to be a burden to me. I constantly reassure her that I love caring for her, and I truly mean it.

But I never noticed how much of a toll caregiving had taken on my body and mind until the day I caught my reflection in the mirror after the aforementioned bath. I was shocked. I looked years older than my mother!

Her wrinkles were shallow while mine were deep. Her cheeks were rosy while mine were pale. Her eyes were flawless and sparkled (even with the dementia) while mine were puffy with dark circles.

It just so happened that I was due for my annual physical the following week. My mother and I have the same primary-care physician, who is well aware of our circumstances.

Most of the doctor's staff was out sick the day of my appointment, so the doctor was the first one to take my blood pressure. I wasn't worried as it's always been within the ideal range; but to the doctor's and my surprise, it was high — concerning enough to require medication.

"Are you still walking every day?" she asked.

"No," I replied somewhat sheepishly. "I haven't been as motivated as I was a while back."

She knew that I had been an avid walker in previous years and seemed concerned that I'd stopped. As we talked, we both realized that my lack of enthusiasm was most likely due to the fact that I was experiencing some depression. Although I had undergone serious bouts of depression throughout my adult life, it had been well-controlled for many years.

While I was not overweight, I had gained about ten pounds, all of which appeared to have taken up residence around my midsection — the area where fat is most concerning for overall health. I was honest about my terrible eating habits. I made sure that Mom had her fresh fruit and vegetables every day along with her gluten-free, home-cooked meals. Why I ate unhealthy snacks instead of those healthy meals was a mystery.

I also confessed that I was easily irritated and very seldom left the house because it was easier to stay home. I spent time on social media talking with my cyber friends because I could do that while keeping an eye on my mother. I had very few friends or acquaintances in the real world.

By the time I left the doctor's office, it was clear that I had completely neglected myself, thinking that I'd get around to it someday. I was thankful for the wake-up call and promised my doctor that I'd find some time for myself every single day.

The moment I got home, I made a list of ten things I was going to do to improve my wellbeing:

1. I will get a family member to come and stay with my mother for an hour or so a few days during the week so I can venture out, even if only for a cup of coffee with a friend.
2. I will learn to say "yes" to invitations that get me out of the house.
3. I will get to bed earlier so I can get up before Mom is awake and resume my daily walking routine.
4. I will eat three healthy meals instead of snacking on junk food throughout the day.
5. I will drink much more water.
6. I will strive to lose or redistribute the unhealthy excess fat around my midsection.
7. I will accept help with my caregiving duties when offered.
8. I will make time to take a hot, relaxing bath a couple of times a week.
9. I will get outside and photograph Mother Nature's beauty like I once did.
10. I will laugh more, focus on the good in others, and be more optimistic.

After making my list, I realized that I was trying to find my way back to the old me. She had gotten lost among all the chaos.

I worked hard to follow my own list of suggestions, making certain to eat better, exercise more, go to bed earlier, accept offers of help to care for Mom, spend quality time outside with my camera, and say "yes" to invitations. In a nutshell, I spent more quality time on me.

Although it has only been a matter of months since I realized the need to alter my lifestyle to include caring for myself, I do feel rejuvenated, healthier, happier and able to give Mom even better care with a genuine, cheery smile.

Since spreading my wings and venturing out, I have met some lovely people — two of whom are also Chicken Soup for the Soul contributors. I am so happy that I said "yes" to joining Samantha and Charles in reading our stories from *Chicken Soup for the Soul: It's Beginning to Look a Lot Like Christmas* at two assisted-living centers in Portland, Oregon. It was a heartwarming experience, and the smiles of appreciation on the residents' faces were priceless — a promise of good things to come.

— Connie Kaseweter Pullen —

Chapter 8

You Deserve It

68

My Own Beat

Find what makes your heart sing
and create your own music.
~Mac Anderson

y pulse quickens as my feet take me closer and closer to the door. In my head, I can hear the words my kids keep telling me, "Do it, Mom. You never do anything for yourself. Just go set it up." I feel my lungs fill with air and release it.

What are you doing here? You're a single mom of five. You're fifty years old! My thoughts fight with my kids' words. Even so, it is as if I have no control over my feet. As if they are being urged along from somewhere deep inside me.

The minute I step into the house, my kids yell, "Did you do it?" Then they see the drumsticks in my hand. They start jumping up and down and then come hug me.

Wednesday comes, and along with it my first drum lesson. I walk through the door and head directly to the seating area in the back. My hands keep fidgeting with the sticks. I keep nervously looking at the time. I try to slow down my breath. I know the teacher will say I'm not the right type of person to play the drums. I turn around to see an older man looking at me.

"Stephanie? I'm Mike, the drum teacher," he says.

He leads me to a room about the size of a large walk-in closet. There are two drum sets, and he tells me to sit at the one closest to the door.

People make me nervous. That's the way I've always been. But Mike has a very calm manner about him, so I relax just slightly. Not only does he not tell me that I am the wrong type of person to play the drums, but he compliments me on how well I hold the sticks and follow along with him. I learn how to read a couple of simple sheets of music, but then my thirty-minute lesson is over.

Walking back to my car, I feel this energy beaming from within me. After taking care of kids and my family since I was twenty-two, it feels scary and amazing at the same time to do something that is purely for my enjoyment, something just for me.

With my practice pad set on top of a bucket in the living room, I practice as much as I can throughout the week. My fourteen-year-old daughter often complained that I never sat down with them, that I was always working around the house. But now with my lesson to practice, I finally sit down with them, talking as I practice my drumming. My second lesson comes, and I play the sheets of music for Mike.

I notice as I play that Mike's concentration becomes more and more apparent. When I finish the whole lesson without stopping, Mike says, "You played that perfectly!" He sounds amazed.

I explain, "Being a mom of five, I am used to moving and doing a lot. But now that my kids are getting older, and two have moved out on their own, drumming gives me something to focus that energy on. I find myself sitting for hours going through the rhythms."

After one week of lessons, I acquire a four-piece used Mapex Orion set. The guy who sold it to me used to tour with some big names and only sold it because he needed money to pay child support. It is big and very loud. I am, by nature, a quiet person — I work at the library — so it seems contradictory for me to pick drumming as something just for me. But I find as I sit in front of my set and beat out rhythms, something sensational happens. I become so focused on the drums that it is as if my expression of who I am comes out with every beat and rhythm. I am not nervous, shy, and quiet. I am a drummer.

As the weeks turn into months of playing, Mike convinces me to play at a blues jam where his band hosts the open mic.

"I'm so nervous. What will I do? What will I play?" I ask.

"You'll be fine. I've seen your self-confidence grow, and I see so much potential in you. It will be a simple beat that you know," he tells me.

How many times have I driven my kids to their competitions and watched proudly as they bravely went in front of judges and audiences? But driving myself to the jam, I realize I'm the one who has to be brave. For an hour, as my teacher's band plays the opening act for the night, thinking of my kids helps me to find strength within me. Clutching my sticks in my hands, I go over and over in my head what I need to play. Soon, it will be my turn.

My teacher goes up to the mic and makes the announcement. He says, "We have a special treat tonight. Stephanie will be on the drums for her first time playing with others and in front of people."

Walking up on the small stage, I inhale deeply and sit at the drum set. As I do, I look up and see that everyone has gotten up to watch me play. It is a little unusual for a woman to play the drums, but that is not all.

I am also a Muslim woman wearing the hijab (head scarf). It is a rare sight to see a Muslim woman playing the drums in hijab.

Facing me, Beau starts playing "Put on Your Red Dress" on his guitar, and soon I join in to keep the beat.

"A little faster," Beau says.

I speed up the beat; he smiles and nods at me.

I miss the first stop, but by the next one I get it. This is great! What a rush I feel when we finish, and everyone is clapping and cheering for me. I did it!

— Stephanie Doerr —

69

Should Today Be a Pajama Day?

The heart wants what it wants, and my heart wants
jammies and me time.
~Kat Helgeson, Say No to the Bro

"Feels like the flu," my husband Gary said as he woke me up one pre-sunrise morning. We'd been here before. I threw on my clothes and dropped him off at the hospital emergency entrance before parking. When you're on chemo and flu-like symptoms present themselves, it can add up to scary infections.

After five hours of antibiotic infusion, I brought my husband home, prepared something for him to eat, ran out to pick up his prescription and… wait for it… reported to work. I was exhausted in every imaginable way.

But if I didn't do my job, it would land on someone else's desk. Or so I reasoned.

There was no resting in this weary, disheartening, cancer-picking-up-speed season. There was only kicking against it in desperation. In Gary's declining months, I fought. I didn't listen to my body. I didn't take care of my soul and spirit. Self-care sounded so self-centered.

My co-workers would have been appalled to know that I showed up at work after being out since 4:30 a.m. "Dear friend, please don't ever do that again," they would have said. "Please stay home on days like this. We've got you covered."

But they had no idea how my day had unfolded.

On that particular day, self-care would have simply meant taking the day off from the office. It would have included brewing a cup of tea and curling up on the couch in the same room with my husband — chatting with him when he was awake, taking an afternoon nap when he slept. Self-care would have meant adding to my gratitude journal and picking up my knitting or a good read as Gary dozed. And those simple things would have refueled me.

Instead, I wore my superhero cape, tattered and dragging in the mud, for entirely too long. I thought I could do it all, and I didn't want to impose on anyone.

A week before Thanksgiving, on a snowy evening, my daughter Summer and I lost Gary.

The thought of all that needed to be done unraveled me. But Summer and I did the oddest thing. We notified immediate family members, put on pajamas, popped some corn, and watched HGTV's *Love It or List It*. I suppose it was our way of coping in the moment, of leaning into the unthinkable, and pushing the details of funeral planning out of our heads. Somehow we knew what to do: fleece pajamas and salty buttered popcorn in front of the fireplace. Self-care.

The next day, we ended up doing another unplanned activity that helped refuel our bodies, souls, and spirits. Based on a meme Summer found — "I live in my pajamas unless I am going somewhere or I know someone is about to come over to my house; even then it's iffy" — we wrote three rules for that first full day without husband and father:

1. Stay in pajamas all day.
2. Don't get off the couch except for coffee and tea breaks… oh, and food and bathroom breaks… and to answer the door.
3. No one was allowed in unless they were wearing pajamas (although we did make a couple of exceptions to this rule).

Ironically, in between the remembering, laughing and crying, Summer and I got quite a bit done from the couch, making lists of everything we needed to accomplish.

By the next day, Summer and I were rested and ready to tackle the items on the lists we'd drafted.

Self-care. It isn't merely something we do for ourselves. We replenish body, soul, and spirit to have a full vessel. To better serve. To be more present in our serving. To be glad and not resentful in the service.

When Gary was on chemo, he was cold all the time. I'd warm a fleece blanket in the dryer and drape it over him as he occupied the hospital bed in our living room. Every time I wrapped a freshly warmed blanket around him he would sigh blissfully.

What if we could wrap self-care around us like a fleece blanket warm out of the dryer? What if we removed our superhero capes and accepted the startling, unexpected grace of others loving on us as we travel life's challenging, noble, heart-wrenching paths?

What if we asked ourselves from time to time: Do I need to stay in my pajamas today?

— Marlys Johnson-Lawry —

70

Just Us

Often we fail to act in our best interests
in the chaos of the present moment,
denying ourselves loving tenderness.
~Elizabeth Gilbert

y landscaper Roy was surprised. I'd just told him, "This year we're going to be home all the time. I want you to put in more flowers than we've ever had before. No one's coming to visit. These are just for us."

Roy said that most of his clients were doing less landscaping, not more, given the pandemic and the fact they wouldn't be entertaining. I explained that the most important people in our home were us — my husband and me. If we were going to be home all spring and summer, we'd better have some pretty things to look at.

That began our spring and summer at home during the pandemic, which first exploded in our part of the country, the New York metropolitan area. We focused on treating ourselves like guests, not only with more flowers but also with everything else we could think of. I had the roof and trim power-washed, something I'd been meaning to do for a decade. I had the painter come and touch up the whole exterior of the house. I had our walkways and patios power-washed, something I hadn't done in years. I bought Sharpie paint pens and refurbished all our black outdoor lights. I had professional window-washers come and do the whole house, inside and out. The electricians came and fixed all the outdoor wiring and circuits, and I even paid them to change the outdoor bulbs, something we could have managed ourselves.

I started using all the nice scented soaps I'd stashed away — the gifts — and then for the first time ever, I ordered boxes of additional expensive scented soaps, for me. Bill started buying fabulous wines and it seemed like UPS was dropping them off three times a week. I had to run downstairs and let the delivery guy see me through the glass at the front door to confirm there was a twenty-one-year-old in the house. On the beverage front, I also treated myself to vast quantities of Spindrift seltzer waters (Bill calls them Spendthrifts). I ordered every kind of dark chocolate bar we wanted to try and brought in enough to treat us for months. We subscribed to every premium streaming service. Bill got me the fanciest, hugest iPad, just because.

I also started throwing away or donating things that I wouldn't have a guest use, like scratchy old towels. If I wouldn't put them out for a guest, why were we still using them? They were welcomed by the local animal shelter. I cut our mug collection in half, removing the ugly and worn ones, and the ones with uncomfortable handles. I finally replaced the yellowed toilet seat in Bill's home-office bathroom. Again, I would never have let a guest see that, so why was it okay for my husband?

We took out our dusty twenty-year-old bikes and had a guy make a seriously expensive house call right to our driveway to service them. Another luxury, but it saved me from hauling them in and out of the car and making two round trips to the bike shop.

How much did all this extravagance cost us? Less than a normal summer vacation at an inn where we would have been treated as valued guests.

And then, surrounded by our spruced-up home and decadent treats, we started using it all. We've never used our hot tub as much as we did this past summer — at least four nights a week we drank our new wine and listened to audiobooks in the hot tub, admiring our flower-filled yard. We rode our fixed-up bikes and shot baskets out by the garage, and of course I bought a new net for the basketball hoop as well, after using the same crusty old one for twenty years.

For the first time ever, in twenty-four years of owning this house, we discovered that the two huge trees in our back yard were tulip poplars. They were covered with beautiful yellow tulips this summer and we finally noticed them because of all the hot-tub time. How had we never known that we had these amazing trees?

When we wanted to see our kids and do something outdoors (i.e. safe) I looked up activities. Everything everywhere was canceled but you could arrange private tours for one family unit. Hence, after a nice donation, we got a private tour of the local Audubon from one of their naturalists. And for another donation we got a private tour of a farm animal sanctuary, complete with petting every kind of animal from chickens to bulls. Thanksgiving will be a different meal this year after I met and petted that turkey whose name happened to be Amy. Did you know that turkeys will lie down and basically beg you to pet them? And pigs will roll over and expose their bellies for a good rubbing, just like a dog?

I bought us beach passes again, and we rediscovered the beach after not going there for a decade. One family excursion to walk the hiking trails at our town's private beach and park cost us more than fifty dollars, but it was worth it to do something different.

Then there was the me time. I'd never been able to exercise as much outdoors, due to my full-time job, but with working at home I could run out for an hour in the middle of the workday. Actually, the pandemic was the impetus for implementing a lot of the advice we dispense through our *Chicken Soup for the Soul* books, advice I always tried to follow: making me time, ensuring we time as a couple, treating ourselves as well as we would treat a guest, experiencing the liberation of less stuff, spending money on things that add joy to our lives. We even stepped outside our comfort zone by putting those old bikes back into action and boy did that improve our fitness. Our neighborhood is very hilly and my legs haven't been this strong in at least a decade.

This was all done with the backdrop of not only the pandemic, but also my fallopian tube cancer, which started inching its way to a relapse. I'm living my life in three-month increments now — the time between scans — while waiting for the day that it recurs enough to force me back into the chemo chair. In the meantime, the pandemic rages and we stay home, treating "just us" the way we would treat our most honored guests. Our latest luxury? Lots of Duraflame logs for our outdoor fire pit now that the hot tub is closed for the winter.

— Amy Newmark —

71

Imaginary Holidays

Take time off. The world
will not fall apart without you.
~Malebo Sephodi

As I was readying my divorce papers, I was also filling out papers for college admission. Like me, lots of my female friends had quit college decades earlier to go to work to support their spouses so they could finish their own degrees. It was what one did at the time, I guess.

"I'll get a job when I graduate," my husband would say, "and pay for you to finish." He graduated with a business degree but never got a job. I had to work to support him and our children, and without a college degree of my own I was forced to work in low-paying jobs, even shoveling snow in the winter to pay our rent. Eventually, I faced the dismal truth: Nothing would ever change.

When I filed for divorce, he asked for maintenance even though he was the one with the degree. "Work," he told the court, "would be, well, just too traumatic!"

I did return to college, and I managed to secure a sedentary job that covered the tuition for one of my college classes. The job was a blessing.

But the pressure of a full-time job, college classes and a divorce case that would stay active for over a quarter-century was overwhelming. My co-workers told me to take some time off (unpaid leave) to go on vacation, but I could not. I had no money, schoolwork was demanding, and the ex just kept getting court hearings and harassing me. I was frazzled, ready to lose it mentally or, worse, quit school yet again.

My co-workers saw my stress and often mentioned I should take a little holiday or vacation. It was care and concern on their part, but it just added to my stress. I knew they meant well, but I would have to figure out a way to resolve the situation myself.

One very busy Friday afternoon, a co-worker asked about my weekend plans. I tried to avoid these conversations because I hated hearing about all the fun they were planning to have. And what would I be doing? I didn't want to be told again to go on vacation. To ward off any further conversation, I said, "Oh, I am taking a mini vacation, just a little weekend holiday." There was surprise but no further conversation.

What a liar I am, I thought. *And they will want details on Monday. It will just stress me more when they all find out that I lied.*

On the long drive home from work, I made a plan. I could pretend I was on vacation and never go anywhere. I stopped at the grocery store to pick up a twelve-pack of Pepsi and lots of snacks.

At home, I put the Pepsi in to chill, pulled down all the shades, checked my messages and shut off the phone. Then I jumped in the shower and put on sweats. The snacks were arranged for easy access on the kitchen counter. I retrieved three books that I had been anxious to read for the past six months. *Well,* I thought as I plopped into an overstuffed chair, *I am on vacation. This can be my imaginary holiday. I will check in with the world on Monday morning.* Then I cracked open the first book.

I read all evening until it was time for bed, getting up to refill my snacks and a bathroom break as needed. The next morning when I woke, I arranged some snacks on the end table and cracked open another Pepsi. Breakfast, even cereal, seemed too tedious and time-consuming to prepare. Saturday was a repeat of Friday night. I read and snacked all day, then took a shower and went to bed. When I got up Sunday morning, I laid out the work clothes I needed for Monday morning and then read and ate snacks for breakfast, lunch and dinner, getting up only for refills and bathroom breaks. By Sunday evening, I was well into the third book.

When the alarm went off on Monday morning, I dressed, had breakfast and went to work. I was busy at my desk when several co-workers came by. "Wow," they said, "you must have had a great vacation. You look so rested." It wasn't until then that I realized I wasn't stressed anymore.

"Maybe," I told them, "it was just an imaginary holiday." They laughed and went off to their desks.

I did graduate from college eventually and got a decent job with some paid vacation. But I still take imaginary holidays where I turn off the phone and electronics, tell everyone that I will be "away," buy lots of snacks and (a little less) Pepsi, and spend a weekend reading in an overstuffed chair.

I have decided that imaginary holidays are one way I can take care of myself. Perhaps that was part of my college education.

— Ann E. Oakland —

72

The Face in the Mirror

The world will see you the way you see you,
and treat you the way you treat yourself.
~Beyoncé

"I look like a burly, hairy man," I said to my husband while leaning over the counter to look in the mirror, inspecting the tragic state of my eyebrows. It was a rare moment of clarity, paired with a (mostly) honest look at myself and who I'd become, inside and out.

He made a sound somewhere between a grunt and a laugh, uncomfortable but smart enough to know at this point that he had to say something in disagreement but not so direct that it'd spark a whole conversation, errr, monologue. Then he wandered back out of the bathroom.

I'd stopped feeling feminine years ago, even though I'd spent my early twenties in heels, blouses, and skirts, and the first few years of motherhood vehemently fighting against "letting myself go." I won that battle only to succumb to depression's attack on my self-care routine at a time when most moms would've been getting their groove back. How ironic that I was a beauty writer for several publications but couldn't be bothered to apply a little eyeshadow. It felt like a dirty little secret.

I continued to study my reflection. I noticed how dry the skin on my face was and how it exacerbated the wrinkles that had developed in my forehead. I rubbed at them as if I could make the skin bounce back. That's when I saw how bad my fingernails looked.

From there, the number of gray hairs around my part and temples came to light. "What happened to me?" I asked myself. The gray wasn't the only problem with my hair. It was dry, growing out in the shape of a pyramid (the curse of fluffy, wavy/curly hair), and the ends looked as frazzled as I'd felt over the last few years.

Looking into the mirror that afternoon was like waking up from a bad dream. I'd convinced myself that my appearance didn't matter because all I did was work from home and drive to and from my daughter's school. I wanted to hide anyway, thanks to the depression and anxiety, and not having any make-up on was a convenient excuse to stay home. No spontaneous trips for me; I was never prepared. Plus, no one could accuse me of being vain, and I saved a lot of money by not buying so many products anymore.

I reached into the bottom drawer by the sink to fish around for my tweezers. One hair at a time, I reshaped my brows to frame my eyes. Some tiny hairs landed on my cheeks. Others fell into the sink or onto the counter. I inspected my work from all angles in the handheld mirror and the larger one over the sink. I felt like a sculptor.

When I saw those old, familiar arches, it lit a spark in me. I pulled out my cleanser, serum, and moisturizer and made a mental note to purchase eye cream.

Once the canvas had been prepped, I applied a full face of make-up, vowing to myself that I would start doing it every day again. It wasn't that hard or time-consuming, really; I just liked to convince myself that it was. I styled my hair, too.

My husband and daughter greeted me with compliments when I made my way downstairs. I felt pretty. I laughed more easily.

A few hours later, I made an appointment for highlights (to blend with the gray) and a haircut. Sadly, I had to wait over a month for my appointment, but that was okay because I had momentum. I gave myself a manicure and pedicure. I promised to take care of myself again — long-term, not just in spurts.

I used to be the girl who was always put together. I never went a day without at least four shades of eyeshadow and expertly applied eyeliner on my eyes. My nails looked nice; my hair had always been styled. My lashes were even curled.

For the past several years, I'd wondered in the back of my mind, *How do I start to feel like myself again? How do I become that happy, friendly, confident person I used to be? And where did she go anyway?*

Oh, I knew where she'd gone. She'd run away to hide after so many major life changes in a row left her reeling, lonely, depressed, and overthinking social interactions so relentlessly that she decided to avoid them — and the stress of rehashing them later — as completely as possible.

I told myself that girl didn't matter anymore, and there was never any point in trying to get "back" anywhere because one can only move forward.

That's not exactly what I would've told my readers. I would've given them hope and encouragement.

The truth (and what I would've told anyone in my predicament, even though I didn't believe it applied to me): Self-care — even when it's as simple as taking time to put on make-up and curl or straighten your hair — isn't selfish, self-centered, or a waste of time. Finally, that began to sink in for me.

My nails haven't been painted every single day since that afternoon because I spend a lot of time typing and the color just chips, but they have stayed trimmed and shaped. My hands and body are drinking in more lotion than they have in years.

Once my hair appointment came around, I bought new color-protecting shampoo and conditioner and started to use a curling iron again. Unless I'm sick, my make-up is on and I'm in "real" clothes instead of my yoga-pants-and-tank-top uniform. I even got a new shadow palette to experiment with, and I feel a rush of delight and creativity every time I open it. Putting myself together each day has become me time — creative time. I may not be painting my lids rainbow colors like I did when I was twenty, but even with neutrals, it's still a form of artistic meditation and a boost I can give myself at the start of each day.

My return to a self-care routine brought about a return to myself. I'm not hiding anymore, from myself or anyone else.

Guess what's happened to my mental health and confidence over the past several months? Major improvement. My social anxiety is all but gone. I'm embracing life and engaging with people with more joy than I have since at least 2010.

That day in the mirror brought a decision with it. From there, I only needed to make smaller decisions to keep the benefits going. Small changes and minor decisions — like adhering to a regular self-care schedule, applying mascara, choosing a lipstick — added up and became one of the easiest ways to change my outlook, future, and mindset.

— Crystal Schwanke —

73

Doing It for Me

There are days I drop words of comfort on myself like falling leaves and remember that it is enough to be taken care of by myself.

~Brian Andreas

With a mask covering my nose and mouth, I stood in front of the pumpkin display at the farmer's market. All I needed were four pumpkins — three round orange ones, as identical in size as possible, to place atop my porch railing, and a giant, warty green pumpkin to set beside the mums by my front door.

I quickly found just what I was looking for, but I hesitated as I reached for the cash in my pocket. Was decorating for fall this year just a waste of time and money?

In the midst of a global pandemic, did it make sense to decorate a house that few folks were likely to drive by, let alone enter? My house was tucked up on a hill next to a patch of woods, barely visible from the dead-end street it overlooked. What was the point of putting out pumpkins? I'd already decided I wouldn't display my smiley-faced electric jack-o'-lantern or hang scary ghosts from the limbs of my dogwood trees. As for putting the witch figurine on my kitchen windowsill or the pair of rubber rats with glowing red eyes on my hearth, it wasn't going to happen. Too much trouble.

I bought the pumpkins anyway.

When I got home and put them in their proper spots, I couldn't help but smile just a little. They cheered things up, especially when complemented by some sprigs of bittersweet I found in the woods. So, despite myself, I kept on going. I found an extension cord and set up the electric jack-o'-lantern. I hung all five scary ghosts from the dogwood trees. My neighbors might enjoy them. So, too, might the postman, the meter reader, and the lady who drives the UPS truck.

But I was *not* going to decorate inside. I live alone. My children and grandchildren live in other states. They were being "COVID careful," and so was I. I wouldn't be visiting them until the virus was under control, and they wouldn't be visiting me. Ditto for the friends I used to invite over for dinner, the members of my knitting group, and my book club.

Why bother decorating?

I settled in front of the TV one crisp fall evening, hoping to find something lighthearted to watch. Scrolling through the cable guide, I found the perfect show: *It's the Great Pumpkin, Charlie Brown.* Previously, I wouldn't let autumn pass without watching it, even after the children were grown and gone. Maybe it was time to have another go at it.

As I watched Linus never lose hope that the Great Pumpkin would show up, I had something of an epiphany. I mustn't give up either. Fall makes me happy. Halloween makes me happy. Even without the hayrides, haunted houses and trick-or-treating, I could still celebrate. COVID-19 couldn't take that away.

I dug around in the storage closet and found the witch figurine, which I placed lovingly on the windowsill. I set the rubber rats on the hearth. I made a bouquet of red, yellow and orange leaves and put it in the middle of the kitchen table. I poured candy corn into a black bowl shaped like a cauldron. I lit an apple-pie-scented candle.

And I celebrated one of my favorite holidays just for me.

I wouldn't let it end there. In November, I would replace the witch with pilgrim and Native-American figurines. I would put away the rubber rats and set a colorful ceramic turkey in their place. The apple-pie-scented candle would keep burning.

And so on with Christmas, Valentine's Day and Easter. Through the pandemic and beyond, I would embrace the changing seasons and holidays with wonder and delight. I would do it for me.

—Jennie Ivey—

74

Time to Play

My childhood may be over,
but that doesn't mean playtime is.
~Author Unknown

'**I**ve been told I was born middle-aged. Sounds about right. I took on a lot of family responsibilities at an early age, which meant putting away childish things long before childhood was over. When you have sensible adult matters on your mind, it's hard to find time for play.

A few months ago, I was listening to a sensible adult podcast about publishing and the book industry. The podcaster's guest had written several books in the self-help genre. During the course of the interview, the host said to the author, "Ever since I read your latest book, I find myself looking for opportunities to play every day."

When I heard a sensible adult podcaster talk about taking time to play, I thought, *Well, that's just silly.*

My reaction to all this talk of play was actually quite visceral. The idea of playing as an adult seemed unappealing in a way I couldn't quite articulate. I was more opposed to it than I had any right to be. It always gets my attention when I feel opposition to a concept without really knowing why.

I guess that's why the idea of taking time to play stuck with me. I didn't want it at the forefront of my mind, so I shoved it to the back. But it certainly stayed there in my consciousness because the desire to play took over a few days later.

It must have been 9:00 p.m., with a starry sky above. I was cutting across the local park, which would have been bustling with children if I'd been there during the day. Now the kids were home in bed, and it was just me in this well-loved playground.

The playground consists of a jungle gym, splash pad, sandbox, swing set, and even a music park that includes xylophones and various other percussion instruments. Those musical instruments struck me as novel, but it was the swing set that really grabbed my attention. When I saw it, I suddenly remembered playing on the swings with my cousin at the park near her house. I recalled the sheer joy of that childhood experience.

During the day, you'd have to wait in line to get on a swing at my local park. And you'd probably get a lot of side-eye from other sensible adults if you were waiting in line with their children. But at night, with no one else around? I saw those swings, and I wanted to play.

I hesitated a bit, but nobody would ever know. So, I got on the swing and pushed off the ground, and my body remembered exactly how to get going. I pumped my legs to go higher, higher, so high I worried I would flip right over the bar. But that giddy fear couldn't bring me down. I spotted the moon over the treetops—a full moon! I hadn't even noticed it before that moment.

The best feelings of childhood burbled up inside me as I flew through the air. It was fun, pure and simple. Swinging was so much fun that I found a smile plastered across my lips. I couldn't stop it.

Of course, that was the moment every dog owner on the block decided to take their pooches for a stroll. I went from having no one in the vicinity to a whole host of neighbours walking by. And did they notice me? You bet they did. It's hard to miss a full-grown adult swinging by starlight. Some of those neighbours even gave me that side-eye that says, "All the weirdos come out when there's a full moon!"

And you know what? I didn't care! Not even a little bit. I was having way too much fun to concern myself with what other people thought of me. My actions weren't hurting anyone. If they thought I was a little loony, oh well. They'd understand the appeal if they tried swinging for themselves.

Eventually, I came down from the swing, but I didn't stop smiling. I couldn't. That smile planted itself on my face, and it wouldn't go away.

Most of the time when I walk through the park, it isn't 9:00 at night, and there isn't a full moon. The playground is packed with delighted young children, and I don't push them out of the way to take a run at the swings.

But there's always a selection of percussion instruments available, so every time I walk by, I pick up the mallets and make a little music. I take the time to play. And you know what? Often, I'm not the only sensible adult tapping out a tune.

— Tanya Janke —

75

Girl's Trip

It is so important to take time for yourself and find clarity.
The most important relationship is the one
you have with yourself.
~Diane von Furstenberg

Starting when I was thirteen and old enough to look after my younger brother, my mother took an annual vacation. Alone. It was just two weeks visiting out-of-town family and perhaps a little sightseeing on the way. And, for those two weeks, my father and the two of us kids were completely and totally on our own.

My teenaged mind couldn't wrap itself around the idea. Why couldn't we go along? Or, at least, why couldn't *I* go along — a real girls' trip? My mother's answer was always blunt and to the point: "I need a break from you guys."

Now, I certainly couldn't understand that reasoning. Were we really that bad? Was it really so hard to live with us that my mother required a two-week respite? I pondered where we might have gone wrong. I helped with housework… sometimes. Didn't she enjoy hearing all about middle-school day after day? What about my brother? He didn't get in too much trouble with the neighbors' kids. And when he did, didn't it give Mom a nice opportunity to connect with their parents? Dad? Well… I wasn't so sure about Dad. He did complain about her cooking once in a while.

Fast-forward twenty-five years. I'm married, hold a job, care for family and aging parents, and am responsible for most of the household tasks. "Where do you want to go on vacation this year?" my husband Bill asks.

I look up from plunging the bathroom sink, clogged again with his whiskers. "Anywhere," I answer, "as long as it's alone."

He doesn't understand. "Don't you like to go away with me?" he asks, looking confused.

"I do," I answer. "But sometimes I want to be by myself." And, really, I do enjoy vacationing with him, just as I enjoy vacationing with friends or other family. Yet, sometimes I feel as though I'm on *their* vacation, compromising with what the majority wants to do when they want to do it, missing out on what may be more important or interesting to me. Exactly like at home. I look down at the stopped-up sink and ask myself, "Is that selfish?" And I answer back, "NO!"

Bill continues to look perplexed. He still doesn't understand. But now I do. I understand the need for every solo vacation my mother ever took. I start planning my own.

***

My first foray was to Bermuda. I lay poolside uninterrupted, reading magazines. I visited the beaches and stayed as long as I wanted, without wondering what I would cook for dinner that evening. I ate when I wanted, where I wanted and as much as I wanted. I went to bed as late as I pleased and slept in as long as I pleased each morning. It was even a break from the cat, who always pawed at my face begging for breakfast.

For five days and four nights, there were no clogged sinks, grocery lists, work deadlines, griping family members, or doctors' visits. Instead, for five days and four blissful nights, there was only peace, quiet and the opportunity to do exactly what I wanted to do. It was glorious. I gained three pounds and came home with a fabulous tan and renewed spirit.

It's been many years since that first girl's trip. I go solo when I can, but travel is expensive and other circumstances don't always allow me the luxury of such a vacation each year. Yet that hasn't stopped me from taking a page from my mother's book. Whenever I feel overwhelmed or like I need a break, I take one. An hour at the manicurist, a long afternoon strolling the mall, or lunch and a movie alone — my choice and my choice only — do well in a pinch. Take it from me and Mom, sometimes we need a little alone time. Understand?

— Monica A. Andermann —

76

Cereal for Dinner

*When you take care of yourself, you're a better person
for others. When you feel good about yourself,
you treat others better.*
~Solange Knowles

I was too tired to make myself dinner. I'd just eat the kids' leftover cereal off the highchair tray. I bet I'd lose some weight doing this anyway. That's how I used to think. I actually thought this was a brilliant plan and called it the "Cereal for Dinner Diet." Back then, I knew nothing about nutrition, and this was one of my misguided attempts at dieting after I had put on some postpartum weight.

Of course, the Cereal for Dinner Diet failed, as did all my other attempts. I knew nothing about how to lose weight in a healthy way. I'd spent years caring for my three children, completely ignoring any self-care. Educating myself about nutrition seemed too lofty a goal when more pressing matters were at hand, such as three toddlers sticking beans in each other's ears and noses.

With two-year-old twin daughters and a three-year-old son, I never took a break. Often, my husband would return from work and find me still in my pajamas, wrestling little bottoms into diapers, with kitchen dishes stacked to the ceiling. One day, he came home and found me lying like a corpse on the kitchen floor with streaks of make-up all over my body. "The kids got into my make-up drawer," I said as I lay there defeated. "I didn't have the strength to stop them."

"It looks like a deranged clown attacked you," he said. "Go out for a while. I'll watch them."

I washed the make-up off and left the house for a walk. I passed a gym in the neighborhood. I averted my eyes. Healthy people went there — people who spent time investing in themselves. This was not me. As I turned to get as far away from that place as I could, I saw a sign advertising a six-month fitness challenge. I continued my fast walk in the opposite direction, but that sign stayed on my mind for the rest of the walk and during the following days.

I can't say what finally motivated me to go sign up for the challenge. Oh, wait. Yes, I can say. It was a ten-minute period in which my son threw his spaghetti plate straight up, lodging noodles and sauce in the overhead light fixture as the twins exploded into their diapers in unison from the startle. I could feel my soul deflate. As soon as my husband got home from work, I said, "You're in charge."

I made a beeline to the gym, marched straight in and said, "Fix me." It was the first time in three years I had chosen to do something for myself.

I was assigned a trainer, Emily. She was young and fit and had the energy of a person who did not have three young children. I wanted an IV with her energy. She asked what my goals were for the six-month challenge. I said, "I want to lose fifteen pounds." I should have said, "I want to take my life back. I want to be healthy so I can be a better mom for my kids. I want to feel powerful." But I could not verbalize such high ambitions at that point in time. I still had spaghetti in my hair.

Emily handed me the heaviest weights I had ever lifted in my life and said, "Okay, so in six months you will compete in a bodybuilding show."

I struggled to push the weights over my head and grunted, "You mean one of those shows where the women pose on stage in little bikinis?" She nodded but was not really paying attention to me. She was looking for a car or a building for me to pick up next. I tried explaining, "No, I don't want to do a show. That sounds scary. I just want to lose fifteen pounds." She pretty much ignored my protests, and we jumped into weeks of strict workouts and nutrition planning. I figured that, at the end of six months, I would just have to disappoint her and tell her I was not going to do that show.

Over the next six months, I learned so much about my body. I thrived in the gym. The pride I felt after my workouts was beyond what I had ever experienced. I watched my body composition change as I learned about food. I ate in a smart way that gave me energy, built muscle, and reduced fat. As it turns out, eating whatever is left on your kid's plate is not a great nutrition plan.

Emily forced me to focus on myself — my wants and my needs. By doing that, I became a much better mother and wife. I had more energy for my family. My lingering postpartum depression lifted. I felt mentally and physically more in control and powerful than I ever had.

At the end of the six months, I looked and felt amazing. Emily handed me a pamphlet for the upcoming show. It was time to break the news to her. "I appreciate all you've done for me, Emily. I really do. I look and feel better than I ever have, but I'm just too scared to do it." For once, Emily stopped trying to locate heavy items, looked me in the eye and said, "The old you is talking."

I thought about the old me, unhealthy and depressed, lying on the kitchen floor and striped with make-up. I compared that old me to the confident, proud woman today who had decided to spend time investing in herself. I thought about which one I wanted my kids to know and which one I would want them to be. My ears could not believe what my mouth was saying when the words "I'll do it" came out.

Emily and I jumped into weeks of preparation. There were posing, hair and make-up, and swimsuit-fitting sessions. By the time the show arrived, I could not believe the woman who confidently walked across the stage. It was a complete transformation of my former self. The mental and emotional benefits that came from this experience enriched me far more than the weight loss I had achieved. I lost pant sizes, but I also gained unwavering confidence and emotional control. Most importantly, there was a shift in how I thought of myself.

In the past, I had put my needs behind all others, but I learned I am a person worthy of investment. This makes me a better person, and those around me are better for it, too.

As the years passed, I became a fitness trainer. I now work with many people who were just like me. I teach them what I learned from taking time to care for myself. I watch these people become powerful, and it is just as rewarding to share this message with them as it was for me to receive it. Cereal for dinner no more!

— Shannon McCarty —

77

It Was a Belly-Binge Kind of Day

Our loving God wills that we eat, drink and be merry.
~Martin Luther

I
t's not often that a day goes my way, but once in a while I get to have a day that is all about myself and my desires.

It was a Monday evening right after supper, and the Gracious Mistress of the Parsonage and I were watching TV. "Oh," my wife said, "by the way, the girls and I are going thrift-store shopping all day tomorrow."

At first, I was a little stunned. I wasn't quite sure why she was telling me this. It's not like she needs my permission to go thrift-store shopping as long as she doesn't take my truck. But, being the veteran husband I am, I did not ask questions.

I have found that after as long a marriage as I have had, when I ask a question, I will get an answer. Most of the time, the answer is not what I really want to hear. So, I keep my questions to the very minimum, to say the least. And, usually, I do say the least.

The next morning as we were finishing breakfast, my wife said, "The girls and I will be going thrift-store shopping today, and therefore you are on your own."

That is the kind of news that I want to hear. I will be on my own? What better day can one have?

"You will have to get your own lunch," she said. "The girls and I will have lunch together."

I almost said (but didn't), "What did you say?" But I knew if I did, I would get an expansive answer that would take time, and I did not want to waste any time.

Trying to hold back a smile, I said, "That's all right. I'm sure I can take care of my lunch."

With that, she joined the girls, and they went off on their thrift-store shopping spree.

I had to sit down a little bit and try to catch my breath. Here I was with the whole day before me to do as I please. Believe me, those days do not come often enough, at least for me.

As excited as I was about the day, I had to sit back and prepare my own to-do list. I got that from my wife. I wanted to put down everything that I could do.

After finishing my list, I looked it over, and then a thought captured my imagination.

What about eating? Did my wife say that I had to take care of my own lunch? Yes, she did! So now, my focus was on what I should eat. I was going to take this very seriously. I could choose whatever I wanted. Of course, at the top of the list was my favorite: apple fritters. As far as I'm concerned, I can't have enough of this "fruit."

Without wasting more time, I got to the neighborhood Publix to do some shopping. I was going to buy everything that I liked, and nobody was going to stop me.

There was one major item missing in my shopping cart: that nasty word starting with the letter V. My whole day was going to be spent without eating any vegetables whatsoever. I was so excited.

Looking at the cart as I went through the check-out line made me hungrier than I've ever been before.

On the way home, and this was before lunch, I stopped at McDonald's and bought a hot-fudge sundae. All this shopping made me hungry, so I thought it would make me happy. And, boy, did that sundae make me happy.

All the way home, I was singing, "I did it my way." I was gloriously out of tune, but it certainly made me happy to sing it.

I got home and started my belly-binge day. I didn't even go to the office. I spent all my time munching on this delicacy and crunching on that delicacy, just enjoying myself.

Then a thought hit me. *If I want to stay out of trouble, and I do, I better make sure I eat all these recently purchased groceries. If my wife sees them, I may be in trouble.*

That was the excuse I used to completely demolish all the food I had just purchased.

As I was crunching the last bite of my belly-binge delicacies, I began to realize that I was stuffed. I'd never eaten so much in my life. I cleaned up the table and kitchen, threw away all the evidence, and slowly walked to my chair to rest.

Sitting in the chair, I began to realize how stuffed I really was. However, I leaned back, smiled as wide as I could, and congratulated myself for taking such good care of myself.

I must have dozed for a moment because the next thing I knew, my wife was coming into the house. The thrift-store shopping day was over.

"I didn't know if you had enough to eat today," she said with a big smile on her face, "so I brought you a sub for supper."

— Dr. James L. Snyder —

Personal Space

78

The Best Mother's Day Gift Ever

Loving yourself isn't vanity. It's sanity.
~André Gide

My one-year-old smeared banana on her highchair tray, then moussed her dark curls with the slimy residue on her hand. Her big sister sat beside her, belting out a new song she had learned in preschool, complete with hand motions, and tipped her milk into her plate. Dinner was over.

I grabbed a dishtowel, thankful my husband was home this evening rather than in his patrol car protecting and serving. "You want dishes or bath time?"

He reached for my empty plate. "I got the kitchen."

"Then I've got the girls." I released the tray and lifted my little one from her seat as her sister scrambled up the stairs chanting, "Bath time! Bath time!" If only I could absorb a smidgeon of the energy surging from her little body. I trudged behind her, listing my remaining duties for the evening: cuddle and story time, prayers and tucking in, lesson plans and grading.

When I finally crawled into bed close to midnight, my husband turned off the TV and moved into his usual position. I snuggled into his shoulder and laid my arm across his chest.

"Mother's Day is next weekend," he said. "Is there something you'd like?"

Only one thing came to my exhausted mind — the best Mother's Day gift ever. But did I dare say it out loud? I tried to settle for a more acceptable answer — a mani/pedi maybe, a gift card, or a piece of jewelry. But I really wanted only one thing… needed only one thing… and I couldn't believe I was actually going to admit it.

I squeezed my arm around him to apologize in advance. "What I want most is for you and the girls to go to your dad's for the weekend."

"What?" I was thankful I couldn't see his face in the darkness. "On Mother's Day? What you want most on Mother's Day is to be away from your family?"

I rolled onto my back and stared at the ceiling fan circling above. "Well, it doesn't have to be on Mother's Day… just… sometime."

He was speechless. I could have told him I wasn't actually his wife but an alien life form from another planet in another galaxy far, far away in another universe, and he would have been less shocked.

But my house, all to myself, for forty-eight whole hours… sounded so good! First, I would sleep until noon. Then I would do a whirlwind declutter so I could relax in semi-cleanness. And then maybe I would grab a book from my books-to-read-when-I-get-to-read-again-someday pile. After that, I would binge-watch a mindless TV series. Better yet, I'd rent all the good movies I had missed since giving birth. I could stay up until the wee hours watching romcoms just like the old days. Of course, I'd find a spot somewhere in my busy schedule to soak in a hot bubble bath and pig out on a pan of under-baked brownies, but not at the same time, of course. Or, maybe at the same time! Heaven on Earth!

I could say all those things to my husband, but he would never understand. He didn't hear exhaustion in my request; he heard rejection. And if I didn't give him a more acceptable answer, he would lie awake quietly hurting while my guilty conscience kept me from much-needed sleep.

"But a gift card would be nice, too. I'd like some new clothes." When he didn't answer, I told him what he really needed to hear. "I love you, and I love the girls. You are my world. I just get tired sometimes."

Twenty years have passed since I asked for the best Mother's Day gift ever. I don't remember what I bought with my gift card, but my husband never forgot my very honest request — which I didn't realize until we were at a restaurant recently, sympathizing with a frazzled mom trying to corral her little ones.

"That time you asked me to take the girls to Dad's..." Apology was in his eyes. His voice cracked. "I didn't know."

I patted his arm. "I know."

He wasn't thoughtless or oblivious when our girls were little. He just wasn't a mom. From his male perspective, our home was a smooth operation. He didn't realize his work schedule — split between day and evening shifts — left me to parent alone half the time. And without grandparents close by to help, I pulled many sixteen-hour shifts solo. Oh, how nice a weekend alone would have been.

Now that our girls are grown and our home is quiet, I've changed my opinion about the best Mother's Day gift ever. The next time my husband asks, I'm going to tell him I want a diamond. I think I've earned it.

— Karen Sargent —

79

The Best View

I took a walk in the woods and came out
taller than the trees.
~Henry David Thoreau

Every room was occupied. The kids were home from school, each ensconced in their room, trying to focus on their online lessons. My mother-in-law was staying for the first three weeks of our national COVID-19-induced lockdown. The dogs flopped in either the lounge or on the veranda. And my husband was working in a room in the vacant house next door, shouting over the wall if he needed anything.

For someone used to hours of peace and quiet, and the space to potter at will every morning, this was a challenge. I had no sooner cleaned all the kitchen counters and popped the stray cups in the dishwasher than another dirty dish would appear. The milk seemed to be more out of the fridge than in, snacks were in constant demand, and doors clattered and rattled.

Just as I sat down to get my own work done, someone would request help or attention. Add to that the stress and anxiety experienced every time I read the news or watched updates on TV. Coronavirus numbers were climbing; deaths were rising. The world was suffering.

I was overwhelmed. I needed to do something, go somewhere. A place with a distant horizon, a wide-open sky and a gentle breeze. My garden. My retreat. My spacious place.

I live in Durban, on the east coast of South Africa, in a home overlooking the warm Indian Ocean. Palm trees wave their branches in the salty sea air, and yellow-billed kites play in the thermals. Pods of dolphins surf the waves below, and whales breach and smack their tails with glorious delight. Little wonder that there, under the palm tree, was my favourite place to rest, recover and recharge.

It was time to head there now. I brewed a cup of strong, black coffee, aromatic and earthy, grabbed the brightly coloured cap I'd bought in Mozambique a few months earlier, and tucked a comfy cushion under my arm. I closed the back door firmly behind me and took the few steps down to the pool area of the garden. Sheltered from the wind and drenched in warm, end-of-summer sunshine, my plastic pool lounger awaited.

I stretched out on the lounger, grateful for the feeling of finally being on my own. I sipped the coffee, gazing over the rim of the cup at the ocean stretched in front of me, blue and peaceful. As I drank, savouring the bitter taste, I began to engage my other senses, taking time to tune in to the sights and sounds around me. Putting down the emptied cup, I began to deliberately notice the ebb and flow of the waves below me, observing the dark of the rocks under the surface. I watched numerous swallows rise and dip in search of food and tried to see the insects that were the object of their desire. I listened to the layers of sound — first, the loud crash and suck of the rolling breakers, then the closest of the birds until gradually I could discern the rustle of the leaves in the tree below me.

I took a deep breath in, one of those stuttering breaths taken by a child at the end of a torrent of tears. I hadn't been crying but must have been more tense and on-edge than I thought, holding my breath tight in my lungs, raising my shoulders nearly to my ears. I took another breath, less shaky this time, and felt my diaphragm stretch and suck air deep within. Exhaling slowly and steadily, my shoulders fell and softened. I settled a little more deeply into my seat.

This practice of observing the wonder of God's creation, of truly looking and noticing, has become a vital aspect of my self-care journey. In doing so, I hear again His whispers, feel His love, enjoy His presence. I am reminded that He is God, and I am not. As such, I don't need to be weighed down with the burdens of the world. He opens the windows of my soul, and the claustrophobic stuffiness is expelled by the fresh wind of His Spirit.

I gathered my coffee cup and cushion and returned to my over-full house. But this time, as I walked through the door, it was different. Or, rather, I was. Now there was space.

— Anna Jensen —

80

Let It Go

This is your moment. Own it.
~Oprah Winfrey

I used to think self-care involved bubble baths, chocolate cake, and monthly manicures. Our consumer culture teaches us that self-care equates to treating ourselves. How often do we tell each other, "Go on, it's self-care. Calories don't count"?

After graduating university, I spent seven years in a fulfilling yet flexible job in the social services. When I felt stressed, I'd buy new shoes, order an ice-cream cone, or sneak out of the office for a massage. Despite bragging about how I regularly indulged in self-care, most of the activities I chose involved spending money I didn't have or consuming calories I didn't need. I really wasn't caring for my "self" at all.

I've always been a bit of a control freak, which likely stems from underlying anxiety. If a group of friends took a limo or taxi downtown, I'd follow behind in my trusty Honda Civic so that I could leave the party whenever I wanted, rather than being at the mercy of the pack.

Whenever I had a negative interaction with another person, I'd spend the day replaying it in my head and dwelling on what went wrong. Conflict terrified me. The sight of flashing lights or the sound of a siren would bring on my anxiety. Sirens meant an emergency was happening nearby, and I had no control over it. A fire could spread; a bad guy could escape; a loved one could be hurt. Indulging in my naïve brand of self-care did nothing to reduce the daily discomfort.

That cupcake or glass of wine just served as a momentary distraction I'd ultimately regret.

Then I did what any control freak with high-functioning anxiety, poor stress-management skills and a fear of conflict probably shouldn't do: I accepted a job as an emergency-room social worker.

By tossing myself into anxiety-provoking, high-stress situations, would I overload and have a nervous breakdown? Or would I find a new homeostasis that would help me cope better with everyday stressors? I essentially became my own science experiment.

The first time I sat down on a stretcher to interview a patient, I was so nervous that my leg bounced around involuntarily and I had to pin it down with my arm. The things I saw in my first few weeks shocked me. Agitated patients screamed and fought while security personnel attempted to negotiate and nurses scrambled for sedatives. Elderly cancer patients huddled under their blankets crying when they realized their final months were in sight. Bruised children. Volatile teens. Brawling families. Grief. Fear. Uncertainty.

It was impossible to plan my day because priorities shifted by the minute and my cellphone rang constantly with pressing new problems. Nothing was predictable, and each scenario was too different to have a cookie-cutter solution.

The uncertainty terrified me at first, but I soon learned to embrace the chaos. I eventually realized that one can find a modicum of predictability in even the most unpredictable scenarios. Helping to care for others in their most vulnerable moments with a cup of water, a good cry, a favourite song, or a comfort object, or helping them to connect with a loved one, reminded me how to get back to basics with my own self-care. Some days, that meant something as minor as eating a strawberry mindfully or wiggling my toes in the grass. One saving grace was reading the daily Chicken Soup for the Soul story I signed up to have delivered to my inbox.

Two months in, instead of feeling paralyzed with fear when the emergency alarm began ringing on the loudspeaker, I felt energized and excited. The trick was getting the surging adrenaline to settle down so that it was useful rather than debilitating. I had to remind my brain there was no saber-toothed tiger attack looming — just some patients and their loved ones needing support. I became one of the people running toward the perceived threat instead of away from it. I may never be fearless, but I aim to fear less.

Most importantly, I learned that anxiety isn't weakness. Showing up to terrifying situations with anxiety is one of the strongest things I've had to do. I learned that the things we can't control are lessons in how to let go. This chaotic job somehow became chicken soup for my anxious soul.

Now, self-care means meal-prepping for the week so I don't settle for subpar cafeteria fast food. It means laying out my clothes so I can sleep an extra ten minutes in the morning. Self-care means clean sheets, tossed salads, staying hydrated, and not checking work e-mail from home. Those fleeting indulgences of manicures and mimosas don't cut it anymore.

Despite handling the chaos well at work, I had a tough time "switching it off" at the end of the day. There was no time to process each crisis before I had to run to the next one, so I spent my evenings reliving my day. I'd heard the advice to "toss your day" into an imaginary bucket to leave behind at work, but it wasn't that simple. The stressors of my day followed me and clattered for attention like tin cans tied to my ankle. One evening, when I poured one too many glasses of wine and lay spread-eagled in the grass hoping the ground would absorb the stress coursing through my body, I realized it was time to come up with a new plan.

Now, when I return home from the hospital, I recite my new mantra: I did the best work I could today. I helped people. Now leave it to others to follow up.

And then I practice a self-care routine they don't teach in any online psychology journal: I log onto YouTube and play my self-care theme song — "Let It Go" — the Disney ditty from *Frozen* that won the Oscar for Best Original Song in 2014.

I belt out that power ballad when I return home after a particularly stressful day. Sometimes, I dance maniacally around, releasing all the pent-up energy. Sometimes, I scream the lyrics into a fan and laugh at my robot voice. Sometimes, I stretch and do yoga poses or ballerina pirouettes while throwing pretend icicles from my fingers. I find myself laughing at my antics, out of breath. But, sure enough, "the past is in the past," and I stop thinking about my workday. For those three minutes, thirty-eight seconds, I run through the day's cases and "let them go and slam the door." By the time the song ends, I've processed the stressful moments from my day and feel no need to dredge them up again.

In the words of Queen Elsa, "It's funny how some distance makes everything seem small...." I leave my workday behind me and move on with my evening.

Now, as soon as the chords of my self-care anthem start up, my body relaxes, and my mind releases the day's struggles. One could say they "become one with the wind and sky."

Sometimes, self-care means letting go.

— Cassie Silva —

81

A More Balanced Life

Some old-fashioned things like fresh air and sunshine
are hard to beat.
~Laura Ingalls Wilder

At my last check-up, the doctor mentioned that my blood pressure was a little high — not dangerously so, but an increase from the past. Rather than put me on medication, the doctor prescribed making time to purposely relax every day. I had never put "purposely relax" on my daily schedule, but I decided that now was the time to seriously consider how to do it.

So how would I attempt to purposely relax? Meditation? Yoga? Deep-breathing exercises? Nope, nothing like that. I went out and bought a hammock.

Yes, I know hammocks are either for cartoon characters, like Fred Flintstone and Homer Simpson, or they're for old guys in general. But I figured now that I was retired, I was officially an old guy, so I deserved a hammock.

There's a shady corner in the back yard, right near the locust trees and the hosta garden, where I hang the hummingbird feeder. It seemed like the perfect spot for a hammock.

It took me a few attempts to get the tension on the ropes just right, and then I had to really work at my balance to get comfortably into the hammock and scoot myself to a stable position. It took a while, but eventually I made it without tipping over.

And it was wonderful. There I was with the latest James Patterson paperback, reclining in the shade, with a gentle breeze moving the air. I read a few chapters, and then I watched the clouds. Finally, I blissfully drifted off into a nap while a cardinal serenaded me from a nearby tree limb. This purposely relaxing stuff was kind of nice.

I must have looked very comfortable snoozing in the hammock because it wasn't long before my cat, Jasper, jumped up to join me. Much like myself, Jasper is no lightweight, and his pounce set the hammock rocking back and forth like a rowboat in the rapids! I was immediately startled awake and grabbed the edges of the hammock for balance.

When we finally stopped tilting, both the cat and I sighed with relief. Then Jasper gingerly strolled over and curled up next to me, where he yawned and closed his eyes.

So, there I was stretched out with my book and the cat, gently rocking in the breeze, when I realized what makes hammocks so wonderful, besides the fact that they're delightfully comfortable. Hammocks are a lot like life.

In a hammock, just like in life, you have to learn to keep your balance. You have to acquire the ability to relax and let go if you're going to truly enjoy yourself. And if someone or something (or some cat) unexpectedly rocks the boat, you have to be ready to adjust quickly and maintain your equilibrium.

So now, every day, despite running all the errands life entails, I make sure to create some time to purposely relax and have a more balanced life with me and my hammock.

— David Hull —

82

Cozy Corner

A little while alone in your room will
prove more valuable than anything
else that could ever be given you.
~Rumi

This weekend I did six loads of laundry, dutifully prepared breakfast, lunch and dinner, and set out healthy snacks to cover the gaps when meals were hours away. I de-greased team uniforms and got them ready to be ruined all over again. And then, of course, there were the drop-offs and pick-ups, beginning at nine in the morning, and the cheering from the bleachers that I managed to squeeze in.

If I remembered or had the time, I'd take a restroom break and grab the granola bar that lay beneath mounds of wipes in my oversized pocketbook that stored everyone's immediate needs. If I was extra lucky, I could wash down the granola bar with the cold coffee in my console.

The start of the work week always required the highest level of organizational skills.

Sunday evening, the week's to-do list was taped on the front door.

I noticed my name never appeared there.

There wasn't time to set aside for myself.

How could I be any good to those I love if I didn't fill my own tank?

I already knew the answer.

So, a new to-do list was placed side-by-side with the family's.

In red marker, the heading read: "Mom's Cozy Corner."

Hours to be determined on an "as-needed" basis.

A coat closet in the hallway was converted into a space that now represents my sanctuary.

I retreat here at least once per day, more when I can sneak away.

To me, it's paradise, a soothing balm for the soul.

A simple piece of plywood sits atop a planter, which makes for a wonderful desk.

An old green throw pillow subs for a chair.

On the wall behind my makeshift desk, I taped landscapes that lift me: lakeside cottages, majestic mountains, thunderous oceans, fresh fallen snow after a storm.

John Denver and James Taylor serenade my old weary bones thanks to my trusty CD player, which my kids make fun of.

The shelf above that used to store winter boots now houses a book collection of childhood favorites, classic masterpieces, and a steamy romance novel or two.

A fresh bowl of lemon and lime peels fragrances the corner.

A thriving cactus sits contentedly next to an artificial candle.

Since the door must remain open for proper ventilation, I place an upright vacuum cleaner in front to indicate that the space is occupied. No admittance, no trespassing unless necessary.

I trained my family well.

I took them on a tour of my cherished retreat and provided explanations of the reasons and rules.

Funny; no one comes near. It's as if the vacuum possesses magical powers.

Every now and then, someone will yell down the hallway, attempting to break the mood.

If everything is all right, I raise the volume on the music and add a minute to my self-care.

On more than one occasion, I have fallen asleep to James Taylor letting me know I've got a friend.

And that's my truth.

I *do* have a friend. In *me*.

I have to take good care of her so that she's able to take good care of everyone she loves.

And thanks to the cozy corner, this mom is nourished and ready to tackle the wonderful life she's been given.

After a quick, refreshing catnap, that is.

— Lisa Leshaw —

One Piece at a Time

*Unplugging helps you refocus on yourself instead
of being pulled in a zillion different directions.
Those directions may all be important,
but you are just as important.*
~Arin Murphy-Hiscock,
The Witch's Book of Self-Care

The newlywed apartment where my son James and his wife Natalie lived was tiny and cramped. That's why I was surprised to see an oversized card table set up in the corner of the living room. On it was a partially worked jigsaw puzzle that pictured several brightly colored hot-air balloons.

Newlyweds working a jigsaw puzzle? The very notion made me want to burst out laughing. I didn't, of course.

"I see y'all are working a puzzle," I said, picking up the box with the picture on it. "A thousand pieces? That's impressive!"

James stretched out on the couch and reached for the remote.

"Not me," he said. "Natalie has done every bit of it."

Natalie dragged two folding chairs from the dining area over to the card table and motioned for me to sit in one. "Want to help?"

"Sure," I said. I settled in to work on the yellow balloon and get to know my delightful new daughter-in-law a little better.

"Have you been working puzzles since you were a little girl?" I asked, remembering how my three kids had loved their ABC floor puzzle.

Natalie shook her head. "Nope," she said, explaining that she had so many brothers and sisters that the family dining table hardly had enough room for plates and food, let alone puzzles. "There wasn't even room on the floor," she said. "I didn't really start working puzzles until I was in law school."

I raised my eyebrows in question. Natalie told me how lonely and lost she'd felt during her first semester. James, then her boyfriend, lived a hundred miles away. She hadn't had time yet to make friends. She didn't have Internet. She didn't have cable TV. And a person can't study all the time.

"I needed to find something relaxing and fun to do, something to take my mind off all the stuff that was weighing me down," she said. So, she went to the dollar store and bought a thousand-piece puzzle, figuring it was the most bang for her buck.

Spreading out the puzzle pieces on her kitchen counter, Natalie went to work. She played classical music on her phone while she constructed the border and fitted the interior pieces together, focusing entirely on the task at hand. A surprising calm came over her.

"For the first time in a long time, I felt relaxed and at peace," she said. "It was incredible."

Natalie eventually made friends. She studied hard. And she never got Internet or cable TV in her apartment.

"I really couldn't afford it," she told me with a laugh. "But the more time that passed, the more I found I didn't need or want it. My law books and my puzzles were enough."

Early on, Natalie began to see a connection between puzzles and the law. In both, you have to look at the big picture first. You find and organize all the facts and all the applicable law. Then you put the case together one piece at a time until you arrive back at the big picture. Once this realization dawned on her, law school didn't seem quite so daunting.

Three years passed. Natalie graduated and got a job, one that challenged and suited her perfectly. She and James got married and, while working on the hot-air-balloon puzzle, she shared her me-time story with me.

And then, James and Natalie added two baby girls, born just fifteen months apart, to their family. Talk about stress! Law school was nothing compared to being a wife, mother and full-time attorney. The family had a bigger house now, with a cozy corner in the living room just perfect for a card table.

"I hadn't given away my puzzles during any of my moves," Natalie said. "So, I got out my hardest one and went to work on it."

These days, more than a decade after graduating, Natalie's still at it.

"A sense of calm still comes over me whenever I work on a puzzle," she told me. "Even if the television's blaring, the kids are bickering, and the dog's begging to go outside, I can usually manage to tune all that out, breathe deep and focus on the task at hand."

Look at the big picture. Concentrate on one piece at a time. And know that, sooner or later, everything will fit together like it's supposed to. That's my delightful daughter-in-law's way to find peace when life gets a little too crazy.

—Jennie Ivey—

The Glad Game

*Once you begin to take note of the things
you are grateful for, you begin to lose sight
of the things that you lack.*
~Germany Kent

The first clue that this isn't going to be a normal summer starts in April when my husband's cardiologist tells him that a leaky valve in his heart needs to be replaced. Since I've been spending the past few summers alone at our New Hampshire lake cottage, this is not welcome news. I rationalize that there will be plenty of time for this operation and recovery before I leave in July. After that, Ray can go back to what he loves best — watching Yankees games on his big-screen TV in our air-conditioned house — and I can return to the lake with its gentle breezes and warbling loons. How wrong could I be? Plenty, as it turns out.

A new procedure for replacing heart valves is offered at some large hospitals. Rather than cracking open the chest, the surgeon threads a new valve through a vein and inserts it into the heart. Before this can be done, there is a long list of Medicare-driven criteria that must be met. First on this list is a vein catheterization to see if it's open enough to insert a new valve. Ray and I spend the day at the hospital — he in a bed, me in the waiting room trying to push the what-if scenarios out of my mind.

We're both tired when we get home at 6:00 p.m. and go to bed early. He wakes me at 3:00 a.m. "I'm having a heart attack." His heavy breathing convinces me to call 911.

"Want to ride in the ambulance with us?" the driver asks me.

"No, thanks. I'll come down once I get changed and walk the dog." I've done this before. *Just another fire drill*, I say to myself. *I won't call the kids. It can wait until morning.*

Ray is admitted to our local hospital for a few days. The doctors rule out a heart attack, saying it's a severe reaction to the dye used for the catheterization.

His recovery takes a week before the other heart-valve criteria can be scheduled. With regret, I flip the page on my calendar to May. I'm still hopeful that he'll recover enough for me to leave — maybe not the first week of July but at least sometime during the summer.

All our conversations now revolve around his health. Will he live? Will he die? He shares with me answers to questions I'd been asking since his stroke twenty years earlier. "Do you want to be cremated or buried? Do you want the funeral to be in Harrison or New Hampshire? Should we buy a cemetery plot?"

I am not accepting this well. Every time I think of what might be ahead, I feel nauseous and need to find a bathroom.

We attend two back-to-back memorial services for friends. I find myself wiping away tears — not for those who've departed but for the possibility that Ray's funeral might be next.

Ray passes all the criteria for the valve replacement. He's given a date at the beginning of June, only to have it pushed back a week because "someone sicker than him needs a new valve first." I understand this, but I am annoyed at another delay.

The operation goes as scheduled. Ray survives it — so well, in fact, that he comes home the next day.

The aftercare directions state that someone needs to be with him for two weeks. There goes my escape to the lake.

I know if this scenario were reversed, he'd do the same for me, but I find I'm beginning to crumble. Friends urge me to take care of myself. I try, but despite long walks, a massage, a facial, and planting a flower garden, I become impatient with my husband. I'm not liking myself, but I don't seem to be able to curb my behavior.

In mid-July, I see a window of ten days with no medical visits. "Would it be all right with you if I go to the lake?" I ask Ray. "I'll come home for the next group of appointments."

He doesn't seem to care. He can now drive himself to cardio-rehab, church, and Stop & Shop. Although he doesn't say it, I sense that he needs a break from me, too.

Unlike in years past, once at the lake, I'm met with challenges. I can't get the electronic garage opener to work, I drop a jar of pasta sauce on the floor where it splatters everywhere. There's a mouse. It rains for four days.

I begin talking to myself, which is somehow comforting. "Stop feeling sorry for yourself, Polly," I shout at the walls. "Life is full of good things, positive things. Find them." Then I remember. When I was a child, I loved reading Eleanor H. Porter's book, *Pollyanna*. Maybe it was because my name is similar, but I think I would have loved this feel-good story anyway. Pollyanna had something she called her Glad Game. I shall play it myself. Here's how I'm going to do it:

1. Every day, I will find three unexpected things to be glad about.
2. I will write a few words about them on Post-it notes.
3. I cannot go to bed until I've written down three.

At first, it is difficult. Sure, I can find three positive things during these days, but my rules say they must be unexpected, which means taking a hike with a friend can't be on the list because I know I'm going to have fun. The first day, I write:

1. Cut open a cantaloupe at its peak of ripeness.
2. Invitation to Bernie's book launch.
3. The woman checking out my groceries said: "Cute shirt."

The next day is easier:

1. Figured out how to change the printer cartridge by going

on the Internet.

2. Opened the lid on a jar of pickles with pliers.

3. Moonlight swim at 9!

I begin experimenting with cooking. One evening, I grill clams. I am not certain if one has opened enough, but before I know it, it is in my mouth. An entry the next day reads: "Didn't get sick from bad clam last night."

Another time, the bathroom light burns out. That night's note reads: "Candles work well in bathroom." I am surprised to receive a dinner invitation from neighbors I hardly know. One Post-it reads, "Ken and Linda's for dinner. Foodies!" The next morning, I smile when two lilies bloom in my garden. That is worthy of another entry, as is "Young man at the dump helped me lift my heavy bag of garbage."

These daily reminders that life can still be good buoy my spirit. When it is time to return home, my mind is in a better place. My five-hour drive gives me plenty of thinking time. I will continue to note the Glad Moments in my life. I don't even need to write them down anymore, now that it's a habit. Recognizing them is enough.

— Polly Hare Tafrate —

Adventures in Meditation

Only those who dare to fail greatly
can ever achieve greatly.
~Robert F. Kennedy

I'm going to get in some meditation time this morning. I've been reading a variety of insightful books on spirituality and self-improvement, and I understand that meditation is a key to self-knowledge and finding peace and tranquility in a chaotic world. It's early Sunday morning and I think I have all the distractions out of the way. The laundry is just about done, I shouldn't get noise from the washer or dryer. I fed the three dogs and the cat. I greeted the husband (John). I medicated the cat. (He's sixteen with a hyperthyroid.) And I changed the linen. I am good to go.

I inform John that I'm going into my office for a little while to do some meditation. He won't disturb me.

I close the door, hopefully cutting myself off from the chaos of life. The ceiling lights are off and the light coming in through the window is soft. I take my seat in state-of-the-art, ergonomic comfort. Feet flat on the floor. Hands, palms up, on my lap. I close my eyes. I breathe deeply in... then out... In... then out... Ahhhhh... Then John blows his nose like a clarion call to arms, cutting through that solid-core knotty alder door like it isn't there.

Okay. No problem. Breathe in... then out... in, then... John trumpets his next nasal blast.

Okay... Still no problem because I've got state-of-the-art Bluetooth-enabled noise-canceling headphones. And I have access to some great meditation music online at Om Harmonics.

First, I have to find my iPhone. Then I need to go to Settings to connect the Bluetooth from the iPhone to the headphones. Then I need to find my username and password for the website. This takes a few minutes, plus a few minutes more to log in. (I live in the country with very slow Internet.)

I log in. I go to the website and choose the FOCUS meditation music. I want FOCUS... oh, on so many levels! I click the PLAY icon and sit back in my chair. Feet flat on the floor. Hands, palms up, on my lap. The music begins. I breathe in...

Music is too loud! I cannot hear myself think, let alone hear my breathing. I must stop, turn down the volume until, perfect! I sit back. Feet flat on the floor. Hands, palms up, on my lap and... breathe in... and out... In... and out... Ahhhhh...

A woodpecker chooses this moment to begin eating my house outside my office window, banging its little beak over and over into the wood siding, effectively overriding the state-of-the-art, noise-canceling features of my headphones.

And now the music is getting on my nerves, too.

I turn off the music, and miraculously it seems that the woodpecker decided to relocate since the percussive beat of its beak has stopped. I feel hope. That's something.

I sigh as I sit back in my chair. Feet flat... I assume the position. I begin to breathe in, and then out, in and out. Not quite as slowly as I think I should be doing. Am I hyperventilating? *Slowly, Phyllis.* In... then out... in... and, what is THIS penetrating the state-of-the-art technology of my noise-canceling headphones?

Very faintly, I perceive a tiny whine from Kitana, my little Jack Russell Terrier, who has planted herself outside my office door, wanting to come in.

A giggle escapes as I get out of my chair. It becomes helpless laughter as I open the door to let in Kitana. In she trots, but as I move to close the door, she darts out, telling me she wants the door open. I'm hysterical now, and tears fill my eyes

Off come the state-of-the-art, noise-canceling headphones. Wiping my eyes, I take one last lingering look at my ergonomically comfortable chair as I slide it back under the desk and think, *The heck with it; I'll write this down.*

There. I meditated!

— Phyllis Abate Wild —

Three O'Clock on Phantom Lake

I could never stay long enough on the shore;
the tang of the untainted, fresh, and free sea
air was like a cool, quieting thought.
~Helen Keller

This time,
I don't give the drain rack a second glance.
Someone else can stack the glasses and
Slide the cutting board back into its narrow cubby.
The plate with eggs baked on by the microwave
Can sit and soak.
I'm out the back door.
The shed smells of mildew from
The left-in-the-rain lifejackets;
Remembered and stowed in September.
And who took apart these paddles?
Just because it's November doesn't mean
I'm in for the season.
It's worth it, these pesky preparations,
To skim along the still waters
And push away the lake fog
with the blunt, blue nose

Of my little kayak.
Let the bills wait.
Leave the cellphone on the kitchen counter.
There will be time enough to grade papers tomorrow.
Here is my peace.
Just me and the sky and this boat.
And sometimes the dog.

—Ilana Long—

Pursue Your Passion

87

Escaping Insomnia

If you do what you love, it is the best way to relax.
~Christian Louboutin

I honestly don't know why I set up the painting table. Even as I put out the paints and brushes, I felt foolish. I was a single parent, pedaling fast to take care of my four kids. I had no family nearby to help and little extra time after work and the kids' sports.

Even after I set up the table in our kitchen, we all knew I wasn't going to paint. It just wasn't going to happen. And it didn't.

All my days were the same. I got up, hustled the kids off to school, went to work, and then picked them up, fitting dinner in around their karate, softball and soccer. At the end of the day, I fell into bed exhausted.

Then the insomnia returned. I found myself wandering around the house at three in the morning. With nothing to watch on television, I cleaned the floors, made the kids' lunches, and tried to catch up on chores. By the end of the week, my checkbook was balanced, and the chores were done. That's when the painting table became more than a rectangular object taking up space in the kitchen. It seemed to call out to me.

I tried to ignore it. I told myself there were other things to do. But in those blurry hours when I should have been asleep, painting seemed like as good an idea as any. It was something to occupy my mind until maybe I could go back to sleep.

One night, I sat down, grabbed my brushes and painted. I did the same thing the following night, and then again, until a week had flown by. Most nights, I never went back to sleep, so it was easy to be dressed and ready for work before the kids got up. Every morning, I returned the brushes to their proper places and put my paints away. One morning — I must have been painting for two or three weeks by then — I sat down at the dining-room table and listened to the kids chatter as they finished their breakfast.

One of my girls turned to me. "Hey, Mom, you're nicer when you paint."

Before I could respond, another spoke up. "Yeah. Nicer."

At first, I was surprised that they'd even noticed. The painting table had become just another piece of furniture taking up space. Then my head swirled as I absorbed their words. Nicer? Did that mean I wasn't nice the rest of the time? My stomach flip-flopped as I pondered the implication. I wasn't a good mom — I was mean. My heart sank as I fought back the tears.

Finally, with a shaky voice, I asked, "So, I'm not nice normally?"

A chorus of voices followed, each child offering up his or her thoughts and explaining what they meant. Somehow, they'd noticed that I had been painting regularly, but they'd also noticed a change in me that I was unaware of.

Painting made me happy. They'd seen that and wanted me to know. Trying to ease my insomnia by filling the time with painting, I'd stumbled on a secret to taking care of me — just by letting my creative self come out of hiding.

And now, when days get long, work is too busy, and life wants to swallow me whole again, I can still hear their voices telling me how much nicer I am when I paint. They'd discovered something I might never have recognized: Doing what I like, even in small doses on a regular basis, is important. It makes me happy.

— Debby Johnson —

88

Wanted: Me

Every secret of a writer's soul, every experience
of his life, every quality of his mind,
is written large in his works.
~Virginia Woolf

I need someone to do my job so I can have more me time. While some writers and creators, including me, consider mine a dream job, it can sometimes be a bad dream. When the printer tells you the press is broken, Kindle Direct is refusing an upload, and you're wondering if you can add an extra couple of days to the month to meet your next deadline, it is stressful. I need me time, but how?

I need to delegate. Here's the want-ad I would like to run:

Wanted: Creative-minded person who is fluent in Adobe Suite, familiar with the English language, and can make entire files disappear with the click of a mouse. Primary duties include editing, graphics, public speaking, and knowing how to smile warmly while biting one's lip.

Secondary duties include heavy lifting, shipping, receiving, handling complaints, handling praise, answering e-mails, and searching for files that have mistakenly been deleted.

Requires long hours, short lunches, lots of travel, and even more in-office time trying to catch up after the travel. Must love dogs and cats, as they will be the closest thing to a personal assistant that you'll get in this office. Sanity optional; three hands a plus.

The company we founded, Greybird Publishers, originally employed only my wife and me (plus a few dogs and cats who are basically lazy and useless). But as our business grew, we had less and less time to get our jobs done. In the past few years, we've added a couple of employees and another dog because it became obvious that trying to do it all ourselves was not only counterproductive but basically impossible.

Before we were able to afford office help, we did delegate the yard work to a local kid. This freed up an extra couple of hours each week, which I used to get more publishing and writing tasks done. That increased revenue allowed us to hire an individual to clean our home offices once a month. That added four more hours of time that we could be doing something else, such as working on *American Digger* magazine or our latest book project. Since I am pretty much a mechanically declined person, auto repairs and the like were already being farmed out, as was gutter cleaning. (Being deathly afraid of gravity, I avoid high places.)

As our business grew, we became better at delegating. It actually gave us more time to make more money, which could pay for even more freedom. I also used this extra time to get ahead in my work, especially that which was deadline oriented. Although staring out the window watching a squirrel chase a cat is a fun thing to do while sitting at your workstation, it is not particularly productive. If you're not productive, you'll never catch up, and if you never catch up, there's no time for "me."

But you say, "I don't own a business! I own a family with kids!" But I can offer you my sincere thoughts and prayers, along with these observations:

You can still delegate to kids, although it's best if they don't realize it. When your children are too young to walk, you have a ready-made system for picking up things from the floor. Just make sure you take anything from them before they put it in their mouths. When the kids are in elementary school, buy a long-haired, low-slung, playful dog — a long-haired Dachshund is perfect — and let the kids chase him all through the house. If the dog is a habitual tail-wagger, so much the better. Voilà, instant floor sweeper!

Once your children are teenagers, plead with them to cut the lawn for free. If they refuse, offer a pittance. Failing that, buy a goat; they are a good investment, sort of like a lawnmower, and they'll do the pruning, too. Once the teens get their driver's licenses, most jump at the chance to get behind the wheel without supervision, which will save you countless time spent chauffeuring other children to functions, picking up random grocery items, and even driving to the hardware store for a gutter-cleaning ladder (after you've convinced them that gravity is only dangerous for older people).

However, if you're a stay-at-home parent, trying to get your own work done, it's hard to wall off any "me time" when the kids are about. There are proven techniques, such as moving to a new home or changing the locks during school hours. Such techniques are frowned upon, and probably illegal, but there are other ways to engage in self-care. Holing up in the bathroom is one answer, a solution long mastered by husbands that I now offer to the wives. Here you can catch up on reading, meditate, take a nap, or Google "laws concerning changing door locks" on your iPhone. Sadly, this solitude ends if someone computes how long you've been in there and starts knocking on the door.

While I don't advocate lying, it is perfectly fine to use the "I have a headache" line on family members other than your spouse. This buys you an hour or two alone as long as you lie on the bed, turn out the lights, shut the door, and occasionally groan to show you're alive. You may also find some me time in the car. Consider running errands alone by sneaking out before anyone knows you're gone.

In reality, your best me time will come between the time your grown kids leave home and the first time the grandchildren visit. Use this time wisely! Travel to peculiar places. Take useless lessons. Dance naked. Do whatever you want to do because, without you, you have nothing.

As for me, I've been there. I've loved my kids and used them wisely. But instead of taking me time when they moved away, I started a business utilizing what I enjoyed most during my me time: writing. I love the written word and all that goes with it, and a lot of my job does seem like me time because I enjoy what I do so much.

That classified ad that I want to run is really my own job description, encompassing all the remaining duties I can't manage to delegate. So, for real time off, I close my work documents, bookmark my edits, save my half-written bi-monthly column, mentally and physically clock myself out from my day job, have a pleasant dinner, and maybe watch some TV. And then, I write. Not for Greybird Publishers but for me. If you like what I write, great; if not, that's fine, too. To me, doing what I love is me time. And I love what I do as me.

— Butch Holcombe —

My Holy Hour

*We need quiet time to examine our lives openly and
honestly — spending quiet time alone gives your mind
an opportunity to renew itself and create order.*
~Susan L. Taylor

Early in the morning, while it's still dark outside, I get up, leave my room, and go downstairs to the facility's dining room where I have found a solitary place in which to write. I love to write and, in those early morning hours before dawn, I can think.

"Is this your hobby?" someone asks as the breakfast cart makes its way to our table.

"Hobby? No. Writing is my life's work. My passion." I repeat myself: "No, it's not a hobby." I believe a lot of residents think I go back to my room, type in "Once upon a time," and send my manuscript somewhere into outer space. And that's it.

"Can we buy the book your story is in?" they ask.

"Perhaps sometime next year," I calculate. "I have to wait and see if a publisher accepts it." Silence falls upon us... and I go on with my day.

I call these couple of hours in the very early part of my day "My Holy Hours." I can think clearly when it's just me and the silence of a soon-to-be-noisy dining room. The lights are on, the tables are set with clean napkins and silverware, and a beautiful centerpiece is waiting to welcome the residents. But, for now, it all welcomes me, and I thrive in knowing that this part of the day is just for me.

When breakfast is over and the day has officially begun, I must sneak moments for writing into my day. While the other residents go to the Activities Room to make birthday cards, play Bingo, or do word-search puzzles, I quietly close the door to my room and remain out of sight and write. These solitary moments I garner for myself take up most of my day, and I like it that way. For a while, my writing world helps me forget the home I had to leave and the life I once had.

One of the blessings of living in an assisted-living facility is that finally, after all these years, I can spend more time doing what I love to do. Gone are the days that I got up at the crack of dawn to prepare breakfast, pack lunches, usher my husband off to work and get my children ready for school. After I packed my daughter and son's book bags and made sure they had the books they would need for the day, I packed my own book bag with the books I would need to teach a class of thirty lively fifth-graders vying for my attention.

Recess didn't offer any time for honing my craft. Fifteen minutes flew by, barely leaving enough time for preparing the next lesson. After-school visits to the orthodontist, basketball practice, and piano lessons didn't offer any spare time for me to construct a phrase let alone a sentence. And then it was time for dinner and bed.

But I miss my family like it used to be. My husband passed away five years ago, and my children are living their dreams in their chosen careers. When my now-grown children used to visit me before the pandemic lockdown, it was hard for me to say goodbye when it was time for them to leave.

"I'll see you soon," I would say as I hugged each one tightly, not wanting to let them go. "Call me when you get home." Tears filled that sacred space in my heart that is reserved "for mothers only."

Then I would close the door behind me, pick up my pen, and write.

— Lola Di Giulio De Maci —

90

Digging Holes

*Self-care has become a new priority — the revelation
that it's perfectly permissible to listen to your body
and do what it needs.*
~Frances Ryan

When my children were young, they had myriad medical ailments and were chronically ill. To make matters worse, doctors often misdiagnosed them, forcing our family to work harder to get to the bottom of their health problems. It was frustrating, stressful and financially draining.

I used many coping techniques to deal with my troubles. I prayed a lot. I wrote about my feelings and struggles, outlining plans to overcome them. I joined support groups and formed friendships with parents experiencing similar difficulties. I escaped from my woes by watching movies, reading books and going on vacations. I celebrated each day that we were alive, trying to maintain a positive attitude and have an optimistic outlook on life despite every bad force that worked against us. I hugged my kids, dog and husband frequently. I cried and laughed often. I ate right, slept six or seven hours each night, and exercised every day.

And there was a strategy that helped me greatly; I dug holes in my back yard.

The rocky, hard soil made for strenuous digging, and that helped me with my stress. Whenever the doctors gave me news I didn't want to hear, I grabbed my shovel and garden gloves, and began surveying the landscape.

"What are you doing?" Patrick asked the first time he witnessed me digging one of my holes.

"I'm going outside to dig a hole," I said sharply.

"Please, not another hole," he begged.

I rested the shovel on the toe of my boot. "I can't think straight until I have wrestled with rocks and immersed myself in dirt." I sighed deeply. "Don't ask me why it helps; it just does." I looked at him with tears welling in my eyes.

He nodded and set down Juliana and Andrea, freeing them to run around the kitchen while I worked in the yard. Patrick kept half an eye on me, probably to ensure I didn't dig halfway to China.

The first thrust of the shovel breaking ground was always the fiercest. Every time, I hit a rock. I worked steadfastly around it, poking and prodding until it was unearthed. The harder I dug, the better I felt. I got a bizarre satisfaction in making a big, round hole.

After an hour or so, Patrick came out to check on me.

"Had enough?" he hollered from the swing set, where the girls were playing.

"Yeah, I'm just about done." I stood back and wiped the hair that blew across my face. "How does it look?"

Patrick walked beside it and peered in. "This would be a dandy place for a tree."

"I would love a lilac bush," I murmured.

He nodded as he thought. "I like lilacs," he said softly. "Take a shower, and I'll cover the hole with a bucket. Tomorrow, we can go to a greenhouse and buy something to plant here. We can't let a good hole go to waste." He smiled as I walked inside.

As I washed away the grime from my body, I thought about how lucky I was to have a loving and understanding husband. Now my muscles were aching in a good way and my worries were gone, at least for that moment. I was able to intelligently sift through the information the doctors had delivered hours before, process it and come to terms with it. I could sleep peacefully at night, knowing I had the girls' medical issues under control. And we would buy a tree in the morning. Patrick had filled in all the other holes I had dug but this new hole had a purpose.

As time went on, we planted lilac bushes, roses of Sharon, plum bushes, and pear and maple trees. It spawned a curiosity about plant life, and I slowly began learning about gardening. I built a small flowerbed with a variety of perennials. Each year, I expanded that flower patch with a wider border, adding new and exciting plants that I got from a nearby farmer's market.

Gardening was something I could control; it gave me a wonderful diversion from my problems. I enjoyed digging in the dirt, but I hadn't realized it until my daughters began having medical problems. Gardening became my daily ritual. It offered me a tranquil place where I could work, think, pray, listen to my heart and clear my head. I could solve my problems in the garden by deadheading flowers and spreading mulch. My hobby was therapeutic. It was good for my yard and my wellbeing: spiritually, physically and mentally.

By the time our daughters entered college, I had dug up enough rocks to build a gigantic rock wall around the perimeter of the yard. I built a fountain pedestal out of the rocks and a shrine to Saint Francis and the Blessed Virgin Mary. I created a tall green wall of lilac bushes with twelve maple trees and ten pine trees dotting the property. The flowerbeds have plants spilling from them, attracting adorable bunnies, scampering squirrels and all kinds of chirping birds.

I never would have believed that my yard could be so relaxing and feel so comfortable. I am blessed that I am surrounded by natural beauty, which was created out of a desire to handle stress. Gardening kept me strong and sane, and it all started with digging a hole, one that my husband filled in!

— Barbara Sue Canale —

91

Me Again

Nourishing yourself in a way that helps you blossom in
the direction you want to go is attainable,
and you are worth the effort.
~Deborah Day

I signed up, then canceled, then un-canceled, then canceled again. The poor woman at the writers' retreat center was probably so frustrated with me. And, I admit, I was anxious — not my most calm and graceful self. But it was my first trip away from my kids ever, and what a decade it had been.

Both of our kids had been born with multiple anaphylactic food allergies and asthma, which can be a deadly combination, triggered by everyday things that are everywhere. The learning curve to navigate these conditions was mountainous, and I knew quickly after our older baby's first terrifying anaphylactic reaction that I didn't want to put their daily lives in anyone's hands but my own. (As one relative commented early on, "Wow, those kids would've died if they'd been born in some earlier era." Yeah, thanks for that.)

So, I'd scratched plans to return to my university job after motherhood, my husband Alex hustled to make up for my income, and I became a full-on, stay-at-home (then homeschooling) suburban mom — and an expert at managing all the landmine situations that come with our kids' diagnoses. I did a little freelance writing, editing, and mentoring from home to help a bit with our bills and my sanity. But my life revolved around our children — and untold hours of hospital visits, doctors' appointments, and midnight research.

After ten years, though, our kids had learned well how to prevent reactions and what to do if they had one. They could read food labels... mostly. Alex and my parents felt more confident cooking for them and navigating those landmine situations. So, when I got excited about a new genre of writing — and a five-day retreat about it across the country — Alex encouraged me to go for it. "You need to get away! You need something just for you!" he told me, like the great cheerleader he is, and the kids joined in.

I wanted to go. It excited me to dive into a new kind of writing, and the retreat looked amazing. Plus, perhaps even more importantly, I'd begun to feel a bit invisible in my life. All the hours of prepping — from meals to medical remedies to homeschool lessons — weren't really seen. I wasn't getting the external rewards and accolades that I'd had in my former job or Alex had in his. The kids weren't exactly bubbling over with gratitude for all my work (which is normal and developmentally appropriate, but still tough sometimes).

I wasn't feeling... awake. I wasn't totally sure who I was anymore in the world outside of "food-allergy mom." Deep down, I knew this retreat could help me kickstart a renewed career, feel visible and enthusiastic again, and get some rewards outside of home while still centered there with our kids.

So why did I keep canceling my spot at the retreat?

My soul was aching for it. My family was supportive. It was *me* who was getting in my own way. Me, and my always-on-alert mode for a decade. Me, and my fears that I couldn't start again, in my forties, in a new genre. Me, and my own health issues, which made travel challenging.

It wasn't all rational, and it certainly wasn't pretty, but it's where I was. Thus, I kept canceling.

Finally, the deadline to register arrived. I had to choose. Could I trust that our kids would be okay without me? That I'd be okay traveling and away from them? That I was worth this investment? That I was ready to grow by doing this? No, yes, no, yes... okay, yes! I would!

I e-mailed the writers' retreat woman once again — this time with my credit card and commitment. Whether she was rolling her eyes at me or perhaps had some compassion for my anxiety, I'll never know. But she gave me a cabin and a spot in the workshop.

Honestly, I was terrified, and my body was a wreck on that cross-country trip. I arrived at the wooded retreat center late at night — to a rustic, remote cabin — and everything in me wanted to turn around and run home.

But I stayed. And I loved it. The genre really was a perfect fit for me; the faculty and fellow attendees felt like kindred spirits. By the fifth day, I was overflowing with gratitude that I'd come.

And when I got home, Alex and the kids had filled the house with signs welcoming me home. Little Post-it notes saying "I missed you!" were on everything from the piano to the sofa to the toilet. They seemed to see a little more clearly all that invisible, behind-the-scenes work I did to support their daily lives.

And today, four years later? I signed with a new literary agent and am working with three publishing houses on five books in my new genre. I'm getting lovely accolades from reviewers and readers. Juggling mothering, homeschooling, health issues, and work is a lot, and sometimes I'm overwhelmed.

But I'm excited. Connected. Visible. Less afraid. And — thanks to taking a chance on me again — I'm more myself than I've been in years.

— Meeg Pincus Kajitani —

92

Reconstructing Me

To practice any art, no matter how well or badly,
is a way to make your soul grow. So do it.
~Kurt Vonnegut

Before I met my late husband, I was very capable. I did a lot of things for myself, including building some of my own furniture. I never really doubted how capable I was. But then I married a guy who was so much better than I was at so many things that I just let him take charge. He was a general contractor and excellent carpenter. And even though I had always loved to garden and was even a garden writer, his green thumb was much greener than mine. He could just look at seeds and "will" them to grow. And then, when the tomatoes, eggplants and peppers he grew were ripe and ready, he could whip up a wonderful homemade meal without a recipe while my culinary skills were greatly lacking.

For the sixteen years we were together, we built many things, including our own home, owl boxes and garden structures for the yard, and two successful careers. But I always felt like he was the lead carpenter in our lives, and I was the apprentice in most things… and not just the construction projects. Of course, I didn't really mind. It made sense to let the person who could just envision a project and make it happen take the lead on most things. Projects would have been a lot slower if I was in charge, even though some things probably would have had a much more artistic flair.

Since he passed away, I have been trying to get my self-confidence back. After letting someone else take the lead for sixteen years, I got to the point where I was afraid to do anything or make decisions by myself.

During 2020, I was going a little stir-crazy being stuck at home during the pandemic. I decided to use all the scrap lumber and other materials I had around the house to build a new structure in my yard to hold orchids. I didn't have any plan to follow. I just looked up some things on Etsy and other places to get ideas. And then I started building. I hadn't built anything that large in a while, and I had to think about every corner, brace and angle — things my husband would have been able to visualize in his head with no problem. And, of course, I didn't really know what kind of lumber I had lying around. I didn't want to buy any because that defeated the purpose. I just made it up as I went along and worked to the point of exhaustion every night.

A million thoughts went through my head. First, I felt proud and accomplished. If my husband were still alive, he would have taken over the project and done it "right." Now, I kind of enjoyed doing it my way. I also know that if he were alive, it would have been done on the first day, and it would have been much more structurally sound but a little less "Bohemian" and arty.

He never would have added the old stained-glass window or the hand-carved wood trim to a project that was just going to be out in the yard. But they were leftover items that had been sitting around in the garage for years, and they fit right in with my creation. I thought a lot about how much I miss having someone in my life to do stuff like this with me. But when the whole project was done, it was completely, uniquely my own. And that feeling of pride and accomplishment made me realize how important it was for me to get back to being me.

It was a breakthrough project for me. I posted pictures of it online and got so much encouragement that it kept me going and made me want to build more things, exactly my way. So, this project was me time in more ways than one. It was not just me spending time doing what I love to do. It was also a project that helped to bring out the real me again.

My husband and I had designed and built the home I live in, but I had somehow forgotten what a huge role I played in that and what an accomplishment it was for me. I had designed the cabinet layouts and the beautiful stone fireplace, and I'd made decisions like using wood trim throughout and putting in huge windows to capture the view outside. I even helped in the actual construction process by putting up cedar siding and helping my husband and his friend do the interior framing. I helped build this beautiful, wonderful home, and yet I felt like I couldn't accomplish things anymore!

I moved my new garden structure right outside a window where I can see it every day. It's a great reminder that I am a strong, capable, creative person in my own right. I'm not the same woman I was when I was part of that wonderful, powerful, successful team that my husband and I created. But I think I'm going to be okay if I just keep reminding myself that part of the reason that team was so strong and successful was because of me.

— Betsy S. Franz —

93

Dancing with the Anxiety Monster

When you recover or discover something that
nourishes your soul and brings joy, care enough
about yourself to make room for it in your life.
~Jean Shinoda Bolen

The alarm rings at 5:30 a.m. I snuggle back under the covers, but the ringing alarm has alerted the monster. I swallow, squeeze my eyes shut, and try to push the monster back into its slumber. But it's too late. It wakes and stretches sleepily, and I reluctantly pull myself away from my bed. I am out of the house in ten minutes.

Once I am at work, the monster stays still and purrs quietly while I have my breakfast. Coffee soothes the beast. Then the school bell rings, the announcements begin, and the monster breathes out its first bubble. I walk briskly to the spectators' stand where the sea of children in pinafores makes the bubble grow ever so slightly. And so my day as a schoolteacher in a secondary school has started.

During my quick break for lunch, a student calls the staff-room phone. "Miss Huang, I need to submit my homework to you." Another one calls: "Miss Huang, I need to meet you to ask questions about an assignment." My lunch goes untouched, gets cold. The anxiety bubble grows. Finally, it's 2:00 p.m., and school day officially ends. A pile of marking awaits. Three o'clock: A committee meeting to discuss an upcoming event awaits. Mark the papers or prepare for the meeting? A phone call. The administrator says it's an anxious parent, calling to talk about her child.

On my laptop, an e-mail alert pings. The lesson plan for next week is needed by a colleague. My mobile phone rings. My mother wants to know if I want cabbage for dinner. A colleague stops by my desk to clarify a detail about a student's project. Then it's 3:00 p.m., and it's off to the meeting. Finally, it's 5:00 p.m., and the meeting has concluded. I never ate my lunch and I throw it out. I have to lug home the papers to be marked. It's Friday, but the anxiety monster is roaring and my head hurts.

A few years ago, I would have surrendered to the anxiety. I would have gone home with a bag of chips and settled in front of the TV, a sense of failure clouding my weekend. But I am smarter and stronger now. On Saturdays, before the monster opens its sleepy eyes, I'm out of bed at 7:00 a.m. My pointe shoes are packed, and my leotard colour is matched to my ballet skirt. I grab coffee and breakfast, and take the train to the ballet studio.

I ignore the anxiety monster when I get there. I place my hand on the warm, teak wood of the barre. The white walls of the ballet studio and the firm but soothing voice of my teacher calm me down. My hair pulled back in a bun, my muscles taut, I release myself to the sweet strains of classical music. The monster takes a few tentative steps and turns into pure endorphin as I dance for the next two hours, freeing myself from the stresses of a work week, dancing my heart out with my friends and laughing at the silly mistakes I make.

I took my first class at age twenty-seven. A failed relationship and my anxiety about work drove me to try something I had always dreamt of — ballet. At first, I looked silly. Seven-year-old flexible children did ballet, not this stiff, pudgy adult. I wanted to bolt. Then the sweet strains of classical music started. Suddenly, I was following the steps, and my mind was a blank. I had to concentrate on moving, and nothing else mattered. It was a sweet zone of Zen as long as the music lasted. The sense of relief had me hooked into ballet for the next three years.

As a child, I had loved dancing, but a mean dance teacher ruined it for me when she said that I, at age five, was too fat for ballet. It is so common now for young people to go onto social media, film themselves performing, and gain a new community online. Growing up in the 1990s, I was just a few years away from such a positive movement, so my well-meaning parents, in a bid to help me recover, enrolled me in everything from swimming to martial arts. Sure, I lost that baby fat, but my love of dancing never died. I was just resigned to dancing behind closed doors, in the living room, following the footwork of dancers on MTV.

I am now thirty-two, which means six years of doing ballet. After my first ballet teacher quit to get married, I left the first studio I started with and enrolled at another studio where I not only became a better dancer, but I also built a family of friends. We have celebrated everything from birthdays to marriages. When work pushed my buttons and I didn't get my promotion, I enrolled in ballet classes three times a week. On days when I cannot go for classes, my muscles feel tight and cramped, and my bubble of anxiety increases. Ballet is my ideal self-care because it is the only thing that I do purely for the joy of it. When I return home after a class, I'm high on endorphins, ready to conquer another work week.

— Juliet Huang —

94

Not Available

*If you're lucky enough to find anything in life that gives
you five seconds, let alone an hour of relief from life,
you should try to do it forever.*
~Jack Antonoff

I've always loved horses, but for years my riding took a back seat to my four kids' soccer games, hockey practices, dance recitals, karate classes, and golf tournaments. As my children became more independent, I decided it was time to put myself on the calendar. After twenty years of being at the beck and call of my family, there's now a standing rule that I will be available to no one on Saturdays until after 2:00 p.m. That's now my barn time, and it's sacred to me.

Since Saturday afternoons are the only time in the entire week that works best for all six of us Smiths to get together, we now schedule luncheons for birthdays and other special occasions at 2:30 p.m. instead of noon. No one complains about a late lunch, though. If Mama's not happy, no one's happy, and this mama is always very happy when she shows up for lunch after her barn shift — happier than after any massage, pedicure, or facial.

I have a work-to-ride lease at a nearby stable and it's the best of all worlds. As soon as I arrive at the stables, I always pause to take a deep cleansing breath or two, inhaling the sweetness of freshly mown hay and the beautiful wild roses growing beside the shower stall.

I get in a little exercise mucking and hauling hay bales for a couple of hours while chatting with other stable hands or listening to a favorite podcast. Then in return for my chores, I get to walk out to the pasture, get my leased horse Tara, saddle her up and go for a joyride. Sometimes, I'm joined by a friend and other times I ride solo, but it's always a reset and recharge of my batteries for another week in the real world.

When I returned from my most recent vacation with my faraway siblings, it felt too short, as always. Feeling homesick for them, I got to the stables bright and early the next Saturday to cheer myself up.

"Did you hear about Heather?" my friend Mary asked with sad eyes as I wiped off my bridle. "It was so unexpected.... She lost her son last week."

Heather's son? I had just met her grandson and granddaughter last month at the stables. They were the same age as my kids, so her son must have been around my age.

"No, how awful," I murmured. "Poor Heather."

"Yes, it's tragic," she said. "I talked to her yesterday. She seemed okay despite everything."

"Yesterday? She was out here?"

"She and her grandkids went for a trail ride. This is the best place to be when you need to get away from real life," Mary commented knowingly.

I nodded silently. Mary's husband had just been through a horrible health scare, and whenever she wasn't taking care of him, she was running out here to take care of herself. We all suffer from various levels of heart-hurt on a daily basis. Our barn is pure escapism — from worry, frustration, hurt, even unimaginable loss.

Relief from real life. We all need it, somewhere, somehow, because life is rough. I'm so glad I've found that horse time can make the hardest landings a little softer. I plan to do this riding thing forever.

— Jayne Thurber-Smith —

We Time

95

A Suitcase and an Adventure

*All life is an experiment. The more experiments
you make, the better.*
~Ralph Waldo Emerson

Our lives had always revolved around our son Bailey's activities. In the early years of child raising, our social calendar consisted of birthday parties, soccer, and homework... so much homework! During Bailey's teen years, when *his* social life gave us our first taste of alone time, we added in dinner dates here and there, but since he was an only child, he seemed to go everywhere we went when it came to vacations. This was a choice we made on purpose as we loved to see and experience new things as a family.

Then Bailey left for college and a new type of adventure began....

George and I made a point of reinventing who we were as a couple. We said yes to adventure whenever the opportunity allowed. We began snow skiing again, hiking, and saying yes to things we hadn't tried before. We found places offering trivia games in the evening and had social dinner parties and barbecues with old and new friends. Our "we time" allowed us to get to know each other as a couple, not just parents, and remember why we married each other.

We took an amazing trip to the Grand Canyon where we hiked

it, flew in a plane over it, river rafted down it, and even rode mules around the rim. What an adventure we had. We said yes to invitations for horse races, polo matches, weekend scavenger hunts in different cities, a trip to the Caribbean and the Bahamas.

Then COVID happened! Life as we knew it completely changed. Like so many, we had to create new excitement. Puzzles and board games became the norm on our dining-room table. We began planning our dinners and cooking together and spending evenings enjoying the back yard and hot tub.

As the gyms closed, we had to find a new way to exercise. The "positive" of COVID we discovered, for us anyway (I am sure the golfers disagreed), was that the beautiful golf course in our neighborhood was closed. Sad for golfers but a welcome opportunity for us to use the beautiful golf course as our daily walking trail. We purchased bikes and took evening rides around the empty town, often ending up at a park just to sit for a time and enjoy our surroundings and each other.

As things started to open up a bit we began discussing a new adventure. We put our house on the market and it sold in twelve hours.

"Now what?" we asked ourselves.

We had lived in the same house for many years and somehow over the course of those years every room and closet had filled with "things." There were things we didn't even know we had. There were others that had no rhyme or reason. I mean, who really needs a clown costume? I realized we had had that clown costume for more than ten years and not once had anyone worn it. And how about those holiday decorations that I bypassed each year because I really didn't like them? Why had I held onto them?

I had every single piece of artwork our son had made and every report card. Was he ever going to look at them? And why if he had not lived at home for five years was his closet still full of clothes, soccer cleats, paintball guns, etc?

You know those old-school photo developer envelopes that contain twenty photos but none you need to keep? After all, the one good one made it into a photo album years ago. But we hold onto all the rest of the photos plus the negatives. How about the twelve wallet-size photos that came with the one 5x7 you wanted from the school photographer? Who even keeps photos in their wallet anymore?

I worried the trashman thought we had lost our minds as we threw away almost the entire contents of our house! Each night I attacked an area or box and found more and more stuff we didn't want. The kitchen appliances and items we got for our wedding twenty-eight years ago — how many times had we fondued? It began to sink in that all these possessions were owning us and not the other way around. A weight lifted with each cupboard or closet that we emptied. At times it was overwhelming, but as I found places to donate the items that I knew would be useful to others a sense of pride came over me.

The Humane Society came to pick up my towels and pillowcases. The new senior center was trying to build a library, so they were excited to take the many books I had accumulated. You know the ones I'm talking about — the ones that you read and planned to someday pass on to a friend.

Now here's where it gets interesting. I sold all our furniture, too — as much as possible to the buyers of the house, and the rest on Craigslist. By the time we were leaving, George and I were sleeping on the couch we had sold to the new people! Our bedroom set was gone already.

Why did I sell the furniture? Because after looking for a place to downsize into in our town, we realized we didn't need to live in our town anymore. Our son's in medical school; he didn't need to come home to this town. He would come home to us wherever we were during his limited vacation time.

I work as the Associate Publisher of Chicken Soup for the Soul from a home office, and George is a firefighter/engineer with shifts that span days on end. We can live anywhere within a few hours drive from his fire station in Southern California. So we decided to try something completely unpredictable. We rented an Airbnb for six months in Lake Havasu City, Arizona. And we put our few remaining possessions in storage and drove to Arizona with just our suitcases!

We have discovered walking waterside and watching the sunset, new outdoor-dining restaurants, and the fun of experiencing a new town and new state after living within the same area for our entire lives.

While I do not miss the possessions and house I left behind, I admit I am a bit homesick for what was familiar. When George is here we have days of uninterrupted "we time" to explore and hike and enjoy winter in Arizona. The days when he's not around are the challenge, but I'm "stepping outside my comfort zone," experiencing "the joy of less," and "making me time," to quote three *Chicken Soup for the Soul* book titles!

I am glad we took the chance — it has shown there is nothing we can't do as long as we do it together. Our adventure and story is still unfolding, so stay tuned… I am sure it will provide a lot of Chicken Soup for the Soul material in the future.

— D'ette Corona —

96

Alone Together

There is no more lovely, friendly, and charming
relationship, communion or company
than a good marriage.
~Martin Luther

"Do you want to go on a date tonight?" my husband Eric asked. "We haven't spent much time alone lately." I sighed and looked down at what I was wearing. It was only 5:00 p.m. but I was already in my pajamas. We'd had company at our house for the past few days. Mere minutes after they'd left, I'd changed and grabbed a book. Playing hostess always wore me out, and I'd been looking forward to a quiet evening at home.

But I'd often complained that Eric wasn't romantic enough. Plus, he's my favorite person in the world, and I love spending time with him. How could I turn down his sweet offer, especially on one of those rare nights when our oldest could babysit? I smiled. "Let me get dressed," I said.

In the car, Eric reached for my hand. "Are you tired, honey?" he asked.

"Not tired exactly. Just… all peopled out."

He chuckled at my explanation.

"I love people, and I enjoyed visiting with our guests, but sometimes I just need time alone away from people and their expectations. I haven't had much of that lately."

"Would you have rather stayed home tonight?"

"No, because you don't count as people," I said. He chuckled again. "You know what I mean," I tried to explain. "Obviously, you're a person, but being with you doesn't wear me out."

"I know what you mean."

I squeezed his hand. "I meant it as a compliment."

He grinned. "'You're not a person' is a compliment?"

"Exactly. Because you're not *a* person. You're *my* person. And that means I can be myself around you. Like our time together still counts as 'me time.'"

He nodded, and this time I knew he really did understand.

We had dinner at our favorite restaurant. After we ate, Eric said, "I'm sorry to do this on our date, but I need to stop by Lowe's for a few things."

I scowled. Eric loved Lowe's, but I hated it. "Can you drop me off at the mall?" I asked. "I can look around there while you're at Lowe's."

He smiled. "That's a win-win because I can't stand going to the mall, and you can't stand Lowe's."

Eric dropped me off at the front door, promising to pick me up in an hour or so. I strolled around my favorite stores. I smelled the new lotions at Bath & Body Works, tried on a few pairs of shoes, and even purchased some adorable new sandals. It was a rare treat for me to shop without my younger kids in tow, and I enjoyed being able to take my time in the stores I wanted to visit.

When Eric texted me that he was on his way to pick me up, I sat on a bench at the mall entrance to wait for him. A lady stopped and asked if I needed any help.

"No, I'm just waiting for my husband. He had to go to Lowe's, so he dropped me off here. But he'll be back any time."

The lady sighed and nodded at the stroller she was pushing. "I haven't shopped by myself in years," she said. "I'm so envious."

I grinned. "It was definitely more relaxing."

When I got back in the car, Eric asked what I wanted to do next.

"Bookstore?" I suggested hopefully.

He grinned and turned the car in that direction. "I knew that's what you'd say."

"I know. It's my favorite place."

We went into the bookstore, each of us heading toward our favorite section. After each choosing a few books to peruse, we met back at a table in the coffee shop. Eric ordered a latte for each of us, and then we sat across from each other, reading and enjoying our coffee. We said very little to one another.

Two hours later, we checked out and headed back to the car.

I sighed, feeling refreshed, more content than I had in days. I thanked Eric for a great night.

"We didn't do much," he said.

"That was exactly what I needed, though," I said with a smile.

The next day, I was washing dishes, and Eric came into the kitchen. "I found a new study I think you'll be interested in," he said. He held up his phone so I could see it. "According to new research, having ample 'me time' is actually more important in maintaining a healthy marriage than going on date nights. I was really surprised by that."

I thought for a minute. "I'm not. Our lives are so busy, and we all need time to relax and not have to worry about taking care of anyone's needs but our own. We all need that, especially when we have children."

"But that's more important to you than going on a date?"

"I don't want to hurt your feelings, but sometimes it is. Having 'me time' makes me a better version of myself for everyone else. It makes me a better wife and mother."

"How do we balance this, though? There aren't enough hours in the day to make sure you get your time, but we still get time together. I think both are important, and I don't want to sacrifice one for the other."

I smiled. "We're balancing it better than you think, honey." At his confused look, I continued, "Last night, when I went to the mall during our date, that was me time. When we went to the bookstore, that was me time, too. That time was pulling double duty. It was good for our relationship, and it was good for me personally. It's me time and us time at the same time."

"It's like we're alone but together — but in a good way," he said with a smile.

"In a great way," I said.

In our marriage, Eric and I have found that including me time in our date nights is a great way to practice self-care while taking care of our marriage.

There's no doubt in my mind that Eric and I are better together. And sometimes, we're better alone but together, too.

— Diane Stark —

97

How Do You Want to Spend Your Time?

Stop allowing time to control you;
instead, take control of your time.
~Marelisa Fábrega

t was the first day of our "Planning Retreat." Sort of like corporate strategic planning but focused on us — my husband and me. I was a little nervous. We had just become empty nesters, and while that was thrilling in a way, I wasn't sure what he really expected. Would he be mad at me if I listed "Go to Paris" *and* "Remodel the kitchen"?

The walls of the small cabin were covered with giant Post-it notes with titles such as:

Top 10 places you want to travel
Most important things to do THIS YEAR
Big purchases this year
Big purchases in the next 5 years
Creative hobbies to do together and separately
New things to try

When we were first married, we used to have weekly "planner days." Back then, we each had a FranklinCovey planner, and part of their method was weekly and monthly reviews of long-term and short-term goals to ensure you were making progress.

In our case, with full-time jobs and five children, some of whom lived with their mother (his first wife), we needed planner time just to coordinate schedules and plan events. Sometimes, we left the house and went to a local coffee shop. From activities with the kids every other weekend and holidays, to graduation, weddings and other major life events, the years went by.

Now, we were trying something new: an annual retreat. "We have to decide how we want to spend our time," he said, "and our money."

We each had our bucket lists. Thanks to a lifetime of trying different methods of organizing my time, I have lists of things I love to do and things I want to do this year, within five years, and maybe in ten years. And they're not just big things like that trip to Paris. Everything I like to do is on a list, from read, dance and nap when I'm tired, to bike, drink wine with friends, and play board games. I also have a list of "things I care about most," which includes global warming, women's rights, wildlife protection, and supporting the arts. I've got a list for projects around the house, such as reorganize the pantry and scan old photos. (This includes our wedding pictures. We've been married for twenty-three years, but that one hasn't made it to the top of the list yet.)

Over the four days of our retreat, we filled in those Post-its and discussed what was most important and feasible. It was four days of planning, brewing coffee in the morning, and sipping wine in a hot tub on the deck in the evening. Both Paris and the kitchen remodeling made the lists; they just can't happen in the same year. We remembered how much we love movies, live theater and concerts. We admitted we also missed seeing our kids.

"Let's create some new traditions," he suggested. How about a beer-tasting night when everyone brings a unique microbrew? How about a family movie-and-book club, and we choose films coming out this year that are based on books? We can go see the movie together and then go out for dinner to compare the movie and the book — or just discuss the movie for people who didn't have time to read the book.

One of my bucket list items was to lead a more creative life: read more and participate more in my own creative endeavors — from playing my clarinet, to mindfulness and yoga, to writing more. He was supportive of all that I was interested in pursuing.

I read a quote once that said: "If you're too busy for your friends, you're too busy."

The same is true of family — parents, siblings, and children. When work prevents you from spending time with the important people in your life, you're not achieving that elusive work-life balance. Even if you love your work, you will be a more efficient, creative employee if you take breaks to rejuvenate your spirit. And the people you love — and the ones who love you back — are an important part of your spirit.

In the past few years, we watched several family members slowly decline. We were fortunate to have the opportunity to say goodbye. I realized that I need to spend time now with the people who will be there at the end of my own life.

As we plan the activities we enjoy, I am going to remember to invite those important people to come along. I may try to become a tourist in my town. Museums, arts festivals, even going for a hike in local parks are all opportunities to spend time with the people who matter most.

Sometimes, the best way to take care of yourself is to take the time to plan your time.

— Melissa L. Weber —

98

Looking Forward to Those Lily Pads

Love yourself enough to set boundaries.
Your time and energy are precious.
~Anna Taylor

I n my twenties, I began my career in Tupperware. I was looking to supplement my husband's paycheck and still be home with our growing family. I earned my Tupperware sample kit and bought a datebook, ready to fill in all the Tupperware parties I was going to hold. There was no doubt in my mind I was going to be successful!

As my datebook began to fill, I found that I was able to encourage other women to join me in this fun and lucrative career. Soon, I became a Tupperware manager, still holding parties and now training the girls on my team — eventually totaling fifty of them.

As my success grew and my datebook filled up, I found I had no time for myself. I was missing events with my children because I was so booked up with Tupperware parties and trainings. If I saw an empty time slot, I filled it, as any successful person would do.

My personal life was suffering, though. When I booked a party on my daughter's birthday, I knew I had to do something fast.

I was ready to quit. I met with my mentor/trainer, and the first thing she asked was to see my datebook. "Well, no wonder," she said. "You have no lily pads."

"What is a lily pad?" I asked.

"They are me-time spaces you block out in your day or week. Spaces in your week that you leap to one after the other for relief from your busy schedule."

I thought a full datebook made me look successful, and that people want to do business with successful people. My lily pads were my children's events, birthdays, manicures, and lunch with my mom or a friend. Even an occasional bubble bath with Calgon bath-oil beads! I started adding entries to my datebook that simply read "Lily P." and the time.

I learned to put everything in my book in code. I had been so afraid to turn down a party or training opportunity with one of my Tupperware dealers, but I found that when they saw that the time they wanted was already booked, they were fine with switching to another time that I offered them. My lily pads were my secret me time and they were easy to protect.

I realized it was up to me to safeguard those special times for me and my family. I learned to schedule my week and stick to my schedule, with lily pads to help me leap through my week with a smile on my face.

— Kristine Byron —

The Sneeze

Three things in life — your health, your mission,
and the people you love. That's it.
~Naval Ravikant

I don't remember what day of the week it was when I sneezed and my life changed. I don't remember what I was talking about or what floor we were going to take the elevator to. I do remember that my students were close behind, notebooks in hand, scribbling words they couldn't define while I talked right over their heads as we waited for the doors to open. I also remember the agonizing pain through my shoulders and neck.

I was a wife and mother of two small kids, juggling my full-time job in healthcare and a second job teaching. My schedule was grueling, but I was a workaholic. All my life I had been Type A. I was always looking to achieve more, earn more, and I put everything and everyone in my life ahead of my own needs.

I was not enjoying my life. I felt disconnected from my husband, bitter toward my employer, and guilty about being too tired to play with my kids. I had this running mantra: "One day, I will get out of this rat race." Friends warned that I was overdoing it. They would invite me out for a bite to eat, but I never had the time. Often, after turning down an invitation, I would feel angry at them. They had time for friends and self-care. They became frustrated with me and eventually stopped inviting me.

The sneeze put an end to it all.

I had been dealing with this pain in my shoulder blades for so long that it just seemed like a normal part of my daily life. It was initially diagnosed as a pulled muscle, so I took some muscle relaxers and eased up on the exercise. It seemed to throb less, although it never went away. I tucked it away in the back of my mind, telling myself it was nothing serious. Work was more important. I would take care of this pain later.

Nearly a year passed. I noticed that the pain had progressed to some numbness and tingling in my hands, so I went to see my doctor. The diagnosis at this visit was "probably a pinched nerve," and I was prescribed physical therapy.

An hour a day, three days a week for four weeks? Absolutely not. I didn't go.

I used ice packs, hot packs, medicated patches, and numbing sprays. I took handfuls of over-the-counter anti-inflammatories. I rubbed my neck and shoulder until my skin was red and raw. I just had to keep going.

Then it happened. I got on the elevator and sneezed — and I knew something terrible had happened. I felt like I had been electrocuted. A lightning bolt ripped through my torso. I lost my balance and almost fell.

An MRI showed that my spinal cord had been severely compressed by some vertebral disks and abnormal bone growths in my neck. The sneeze had forced the disks into my spinal canal. Within hours, I had lost feeling in my legs and could no longer walk. I had emergency surgery to decompress my spinal cord followed by months of rehab to walk again.

My recovery was the most difficult thing I have ever been through. I didn't know how to rest. I didn't know how to slow down, but I didn't have a choice. Taking care of myself was about to become my only responsibility.

I rediscovered my love of reading in those first few weeks. I was feeling very sorry for myself, so I tried to read books that lifted my spirits like *The Art of Living* by Thich Nhat Hanh and *Daring Greatly* by Brené Brown. Reading filled my soul in a way I hadn't experienced since high school.

I discovered meditation and visualization. They became daily practices. I would lie in bed upon waking and visualize myself up and running again without any balance issues or walking aids. I meditated only five minutes at first but found eventually that thirty minutes of meditation before going to rehab actually made me feel stronger and more positive that I would make progress.

As my legs got stronger, I found joy in taking long, hot showers. I would massage lavender lotions into my skin before bed. The scent brought me right back to those early days after my babies were born, when I used lavender to help them sleep. It felt delicious to take care of my body. I would never have guessed that something so simple could have such a calming effect on my mind. I slept peacefully, often dreamlessly, and I would awaken in a positive mood with a clear head.

All this deepened my connection to my husband, children and some very dear friends. I sat with my kids nightly to help with homework or to read together. They told me stories about their day at school, and I reveled in getting to be fully engaged and present in the moment with them.

My husband, who had previously been a stay-at-home dad, divulged that he often felt uncomfortable that I was the breadwinner. He was glad to go back to work, happier, which renewed some of the passion in our marriage. Connection to my family became the cream of the "self-care crop." I felt amazingly complete and content when I was surrounded by them.

My life is so different now. I no longer live in the rat race. I won't engage in any activities that make me feel stressed. The wellbeing of my mind, body and soul is finally my first priority, and every other aspect of my world has benefited. I've learned that self-care is not a luxury; it is a necessity.

— Anne Wandycz —

100

Cabin Life

*Deny yourself the connection to the wild places
that your soul craves and the fire inside you
will slowly turn to ash.*
~Creek Stewart

When I was a child, I had a teacher who played the sounds of the forest during our nap time. It was relaxing to hear bubbling brooks, light breezes in the trees, and wildlife calls.

Many years later I adopted my first dog, a German Shepherd coyote mix who came from the woods. Because my townhome was not ideal for him, I searched for a place I could bring him that suited him better. I found a rental cabin in the Blue Ridge Mountains.

Baxter and I spent many seasons exploring the surrounding woods, admiring the wildflowers and watching clouds of ladybugs swarming like tiny tornadoes as they passed us on our trek. I learned to identify tree frogs, golden flies, and peacocks from their sounds.

Baxter was a wild one, but also fiercely protective. He always stayed close by, and I never had a flutter of fearfulness with him there.

He was from those woods. He was part of that wildlife. Before coming to live with me, he'd been hit by a truck. A Good Samaritan rescued him from certain death. No one would adopt him due to his injury and wild nature. Then we met and became best friends. But deep down, I always knew he belonged to these woods, more to the woods than to me.

Eventually, he and I brought our other dog on vacation with us, a yellow Lab that I often called My Sunshine Girl. Her favorite pastime was sitting on the screened-in porch snoozing while I spent the day nearby on a swing reading. Once, I found a copy of *The Phantom of the Opera*, and I read it from dawn to dusk as I lay on that swing lazily, completely content with my life under blue skies.

I've been to that cabin as thunderstorms threatened. I've stayed there on moonless nights when it was so dark that you couldn't see your own hand directly in front of your face. I have woken up there as early morning mist has risen from the depths of these mountains like hallowed spirits. There have been bone-chilling days when I sipped piping-hot coffee while watching the sun come up over the horizon. I have decorated a Christmas tree while nibbling on homemade treats and listening to holiday music before watching a classic Christmas movie.

I have taken hours-long bubble baths in sweet silence there, spending some quality time with my own thoughts. There have been days I cooked like a pro and then sampled my efforts while happily sipping on a favorite glass of wine or, even better, a glass of sweet orchard cider. Later, there would be a good movie to watch while cuddled up under several blankets, sometimes sitting beside a roaring fire that I proudly started myself with kindling I'd collected and the logs that were piled up outside for guest use. At night, I'd fall asleep with the stars so clearly visible overhead in that dark mountain sky. Sleeping well is never a problem there.

I have visited this cabin in good times and bad. It's been a sanctuary when I've needed it, like when Grandpa Ben passed away. I've been to these woods seeking refuge from exhaustion and sudden illness, to recover and rest. I've come to celebrate milestones in my life and to have a porch party with friends. Other times, I've gone there to mourn the passing of a friend. I recall sitting on the porch that Baxter and I shared for so many seasons, reading *Chicken Soup for the Pet Lover's Soul* with tears streaming down my face since I had just released his ashes in his favorite place. And yet there was a smile on my face.

Sometimes, when I return to the cabin now, I am overwhelmed by too many memories, but then I imagine the familiar pitter patter of his paws and I realize he'll always be there with me. This is our place, available when I need it.

The cabin is my church, my sanctuary. and my escape. When I leave the cabin, it often rains, just lightly, as if the woods are sad that I have to go. But as I look over my shoulder, at what's fading from view behind me, I always whisper, "I'll be back," because this is where my heart is, and this is where my spirit feels most free, at Mile Marker 13, Highway 5, in Northwest Georgia.

— Tamra Anne Bolles —

101

My Ladies of the Lake

One's friends are that part of the human race
with which one can be human.
~George Santayana

The women who make up the Philia Bridge Club have been together longer than some of us have been married. We've been playing bridge once a month for about forty-five years. Once each summer, we rent accommodations at Lake of the Ozarks, Missouri, and spend the weekend playing bridge, talking, and solving the world's ills. We have been through births and deaths, marriages and divorces. We have helped raise each other's children, celebrated success and supported one another through failure.

We are bonded in a way that is uniquely feminine. We have now come to the point where we need each other more than we need the cards. To say that we love each other does not even touch what we have. We love what each of us becomes when we are together. The sum is truly greater than its parts.

When we started playing, back in the early 1970s, we were rabid bridge players. We would start around 7:00 p.m. (most of us worked outside the home), and dessert wasn't served until midnight. We rode the cards lean and mean, and "a card laid was a card played." But — and this is important — there is more to the game than the game. The company has gotten better as the cards have gotten worse.

Each of us has had evenings at the bridge table that weren't our best moments. There was the month I hosted when I was broke. I had to serve iced tea and popcorn for snacks. There was another time when one of our most harried women, the busy mother of four children, got confused about which week she was hosting and was at a school meeting when we showed up at her house. Her children found nothing strange about the "bridge ladies" showing up at the front door. They found a box of cheese crackers for us and emptied the fridge of all the sodas. When their mother returned around 9:00, she found that her poor husband had been pressed into service as a substitute.

Those of us who are married find our husbands fleeing to the most remote part of the house when bridge club comes to their castles. They sneak in for dessert and then retreat as quickly as possible. Their attitude is summed up by one man who was asked to bring the coveted, floating trophy to another woman's house because his wife had forgotten to bring it. He drove the entire length of St. Louis to bring the trophy to the host, handed it to the husband who answered the bell, and said only one thing before getting back in his car: "So, you're the lucky guy this month."

One of our favorite pictures shows four of us at the bridge table during one of our weekends at the lake. One of us is in pajamas, two are in sweats, and one woman has a bag of frozen peas on the back of her neck to help cool her hot flashes. It is a testament to our alignment. Whether it's bifocals, hormones, the angst of raising teenagers, or separation anxiety when our children left for college, we have helped each other through our common milestones.

We used to make bad jokes about our intent to play bridge on our deathbeds. That stopped being a joke when one of us got cancer. Margie had never smoked but was being operated on for lung cancer when they found that her lungs were the victim of the ovarian cancer that was marching through her body.

Margie entered hospice during the month it was her turn to host bridge club. She asked if we would come and play at hospice for as long as her strength would allow. Every few days, three of us would come and deal cards until Margie called it a night. Our friend played her last game the night before she died. There was laughter every night, including that one.

Some people wisely play games to relax. I play bridge with my Ladies of the Lake because of them. I can't imagine not playing bridge with these women. The cards keep my mind and fingers nimble, but the ladies keep my heart light and my soul a softer, quieter thing.

— Louise Butler —

Meet Our Contributors

John Kevin Allen, DMin, is ordained in the United Church of Christ and serves as a hospital chaplain and clinical pastoral education educator in St. Louis, MO. He is compiling a book of spiritual exercises that will help readers cope with stress and turmoil. John and his wife Carole love to travel — it keeps their marriage lively and fun!

Monica A. Andermann lives and writes on Long Island where she shares a home with her husband Bill and their little tabby, Samson. Her work has been included in such publications as *Sasee*, *Guideposts*, *Woman's World* and in several other *Chicken Soup for the Soul* books as well.

Joan Bailey is a freelance writer currently living in Japan where her work focuses on food, farming, and farmers' markets. She lives near the mountains with her husband and two cats.

Lauren Barrett received her Bachelor of Science in Deaf Education, with honors, from Indiana University of Pennsylvania and her Master of Arts in Reading Education from East Carolina University. She has a toddler son and teaches and coaches in Raleigh, NC. She enjoys visiting MLB baseball stadiums with her husband, running, and writing.

Brenda Beattie is a retired letter carrier and chaplain. She writes for *The Mountaineer* and her church's devotional. She has published two books: *Finding Sacred Ground in the Daily Grind* and *The Case of the Missing Letter*. She's retired and living the dream in Florida. E-mail her at 1955beachbabe@gmail.com.

Anneliese Rose Beeson is a writer, poet, crafter, ukulele player and lover of nature. Having sold her house and possessions, and bought a motorhome to live in full-time, Anneliese devotes her life to home educating her two children and traveling the world. Follow the Beeson family at @themigratorybees on Facebook and Instagram.

Tamra Anne Bolles received her Bachelor of Arts in Journalism from the University of Georgia in 1988, and Master of Education from Georgia State University in 2000. She teaches for the Cobb County School District and enjoys kayaking and exploring nature. She plans to retire from teaching soon and move to Blue Ridge, GA.

Louise Butler is a retired educator. She has advanced degrees in administration and economics and was a speaker at the Global Summit on Science and Science Education. She now enjoys the life of a writer. She is active in her community where she enjoys good books, golf, playing bridge, and mahjong.

Jack Byron received his degree in illustration and has published art criticism in addition to writing for the *Chicken Soup for the Soul* series. Always encouraging others to write, he believes that the best stories are written first in our daily lives before ever being committed to paper. Follow him on Twitter @jackbyron13.

Kristine Byron retired from Tupperware Home Parties. Now she spends her time traveling with her husband and enjoying time with family and friends.

Award-winning author **Barbara Canale** has published three devotional books, including: *Prayers, Papers, and Play: Devotions for Every College Student*; *To Have and to Hold: A Daily Marriage Devotional*; and *Hope and a Whole Lotta Prayer: Daily Devotions for Parents of Teenagers*. She is a frequent contributor to the *Chicken Soup for the Soul* series.

Phyllis Cochran retired early from a career in business and became a freelance inspirational writer. Her work has appeared in *Woman's World*, *Grit*, *Focus on the Family* and a number of other magazines as well as several anthologies. She has taught writing for publication and memoir classes. Phyllis enjoys caring for her grandchildren.

D'ette Corona received her Bachelor of Science degree in business management and is the Associate Publisher of Chicken Soup for the Soul.

D'ette and her husband of nearly thirty years recently downsized and look forward to their new adventure. Their son is currently attending medical school in the Caribbean.

Amber Curtis is a Western Wayne High School and Temple University graduate. She resides in Connecticut with her black cat, Sombra. She is still dating her boyfriend Sam, whom she mentioned in her story, which took place seven years ago. Since her first race, she has run many others, including two marathons, all by the grace of Jesus.

Barbara Davey is an adjunct professor at Caldwell University where she teaches the process of writing to undergraduate students. She is a graduate of Seton Hall University where she received her bachelor's and master's degrees in English and journalism. A yoga enthusiast, she and her husband live in Verona, NJ.

Lola Di Giulio De Maci is a retired teacher whose stories have appeared in numerous titles in the *Chicken Soup for the Soul* series, *Los Angeles Times*, *Sasee*, *Reminisce* magazine, children's publications, and in newspapers as a columnist. Lola has a Master of Arts in Education and English. She writes overlooking the San Bernardino Mountains.

Cosmo DeNicola manages a diverse portfolio of global businesses serving seventeen countries including technology, healthcare, professional football and talent management. He actively manages humanitarian initiatives that impact positive, global change. He has been married to his wife Janet for forty-six years and has two children and two granddaughters.

Stephanie Doerr received her Bachelor of Science in 1993 from Metropolitan State University. As a mother of five, she has homeschooled through high school. She currently works as a material handler at the library system in Colorado and enjoys playing the drums in her free time.

Dana Drosdick is a marketer living in Saratoga Springs, NY with a passion for all things related to stewardship, faith, wellness, and personal enrichment. Her work has been featured in various *Chicken Soup for the Soul* anthologies, *Peaceful Dumpling* magazine, and *The Banner*. Follow her on Instagram @danadrosdick.

C. Ede is completing her B.A. in Studio Art at UW-Eau Claire and will begin an M.A. in Art Therapy at Saint Mary-of-the-Woods College in fall of 2021. She looks forward to a career helping people through the healing power of art. She is the proud mother of three children who span from twenty-one to three years old and she is a lifetime Girl Scout!

Melissa Face is the author of *I Love You More Than Coffee*, an essay collection for parents who love coffee a lot and their kids... a little more. Her essays and articles have appeared in *Richmond Family Magazine*, *Tidewater Family* magazine, and twenty-two volumes of the *Chicken Soup for the Soul* series. Read more at melissaface.com.

Carole Brody Fleet is a multi-award-winning author, media contributor and six-time contributor to the *Chicken Soup for the Soul* series. An expert in grief and life-adversity recovery, Ms. Fleet has made over 1,200 radio appearances and has appeared on numerous television programs, as well as in worldwide print and web media.

Kim Forrester is an award-winning author, holistic well-being educator and consultant. Kim blends science with spiritual philosophy to inspire fullness of living. She is the host of the Eudaemonia podcast, interviewing world-class experts about the traits and practices that allow us to flourish in life. Learn more at www.kimforrester.net.

Betsy S. Franz is a freelance writer and photographer specializing in nature, wildlife, the environment and both humorous and inspirational human-interest topics. You can visit her online at www.betsyfranz.com, on Facebook at www.facebook.com/thenaturelady, or e-mail her at backyarder1@earthlink.net.

Pam Gibbs is an author and spiritual director who lives just outside Nashville, TN with her husband and teenage daughter. She is currently working on her first fiction novel, a mystery set in the South. One day she wants to scuba dive off the Great Barrier Reef.

Kat Gottlieb is a writer and artist whose stories and creativity encourage others to discover their most authentic, joyful, soulful existence. Gottlieb enjoys sharing life with her husband, six children, three horses and two dogs. See more of her work at KatGottlieb.com.

Annette Gulati is a freelance writer and children's author living in Seattle, WA. She's published stories, articles, essays, poems, crafts, and activities in numerous magazines, newspapers, and anthologies. She also writes books for children's educational publishers. Learn more at www.annettegulati.com.

Gina Gutzwiller is a lawyer from Switzerland who loves learning difficult languages, traveling to cold places, finding herself in a new book, and walking the ghost of her dog (she really misses her). She's still trying to prove that her partner trained the dog to steal all her winter hats. Also, she's working on a novel.

Marilyn Haight has written four how-to books and one book of poetry. As a result of surprising DNA test results, she has also become an amateur genealogist. Visit her website at www.marilynhaight.com.

Wendy Hairfield has a B.A. in journalism from Temple University. After years in public relations promoting environmental programs, she is now a freelance writer who enjoys photography, biking, hiking, and gardening. She has a daughter and stepson and lives in the Seattle area with her husband and two tortoises.

Terry Hans, a retired dental hygienist, is compiling an Erma Bombeck–style collection of stories told to her by patients in the exam room. A previous contributor to the *Chicken Soup for the Soul* series, Terry enjoys spending time with her family. Most days you will find her and her husband cheering at one of their four grandsons' sporting events.

Kim Hanson is a quilt designer and writer, contently spending many hours working in her home studio. She is a married grandmother who has been blessed with three beautiful children and two precious grandchildren who both have her heart. She blogs regularly on her website at www.KimHanson.ca.

Butch Holcombe resides in his hometown of Marietta, GA where he works at *American Digger*, the magazine he founded in 2005. While most of his time is spent editing the works of others, he still finds time to write. E-mail him at publisher@americandigger.com.

Kristin Baldwin Homsi lives in Houston, TX with her husband and three small children. Kristin began writing after the premature birth of her twins drastically altered the trajectory of her life. She chronicles her attempts to manage a career with three babies in her blog RaisingTrinity.com.

Juliet Huang is a teacher in Singapore with a dance obsession. Dancing has helped her appreciate the arts, cope with stress and be more creative. She is also reminded of the pains and joys of being a dance student as an adult! She enjoys reading historical fiction and writing short stories in her free time.

David Hull is a retired teacher who lives in upstate New York. He enjoys reading, writing, working in the garden and he watches too many *Star Trek* reruns. He has been published in many other titles in the *Chicken Soup for the Soul* series.

Jennie Ivey lives and writes in Tennessee. She is the author of several works of fiction and nonfiction, including stories in numerous *Chicken Soup for the Soul* books.

Tanya Janke has worked in three schools, two shopping malls, a theater, a market research company, and a berry patch. She now spends her days writing. Her first play, an adaptation of *The Little Prince*, was produced in Toronto in 2010.

After a career in education, **Susan Jelleberg** has embarked on a career in visual arts and writing. She taught art in North Dakota before earning her master's in guidance and counseling from Northern State University in Aberdeen, SD. She enjoys anything creative. Susan has two children.

Anna Jensen is a British ex-pat who has lived in South Africa for a little over twenty years. She lives with her husband and two teenage children a few miles north of the city of Durban on the east coast, where she watches dolphins and whales at play from her home. Anna writes Christian devotions and inspirational poetry.

Maggie John lives in Northern California with her husband of thirty-five years. Her most joyous days are the many weekends and holidays she gets to spend with her two grown children and growing family. She edits and writes for local newspapers and magazines and has written a children's picture book. She hopes to publish more!

Debby Johnson — Wife. Mother. Karate instructor. Just a few of the labels she proudly wears. As the mother of five she has plenty of tales to tell. Debby has been writing for as long as she can remember and has published several children's books. She loves to hear from her readers so e-mail her at debby@debbyjohnson.com.

A speaker and award-winning writer, **Marlys Johnson-Lawry** has a passion for repurposing old junk into cool new stuff and an even greater passion for showing people how to navigate life's challenges. Her free time is filled with hiking tall mountains, snowshoeing through powder, and sipping chai tea while reading through stacks of books.

Meeg Pincus Kajitani is a writer, editor, and educator. Her work has appeared in books, including several in the *Chicken Soup for the Soul* series, the anthology *Mama, PhD*, and publications such as *The Chronicle of Higher Education* and *Mothering* magazine. As Meeg Pincus, she also writes nonfiction books for children.

Jill Keller is a novelist and lives in a small town of Southern Indiana with her husband, two children, and cat named Italics. When not writing, she enjoys pursing her passions for cooking, running a small business, perusing the library aisles, baking pie, and reading to her children. Learn more at kellerjf.wixsite.com/authorjillkeller.

Wendy Kennar is a mother, writer, former teacher, and Los Angeles native. She prefers sunflowers to roses and silver to gold. This is Wendy's second story published in the *Chicken Soup for the Soul* series. Wendy writes about books, boys, and bodies — primarily living with an invisible disability — at www.wendykennar.com.

Robert Kingett is a totally blind author who writes essays and fiction in which disabled characters live normal lives. When he's not writing, he loves to listen to fiction podcasts. Learn more at www.blindjournalist.wordpress.com.

Lynn Kinnaman is a writing instructor at Montana State University and the author of several books and numerous articles. She's been publishing since college and loves to tell stories, teach people, and create connections. She's a creativity coach for writers and offers workshops and classes. E-mail her at Lynn@LynnKinnaman.com.

Margaret Lea is an avid reader, but this is her first time to have a story published. She lives in Texas with her amazing husband and three beautiful daughters. She plays piano, clarinet, sax and flute. She loves live theater, movies and board games. She has traveled to forty-nine states and twenty-two countries and has completed three marathons.

Barbara Lehtiniemi is a writer and photographer from rural eastern Ontario, Canada. She has published many articles in Athabasca University's student magazine, *The Voice*. She has also contributed articles to *The Review* newspaper and other publications. When not writing, she enjoys knitting, birdwatching, and long walks.

Lisa Leshaw is keeping a pledge she made to herself following retirement: to write every day and pray that her work lands in a prestigious space like the *Chicken Soup for the Soul* series. She spends her days churning out short essays on everything from "finding quiet heroes among us" to "the hidden secrets of peanut butter after 9 p.m."

Ilana Long loves to share her life stories in the *Chicken Soup for the Soul* series. She is a parent of twin teens, a teacher, an adventure traveler, a long-distance swimmer, and sometimes a stand-up comic. Ilana is the author of *Ziggy's Big Idea*.

James C. Magruder is the author of *The Glimpse*, an inspirational novel, as well as many reflective essays. He has been published in nine *Chicken Soup for the Soul* books and many national publications. Visit his website at jamescmagruder.com to read his blog and sign up for his inspiring newsletter, *Pause More. Rush Less.*

Brynn Mahnke is a freelance writer specializing in writing articles for websites and blogs. She resides in Nebraska with her husband and seven children and enjoys distance running, kayaking, and spending time outdoors.

Dawn Marie Mann is a high school English teacher and mom to two teenagers. She is passionate about photography, reading, writing, and her morning cup of coffee. Dawn finds serenity in long walks on the beach, and in breathing through yoga.

Joshua J. Mark is an editor/director and writer for the online history site Ancient History Encyclopedia. His nonfiction has also appeared in *Timeless Travels* and *History Ireland* magazines. His wife, Betsy, passed on from cancer in 2018 and he now lives with his daughter Emily and their dogs in upstate New York.

Laura M. Martin resides in South Carolina with a Basenji and a very lively sourdough starter. She teaches writing at Lander University. Her essay "Dead Horse Bay" was a semi-finalist for the Brooklyn Nonfiction

Prize. You can find her essays online at *New South, The Smart Set, The Eckleburg Review,* and *Luna Luna.*

Timothy Martin is an author and screenwriter living in Northern California. He has contributed to over two dozen *Chicken Soup for the Soul* books. His young adult multicultural novel *Scout's Oaf* is due out in Spring 2021. E-mail him at tmartin@sitestar.net.

Shannon McCarty writes humor articles to keep herself sane. She is a software trainer by day and wine mom by night. She has three lovely and spirited children: Tess, Tabitha and Riley. Shannon and her family live in Austin, TX.

Courtney McKinney-Whitaker is an award-winning author of novels, poems, and essays. She reads and writes with her family in Pennsylvania. Follow her on Twitter @courtneymckwhit or visit courtneymck.com.

Ann Morrow is a writer, photographer and seventeen-time contributor to the *Chicken Soup for the Soul* series. Additionally, her work has appeared in online publications and national magazines. Ann's passions include dogs, hiking and bookstores. She is currently working on a memoir.

Haley Moss is a Florida attorney, author, and advocate for autism who is passionate about neurodiversity and disability work. Outside of writing and inclusion-related activism, Haley enjoys drawing and painting, reading, playing video games, and blasting her music a little too loudly. Follow Haley on Instagram @haleymosssart.

Jonet Neethling lives in a small town in South Africa. She spends a lot of time outdoors and with her pets. Writing and reading are some of her hobbies. Running and cycling is the best time to think about stories and put them later on paper and then hide them for no one to read. Jonet is a loner and dreamer.

Stephanie Nikolopoulos is a writer and editor based in New York City. She is the coauthor with Paul Maher Jr. of the biography *Burning Furiously Beautiful: The True Story of Jack Kerouac's "On the Road."* Learn more at StephanieNikolopoulos.com.

Ann E. Oakland believes that the best defense of a mundane life is her imagination. Life is too precious to ever be bored.

Sister Josephine Palmeri has been teaching teens for over five decades in Pennsylvania and New Jersey. She has a master's in Spanish and one in theology, loves reading, walking, singing, biking, Scrabble, puttering in the kitchen, and telling jokes. Sister has published two joke books in memory of her dad, a professional comedian.

Noam Paoletti is a writer and an almost-graduate of San Jose State University. He lives in Denver, CO, where he spends his spare time hiking, camping, and traveling.

Kristiana Pastir graduated from Syracuse University's S.I. Newhouse School of Public Communications with a bachelor's degree in magazine journalism. She freelances for Chicken Soup for the Soul when not chasing after her kids. Kristiana lives with her husband and their children in Connecticut. She enjoys reading, baking, running, CrossFit, and having an uninterrupted conversation.

Jon Peirce is a retired professor and union labour relations officer living in Gatineau, Quebec. In addition to writing essays, plays, fiction, and mentoring younger writers, he acts in community theatre productions. Check out Jon's approach to mentoring at www.jonpeirce.ca.

Connie K. Pombo is a freelance writer and frequent contributor to the *Chicken Soup for the Soul* series. She and her college sweetheart, Mark, just celebrated forty-five years of marriage and enjoy their salty, sandy and happy life on the Gulf Coast of Florida where they dive for sand dollars. Learn more at www.conniepombo.com.

Wendy Portfors is a previous contributor to the *Chicken Soup for the Soul* series. She has several published short stories and a book, *Remembering Love*, which is a personal memoir. Wendy is a member of the Writers' Guild of Alberta. Now remarried, Wendy and Dave enjoy golfing and travelling. They reside in Turner Valley. E-mail Wendy at wportfors@gmail.com.

Connie Kaseweter Pullen lives in rural Sandy, OR, near her five children and several grandchildren. She earned a B.A. with honors at the University of Portland in 2006, with a double major in psychology and sociology. Connie enjoys writing, photography and exploring nature. E-mail her at MyGrandmaPullen@aol.com.

Rebecca Radicchi is a freelancer writer who lives in Atlanta, GA with her husband and four kids. She writes about adoption, faith, and parenting. She's written for *Today's Parents*, *No Hands But Ours*, and *iBelieve*.

Ankit Raghuvir Rao counsels and coaches those with mental health issues. He was inspired to work in this field after the passing of his dad, who himself helped others and put smiles on their faces. He misses his dad every day.

Tyann Sheldon Rouw lives in Iowa with her husband and three sons. Her work has appeared in *Yahoo!Life*, *The Huffington Post*, *Scary Mommy*, *The Mighty*, and several newspapers. In her spare time, she enjoys managing chaos, deep breathing, and wearing her old blue robe. Follow her on Facebook at www.facebook.com/TurnUptheVBlog.

Anne Russ is an ordained pastor in the Presbyterian Church. She is the creator of the online faith community "Doubting Believer" and the *Bible Stories for Big Kids* podcast. She is married and has a daughter studying musical theatre at Syracuse University. Anne is a displaced Southerner currently living in New York City.

Judy Salcewicz loves being a grandmother, a gardener, and a volunteer. After a satisfying teaching career, she's excited about pursuing her lifelong love of writing. Judy's a cancer survivor who has learned to share the load and praise the good.

A recently retired educator, **Karen Sargent** gets her teaching fix by equipping aspiring writers. Her novel *Waiting for Butterflies* is the 2017 IAN Book of the Year. She is a *Guideposts* writer-for-hire, a contributor to the *Chicken Soup for the Soul* series, and is joyfully at work on her third novel. Learn more at KarenSargent.com.

Crystal Schwanke is a freelance writer, blogger, and author who lives in Atlanta, GA. When she's not writing for clients or working on her website, thatoldkitchentable.com, she's reading, trying a new coffee, or exploring a new hobby.

Jonney Scoggin retired from the Los Angeles corporate world in 2011. He now lives on a forty-acre forest in southern Mississippi with his two Collies and spends his time working on his writing craft and capturing the world around him with photography.

Lori Shepard lives on the Space Coast in Melbourne, FL with her precocious cat, Libby. Since retiring from the library, Lori enjoys traveling the world. Her goal is to visit all of the national parks in the U.S. In her free time, she reads to kids in elementary schools and performs improv comedy.

Cassie Silva lives and works near Vancouver, BC. This is her fourth story published in the *Chicken Soup for the Soul* series. E-mail her at cassiesilva@ymail.com.

Dr. James L. Snyder lives with his wife in Silver Springs Shores. Through forty-seven years of ministry, he and his wife, Martha, have been involved in three church planting projects prior to their current ministry at the Family of God Fellowship in Ocala, FL. E-mail him at jamessnyder2@att.net.

Judee Stapp loves to share her life experiences in an engaging way to inspire others. She has had seven stories published in the *Chicken Soup for the Soul* series and a one-syllable story in *Short and Sweet*. Judee is a wife, mother of three and grandmother of four who loves reading, writing and travel. E-mail her at judeestapp@roadrunner.com.

Diane Stark is a wife, mother, and freelance writer. She is a frequent contributor to the *Chicken Soup for the Soul* series. She loves to write about the important things in life: her family and her faith. E-mail her at Dianestark19@yahoo.com.

LaQuita Jean Starr received her Bachelor of Science degree from Texas State University in San Marcos, TX. LaQuita and her husband, Youthel, have been married for almost sixteen years. Her living hero is her mother, Mrs. Emma Elie. LaQuita enjoys speaking, traveling, volunteering and tending to her garden.

A native Texan, **Wanda Strange** resides in Bluff Dale, TX. Her active life prioritizes faith, family and friends. Actively involved in church and community, she devotes time to reading, writing, music, and volunteering. Her passion for people provides motivation to share stories of God's faithfulness.

Still a beach girl, **JC Sullivan** tries to make me time and often meets friends for walks. She feels that by encouraging others, we can keep each other on a healthy track, which is more important than ever. Small steps day after day add up to make a big difference, so please walk or (favorite exercise) on! E-mail her at poetrybyjc@yahoo.com.

Lynn Sunday is a writer and animal advocate who lives near San Francisco with her senior rescue dog. More than a dozen of Lynn's stories have appeared in the *Chicken Soup for the Soul* series as well as other publications.

After **Polly Hare Tafrate** retired from teaching first graders how to read, she became an eclectic freelance writer publishing numerous articles on education, travel, parenting, health, volunteering, German Saturday schools, grandmotherhood, Appalachian Trail Angels, and whatever else piques her interest. E-mail her at pollytafrate@hotmail. com.

Jayne Thurber-Smith is an international award-winning freelance writer for various outlets including *Faith & Friends* magazine, *Sports Spectrum* and writersweekly.com. She loves tennis, swimming, horseback riding and being included in whatever her husband and/or their four adult children have going on.

Anne Wandycz is a wife and mother of two living at the Jersey Shore. She is a respiratory therapist and an educator who dreams of making a living as a writer. Anne loves the beach, laughing with friends, cooking and spending time with family. E-mail her at Anmaro512@ gmail.com.

Melissa L. Weber is a lifelong Ohioan with a B.A. from Bowling Green State University in radio-TV-film. She has a master's in journalism from Ohio State where she spent twenty-seven years in communications. Married with five adult kids, she loves talking, writing, reading, yoga, hiking, and playing with her cat and dog (but not together).

Phyllis Abate Wild graduated *magna cum laude* with a B.A. in journalism from San Francisco State University in 1985. Among other things, she's worked as a journalist, teacher, paralegal, real estate broker. She built and currently runs a volunteer non-profit program to bring socialization to isolated and homebound seniors.

Pauline Youd is the author of twenty-three Bible story books for children and adults. Her background includes public school teacher, musical theater, and church choir and musicals director. She has served her community as a reading and writing tutor. Her family includes her husband, three adult children and four grandchildren.

Jeanne Zornes earned her M.A. at Wheaton College and is a seven-time contributor to the *Chicken Soup for the Soul* series. She has written seven inspirational books and more than a thousand articles and short stories. She blogs weekly at jeannezornes.blogspot.com. She and her husband have two adult children and four grandchildren and live in Washington State.

Meet
Amy Newmark

Amy Newmark is the bestselling author, editor-in-chief, and publisher of the *Chicken Soup for the Soul* book series. Since 2008, she has published 174 new books, most of them national bestsellers in the U.S. and Canada, more than doubling the number of Chicken Soup for the Soul titles in print today. She is also the author of *Simply Happy*, a crash course in Chicken Soup for the Soul advice and wisdom that is filled with easy-to-implement, practical tips for enjoying a better life.

Amy is credited with revitalizing the Chicken Soup for the Soul brand, which has been a publishing industry phenomenon since the first book came out in 1993. By compiling inspirational and aspirational true stories curated from ordinary people who have had extraordinary experiences, Amy has kept the twenty-seven-year-old Chicken Soup for the Soul brand fresh and relevant.

Amy graduated *magna cum laude* from Harvard University where she majored in Portuguese and minored in French. She then embarked on a three-decade career as a Wall Street analyst, a hedge fund manager, and a corporate executive in the technology field. She is a Chartered Financial Analyst.

Her return to literary pursuits was inevitable, as her honors thesis in college involved traveling throughout Brazil's impoverished northeast region, collecting stories from regular people. She is delighted to have come full circle in her writing career — from collecting stories "from the people" in Brazil as a twenty-year-old to, three decades later, collecting stories "from the people" for Chicken Soup for the Soul.

When Amy and her husband Bill, the CEO of Chicken Soup for the Soul, are not working, they are visiting their four grown children and their grandchildren.

Follow Amy on Twitter @amynewmark. Listen to her free podcast — Chicken Soup for the Soul with Amy Newmark — on Apple Podcasts, Google Play, the Podcasts app on iPhone, or by using your favorite podcast app on other devices.

Chicken Soup for the Soul

Thank You

We owe huge thanks to all our contributors and fans. We received thousands of submissions for this popular topic, and we spent months reading all of them. Our editors Laura Dean, Crescent LoMonaco, Jamie Cahill, and Kristiana Pastir read all of them and narrowed down the selection for Associate Publisher D'ette Corona and Publisher and Editor-in-Chief Amy Newmark.

Susan Heim did the first round of editing, D'ette chose the perfect quotations to put at the beginning of each story, and Amy edited the stories and shaped the final manuscript.

As we finished our work, D'ette Corona continued to be Amy's right-hand woman in working with all our wonderful writers. Barbara LoMonaco, Kristiana Pastir, and Mary Fisher, along with Elaine Kimbler, jumped in at the end to proof, proof, proof. And yes, there will always be typos anyway, so please feel free to let us know about them at webmaster@chickensoupforthesoul.com, and we will correct them in future printings.

The whole publishing team deserves a hand, including our Senior Director of Marketing Maureen Peltier, our Vice President of Production Victor Cataldo, and our graphic designer Daniel Zaccari, who turned our manuscript into this beautiful, inspirational book.

Sharing Happiness, Inspiration, and Hope

Real people sharing real stories, every day, all over the world. In 2007, *USA Today* named *Chicken Soup for the Soul* one of the five most memorable books in the last quarter-century. With over 100 million books sold to date in the U.S. and Canada alone, more than 250 titles in print, and translations into nearly fifty languages, "chicken soup for the soul®" is one of the world's best-known phrases.

Today, twenty-seven years after we first began sharing happiness, inspiration and hope through our books, we continue to delight our readers with new titles, but have also evolved beyond the bookshelves with super premium pet food, television shows, a podcast, video journalism from aplus.com, licensed products, and free movies and TV shows on our Popcornflix and Crackle apps. We are busy "changing your world one story at a time®." Thanks for reading!

Share with Us

We all have had Chicken Soup for the Soul moments in our lives. If you would like to share your story or poem with millions of people around the world, go to chickensoup.com and click on Submit Your Story. You may be able to help another reader and become a published author at the same time. Some of our past contributors have launched writing and speaking careers from the publication of their stories in our books!

We only accept story submissions via our website. They are no longer accepted via mail or fax. Visit our website, www.chickensoup.com, and click on Submit Your Story for our writing guidelines and a list of topics we are working on.

To contact us regarding other matters, please send us an e-mail through webmaster@chickensoupforthesoul.com, or fax or write us at:

Chicken Soup for the Soul
P.O. Box 700
Cos Cob, CT 06807-0700
Fax: 203-861-7194

One more note from your friends at Chicken Soup for the Soul: Occasionally, we receive an unsolicited book manuscript from one of our readers, and we would like to respectfully inform you that we do not accept unsolicited manuscripts, and we must discard the ones that appear.

Changing the world one story at a time®
www.chickensoup.com